"As you read through, "I Didn't Want to be That Girl! A Look at the Life of Eve," I pray that you are encouraged and challenged to look at your own LIFE through the eyes of your Heavenly Father. As you realize things don't always work the way you want, I hope you will accept God's Timing is perfect...as is His Love."

Missy Wilson
Executive Director
myLIFEspeaks, Neply, Haiti

"I have known Sue Allen for more than twenty years and she exemplifies everything it means to be a humble and Godly woman, wife and mother. With many insightful personal anecdotes, rich applications of scripture, and easy to read devotionals, this Bible study will quickly become a treasured resource for all women."

Al Hassler
Pastor of Rockhills Church, San Antonio, TX
Speaker and Successful Trial Attorney

"Grab your girlfriends, the Bible, a cup of your favorite beverage and this book. Sue Allen will lead you into a study that can change your life and help you learn to be the woman God intends you to be."

Deanna Ellisor
Editor and friend

I Didn't Want to Be That Girl!

A Look into the Life of Eve

Sue A. Allen

WestBow
PRESS®
A DIVISION OF THOMAS NELSON
& ZONDERVAN

Cover illustration by Emily Allen.

WestBow Press books may be ordered through booksellers or by contacting:

WestBow Press
A Division of Thomas Nelson & Zondervan
1663 Liberty Drive
Bloomington, IN 47403
www.westbowpress.com
1 (866) 928-1240

ISBN: 978-1-5127-0173-9 (sc)
ISBN: 978-1-5127-0174-6 (e)

Library of Congress Control Number: 2015920113

Print information available on the last page.

WestBow Press rev. date: 02/23/2016

CONTENTS

INTRODUCTION

I wonder if any of us could say that our lives turned out exactly how we planned them to be. I seriously doubt it—or at least I haven't met anyone who could say so. Speaking from my own experience, I dreamed of a life without any hiccups. I envisioned a perfect life without any roadblocks, without serious illnesses or unforeseen catastrophic events. And although I knew, even as a child, that unfortunate circumstances probably could not be avoided, I also deep down wished that I could pick and choose the ones that I would encounter. Because I grew up in a generation with a myriad of fairy-tale princess stories, my imagination could not help but dance off into one for my own life. I can remember dressing up in a homemade princess dress. I wore that dress proudly and would dance around the living room almost on a daily basis. I did not have a care in the world. I thought the world revolved around me. I was happy through and through. I felt beautiful as I twisted and turned, watching my dress swirl all around me. At that moment, my life seemed perfect and complete. But then again, I was only four years old.

Fairy-Tale Moment

What I realized later in life is that my fairy-tale bubble would burst, and my life did not turn out at all as I had imagined. I did not always get my way. Things did not turn out perfectly. Not everyone liked me or even wanted to be around me. I could not predict the sudden twists of fate or onslaught of difficulties. There were times when unforeseen events would toss me completely out-of-control, spiraling downward into a pit of anger, self-pity, or complete bewilderment. To be completely honest, I didn't like it. I didn't like it at all. I didn't like not being the one calling the shots. I didn't like the feeling of being out of control.

It all boiled down to the fact that I didn't want to be *that* girl. I didn't want to be that elementary child who was the last one picked for the kickball team at recess . . . that teenager who sat all alone at the lunch table . . . that girl who overheard snickering and whispering when she walked into the room. I didn't want to be that girl who never heard the words *I love you*. I didn't want to be that girl who had a slew of bad relationships. I didn't want to be that girl who could not keep a friend to save her life.

I know so many women who would say the same thing about their own lives—"I didn't want to be *that* girl!" I didn't want to be that girl who had a rebellious child. I didn't want to be that girl who carried around a big "D" for divorce. I didn't want to be that girl who had to move. I didn't want to be that girl with illness or debt piled higher than her head. I didn't want to be that girl who struggled with her weight. I didn't want to be that girl who was anxious and worried. I didn't want to be that girl who was at the end of her rope. Oh, Lord, I didn't want to be *that* girl!

We all can think of something about our lives that did not turn out how we expected. So, if you were allowed to fill in the blank, what would it say? And maybe some of you are thinking, as am I, that you need much more than a mere blank. I surely need an entire blank page—or enough pages to fill a book. But for starters, what would you say? "I didn't want to be that girl who _____." I'm sure there has been a time when you felt cheated for the way things turned out. You probably have a few regrets. You certainly have gotten the raw end of the deal. There has been a time in your life when, like it or not, you have been that girl—the girl who is struggling with her identity, the girl who doesn't know which way to turn, the girl who feels like she has no purpose, the girl who is having a total meltdown and is an emotional wreck, the girl who is on the never ending roller coaster ride and frantically trying to hang on for dear life, the girl who is barely able to hold her head above the waves that keep crashing all around her.

It's during these times that I have a hard time believing God's Word is true, for it says in Romans 8:28, "And we know that in all things God works for the good of those who love him, who have been called according to his purpose." Within the deepest part of my being, I want to believe that it is true, but as I look straight on at my circumstances, I certainly would not call them *good*. God's Word says that He is good. Psalm 119:68a says, "Thou art good, and doest good" (KJV). Despite what I am able to see with my own two eyes, God is somehow still good.

It is difficult to understand how our pain and suffering could possibly be good or used for good. It seems like such a contradiction. And so it is, for Isaiah 55:8–9 clearly tells us that our thoughts are not God's thoughts, and our ways are not God's ways. Therefore, we cannot be expected to understand all that happens in this world.

I listened to an interview with Lady Gaga, the pop-rock singing sensation, this morning. Lady Gaga is well known for her bizarre sense of fashion and outrageous performances and music videos. As of October 2011, she has garnered numerous achievements, including five Grammy Awards,[1] one American Music Award,[2] and the estimated sale of 23 million albums and 64 million singles worldwide.[3] *Billboard* named her both the "Artist of the Year" in 2011 and hailed her as the person with "the most influence on entertainment and culture in 2011."[4] *Time* magazine has named her the second most influential person of the past decade.[5] Forbes has included her on its list of "The World's Most Powerful Celebrities" list.[6]

She had completed all of this by the age of 25. I was dumbstruck when I heard Lady Gaga refer to herself as a "loser."

She certainly would not be considered a loser based on her musical talents and accomplishments or the amount of cash that she has been able to stash away. And from the portraits that I have seen of her, she is in no way, shape, or form ugly. I think it would be pretty harsh criticism to consider her even remotely close to being a loser. Lady Gaga went on to explain that she regularly feels that she has been misunderstood and unaccepted. She has made it a routine to meditate for a minimum of five minutes each day with encouraging and self-acclaiming thoughts in order to battle her poor self-image. She explained that she lives about 50 percent of her time in a fantasy world, just pretending to be this person that she wants to be.[7]

And so I wonder, if Lady Gaga, despite all her successes, has had this struggle, how many of us share this struggle too? Do we find ourselves living in fantasy worlds, just pretending to be these people that we want or are expected to be? Or is our reality so scarred and unacceptable that we live our lives pretending that we have it all pulled together, everything is wonderful, and our lives are as perfect can be? And has this attitude infiltrated the church to a point that it turns unbelievers away? Churches are filled with people just pretending to worship God, proclaiming

1   "List of awards and nominations received by Lady Gaga," *Wikipedia, The Free Encyclopedia*. Last updated August 4, 2013. *Wikimedia Foundation. Inc.: http://en.wikipedia.org/wiki/List_of_awards_and_nominations_received_by_Lady_Gaga#Grammy_Awards* (August 4, 2013).

2   Ibid.

3   "Lady Gaga to perform at Belfast MTV awards," *BBC News: Northern Ireland*. Last updated October 17, 2011. *BBC: www.bbc.co.uk/news/uk-northern-ireland-15340049* (November 8, 2011).

4   Keith Caulfield, "Lady Gaga Is Billboard's 2010 Artist of the Year, Ke$ha Takes Top New Act," *Billboard News*. Last updated December 9, 2010. *Billboard.com: www.billboard.com/articles/news/949522/lady-gaga-is-billboards-2010-artist-of-the-year-keha-takes-top-new-act* (August 4, 2013).

5   "Time 100 Faceoff: The Decade's Most Influential People," *Time Online*. Last updated April 17, 2013. *www.time100.time.com/2013/04/11/face-off-whos-the-most-influential/?iid=time100-page-lead* (August 4, 2013).

6   "Lady Gaga Profile," *Forbes*. Last updated June 26, 2013. *Forbes.com LLC: www.forbes.com/profile/lady-gaga* (August 4, 2013).

7   Marcus Barnes, "'I still feel like that loser kid in high school': Lady Gaga reveals her insecurities with a flood of tears during HBO documentary," *Daily Mail*. Last updated April 26, 2011. *www.dailymail.co.uk/tvshowbiz/aritcle-1380362/Lady-Gaga-reveals-insecurities-flood-tears-HBO-documentary.html* (August 5, 2013).

loudly that Jesus means the world to them. Meanwhile, our hypocrisy is so evident in how we live our lives, spend our paychecks, and manage our time.

As time has passed, there have been many times I wished I could put the fairy princess dress on again and dance my troubles away. I wish to be carefree and free of pain and sorrow. If only we could live in a fairy tale world. How different our lives would be.

Eve lived in paradise. She lived in a carefree, pain-free, sorrow-free world. She lived in Eden, a place synonymous with perfection, in fellowship with her Creator, God, and her husband, Adam. This girl appears to have had everything, and yet it was not enough. As humans, we have looked at Eve and forever labeled her with her infamous sin. However, God looks at Eve and sees her as His bride.

Please join me for this eight-week study of Eve's life. Eve was someone who honestly didn't want to be *that* girl! In spite of having it all, she did not like her situation or circumstances. May we discover some commonalities with Eve and admit that we, too, didn't want to be *that* girl! But oh, instead, we are so blessed to be called His!

USER'S GUIDE

I Didn't Want to Be That *Girl!* is a Bible study designed for women, both single and married alike. Topics in this Bible study include God's silence, the goodness of God, humility, struggles with sin, lying lips, learning to hear God's voice, holiness, insecurity, motivations of the heart, restoration, forgiveness and much more. Here are a few suggestions to make your study time more effective.

First, this is an eight-week Bible study broken down into daily devotionals. Each week is comprised of five daily devotionals, consisting of homework with interactive questions. At my age, I don't like the sound of homework, either. I get my fill helping my children complete their schoolwork. However, I have learned over the years that if I merely rush through my daily Bible reading without taking the time for some personal reflection, my spiritual growth is greatly hindered. So don't let the homework scare you, but rather allow the Holy Spirit to use it to pierce your heart and draw you closer to God.

Second, this study can be completed in the comfort of your own home, with coffee mug in hand. It can certainly be used as an independent tool for personal spiritual growth. However, my hope is that you would take your French roast to go and share what God has revealed to you with other women. Share with them in the comfort of your own home, at Starbucks, in a church classroom, or wherever. I cannot begin to tell you how much I have benefited from the spiritual wisdom of other women!

In the hope that you would be encouraged to find some women to study with, I have highlighted one question each day. The highlighted questions are meant to spark conversation and foster community within your group. There will be five to six highlighted questions for each week. Knowing how women like to talk (or at least I do!), this should be sufficient for a lively, weekly discussion. Nevertheless, please don't feel constrained by the highlighted questions. Follow the Holy Spirit's leading to promote heartfelt, sincere conversation. Be honest with yourself and each other.

This is a conversation-led study. Therefore, it is not necessary that there be a single-leader, though I am certainly not opposed to that format. However, there doesn't need to be any thumb wrestling to see whose turn it is to lead. Everyone can pitch in and be a part of the study. Everyone should have something to say. If there is ever a lull in the conversation, I have found that you can break the ice by being vulnerable and sharing something personal. You may be surprised to find out that a little humility can go a long way!

The highlighted questions are shaded and will look like this:

Highlighted Question for Group Discussion

Third, each devotional ends with a time of daily confession and repentance. This time is intended to be just between you and God. You will not be required to share this information with your study group, unless you so desire. There is space at the end of each lesson for you to reflect on the material and personally apply it to your life. This section begins with my own personal confession and is denoted by the following symbol:

My dear friend, I'm excited to have you journey with me in this study! May God bless you for your effort. May you be diligent to persevere to the very end. May you discover that you, too, are a part of a much bigger story.

Your humble servant and friend,

Sue

WEEK 1: OUT OF FOCUS

Day 1—In Awesome Wonder

Day 2—The Abruptness of Silence

Day 3—Is God Really Good?

Day 4—Where Will My Rest Come From?

Day 5—Clay in the Potter's Hand

IN AWESOME WONDER

Week 1: Day 1

This is a Bible study about the very first woman, our gracious and sweet Eve. You might detect a hint of sarcasm in that turn of phrase, because none of us has come to define Eve with those terms. At the sound of her name, the words *gracious* and *sweet* certainly do not instantly come to mind. And even if this is your first time to read the Bible or attend a study such as this, I bet you've heard of the story of Adam and Eve. It has been highlighted in movies, cartoons, books, and novels—and certainly has been passed down from generation to generation for all to hear. It has been a familiar passage discussed in many Sunday school lessons and sermons. So, just out of curiosity, what words do come to mind when you think of Eve?

Before we jump into Eve's most infamous debacle, I would like us to be sure we have a good picture of her circumstances and a solid background for understanding what led up to one of the most famous sins of all time. Today we are going to start by reading the entire first chapter of Genesis. Since it is such a familiar passage, one that we would easily be tempted to gloss over or speed-read through, I want to really challenge you today. As you read, step into the verses using all your senses. God's Word was meant to involve all our human senses: sight, hearing, taste, smell, and touch. When we read God's Word, we should read not only with our intellects, but also with our hearts, allowing emotions and feelings to touch us so that God can spur us into action. Therefore, please read this passage of the Scriptures today, asking and allowing the Holy Spirit to speak to you. Another suggestion is this: if you are able, go somewhere outside—maybe a park or your backyard—where you may take in some of the splendors of God's creation as you read and meditate on these verses.

What do the verses of Genesis 1 teach you about God?

Were any of your senses inspired as you read God's Word today? Which ones and how?

I can't think of a passage of the Bible better able to stir up emotions and feelings within us. I've always been a sucker for the great outdoors, and I am absolutely drawn to it. I have even decided to take my laptop outside with me today to write. I am blessed to live in the beautiful city of Austin, Texas, where I am so easily reminded of God's incredible creativity, attention to detail, diversity, magnificence, and so much more. The outdoors is simply amazing and breathtaking. We cannot help but be drawn to God, our Creator, as we examine the intricate design and order of His creation. Even as I write, several species of birds have come and perched on our bird feeder. They are all absolutely breathtaking in their detailed design and beauty. And I cannot help but marvel at the intellect of the Maker, God Himself, for He has handcrafted each bird so specifically in its own unique design.

What words would you use to describe God's creation?

The loud clap of thunder works to awaken us to God. The soft sand beneath our feet allows us to touch the handprint of God. The height of the highest mountain and the depth of the deepest sea allow us to see the power of God. The tulips and freshness of spring smell of God's goodness. The taste of fresh garden produce reminds us of God's provision.

Does God's creation cause you to recognize Him? What attributes of God do you notice?

Read Psalm 19:1–4.

While the order and design of creation provide proof of God's existence, others who do not believe attempt to explain God away. Several scientific theories have tried to explain how the world began. As believers, we can so readily see how creation points us to God, and yet we stand baffled as our unbelieving neighbors, friends, and coworkers remain unimpressed by the work of His hand. We cry out for them to see God at work all around them. Do not the heavens declare the glory of God and the skies proclaim the work of His hands (Psalm 19:1)? I cannot fully grasp why others are not so quickly persuaded. Some will spend their entire existence on the work of explaining God away. Why, even my daughter's science teacher said last year that he did not believe in God. He was convinced, rather, that the stars in the heavens gave him signs. As an astrologist, he felt persuaded rather to worship the stars and the heavens above, unwilling and unable to consent to the existence of God, the one true Maker.

It would be so easy for me to poke fun at such behavior. For me, it seems so simple, so explainable, that there is a God who spoke us into existence. But then again, as I sat outside today basking in God's splendor and glory, I was so quickly reminded of how often I take my eyes off of God as well. How many times I forget about the Maker! It is so easy for me to worship the music rather than the Musician. I worship the invention rather than the great Inventor. I worship the architecture and design rather than the true Architect. There are so many times when I've been so close to worshiping and fully trusting God, but instead I've lost sight and put my trust in something or someone else.

I forget that He is in charge. I forget that with just words—just mere words—He spoke the entire universe into existence. Then I take my eyes off of Him and choose instead to focus on my little world, my life's circumstances, and my own personal challenges. I so readily forget that He's got this thing under control.

My heart is so quickened to repentance as I peer within my own soul. And although I may have taken my eyes off of Him, He has never taken His eyes off of me.

Read God's promise in Matthew 6:26. What does it say to you?

Like me, have you taken your eyes off of God? Is there something in your life today that seems too big for God to handle? Have you been simply living life without a constant awareness of God's presence?

> *Lord, I confess, I didn't want to be that girl who took her eyes off of You. I didn't want to forget about the splendor of Your glory and the work of Your hands.*

Write your own personal response to God in the space below.

I believe in a God who does exist, who is real, and who cares. Spend the remainder of your quiet time today worshiping God simply for who He is.

> *But God made the earth by his power; he founded the world by his wisdom and stretched out the heavens by his understanding.*
>
> —Jeremiah 10:12

THE ABRUPTNESS OF SILENCE

Week 1: Day 2

I confessed to my husband just yesterday that I had been feeing somewhat lost, almost as if the rug had been pulled out from under my feet. I can't really put words down on paper to describe this empty feeling that has permeated my thoughts and my mind. I'm not talking about a literal, physical sense of being lost. Although my state of being lost is called into question frequently, today I can say that I do know where I am, and thankfully I'm not driving aimlessly around in my car. I'm also not talking about being spiritually lost. I know the Lord as my personal Lord and Savior and gladly declare Him as such.

I've searched inwardly to come up with an explanation for this void I feel. One easy explanation may be that we moved away from our home in Houston, and I'm still dealing with the newness of living in an unfamiliar place. Others may say that I need to put down some roots and make more of an effort to develop new friends. A dear friend offered me advice: put down roots wherever you live . . . even if you know you will be there for just a short time. I deeply value this insight and wisdom. On one of my first attempts to do so, though, the response I received was a bit jolting. I actually had a woman say to me, "I don't need any more friends." Her life was so busy with her current circle of friends and wrapped up with her work, her kids' schedules, her husband's expectations, and her unending list of chores and errands to run, that she didn't see how she could possibly have time for any more friends.

After that abrupt encounter, I decided I would not deliberately seek new friends; rather, I would find friends along the way. Rather than focusing on finding a friend, I would search for something that I liked to do. If I could not fill this feeling of a void with a friend, then at least more activities could nullify the empty hole.

Shortly thereafter, a woman invited me to a Thursday morning Bible study. For the past four weeks, I have made the most concerted, sincere effort to attend. I cannot tell you how much I believe in studying God's Word and living in fellowship with other Christians. After all, I would not be sitting here writing a Bible study if it were not so. I do not want you to misunderstand or misconstrue what I am about to say. Studying God's Word is of utmost importance. However, try as I might to attend this particular Bible study, I have had the strangest last-minute predicaments arise to the point that I could not physically even get there. I kid you not: the very first week I set out to attend, I had a flat tire. The second week, I was running a fever of 102 degrees. The third week, my daughter's soccer coach called as I was pulling out of my driveway with an urgent request that needed to be addressed by noon. And then last week, as I was pulling into the parking lot of the Bible study, my daughter frantically called from school, requesting me to bring her forgotten homework before her next class period would begin.

My schedule has been cleared out for reasons beyond my control. Even as I have made attempts to fill this void, it is as if God keeps shutting those doors. I've had to resign myself to the fact that I'm not in control; rather, it is God who reigns most high. And in the midst of my disliked, unavoidable, unpredictable, unknown quietness, I must consent that God is still there.

Reread Genesis 1:1–3. How did God create this world?

What words are used to describe the earth in verse 2?

Have you had a time in your own life that seemed "formless and empty"? Describe that time here:

Not many of us growing up in the fast-paced American culture appreciate quiet. Sure, we say that we do, and we certainly enjoy short stints of it. We relish in our vacations on the beach or quiet afternoons without the kids. But when our short stints seem unending, and suddenly we find ourselves in a season of quiet, we do not know what to do. Rather than turn ourselves over to God, our nature is to create things to do. We indulge in work commitments, school activities, hobbies, fitness regimens and even church activities. If we are not self-sufficient in concocting something to do, we quickly fill our plates by saying yes to everything that crosses our paths. We don't like the silence. In an effort to muffle it, we have constant background noise: car radios playing, televisions turned on, etc. To be alone with merely our thoughts can be stifling. How often have we found our identities and value in our busyness? We don't like sitting life out on the sidelines. And we certainly don't like feeling uninvolved or excluded.

Skim back over Genesis chapter 1. What was God doing in the midst of silence?

Although we may not always think that God acts promptly, we can rest assured that He always does hear. (See Psalm 34:15–17, Micah 7:7, and Psalm 65:2.)

I think we often find it difficult to rest in our places as the creatures rather than the Creator. It is difficult for us to grapple with the fact that we are not in charge and really have no control over how this whole journey called "life" is going to work out for us. We cannot predict what is around each corner. We have no idea what is around the next bend. We attempt to take control and put bandages on inflicted wounds and fix broken things. But, ultimately, we must relent to the fact that we are not in control.

Read Proverbs 16:9. Who is ultimately in charge?

Only God knows the beginning from the end. Only God could speak the world into existence. Only God can control what happens next. Only God knows when your current suffering will end.

Only God knows how your current situation will work for His good. How does it make you feel to simply . . . not know?

I love the opening statement quoted from Mickey Mantle in the movie *Moneyball*: "It's unbelievable how much you don't know about the game that you've been playing your whole life." Just when you think you've got this thing figured out, you are thrown a curveball. Many of you reading this study have grown up in Christian homes and attended church your entire life. You may be thinking to yourself, "What can yet another Bible study teach me? I've heard it all." However, we fail to recognize that God is never finished with us. He desires to draw us deeper in relationship with Him every step of the way.

For the past year and a half, I have felt God tugging on me to write a Bible study. I had just completed my first Bible study for my women's ministry group at Second Baptist Church in Houston, Texas, and immediately was asked by several women when the next study would be coming out. It seemed like one excuse after another would roll from my tongue: *I don't know what to write about. I don't have the time. I need to spend more time with my kids and husband. I have to run errands. I have to pack for our move to Austin. I have to . . .*

What excuses have you made to avoid what God is calling you to do?

About a month ago, I was asked to speak at my home church. Around this same time, the Holy Spirit began heavily pressing in on me about writing a Bible study. I had been avoiding the subject and sidestepping it for months until finally the moment came when I was just sick of running. I prayed that God would give me clarity about whether or not, once and for all, I was supposed to spend my time writing. And to my shocking surprise, He did. After I finished speaking, a dear friend of mine, Dorothea Caldwell Pickens, looked me straight in the eye and told me, "Girl, you've got to write a book." I gave her the most bewildered look that you can imagine because I had not told anyone, not even my sweet husband, about my specific prayer request to the Lord that week. My response to her was one of complete shock, so much so, that she had to repeat herself again, "No, I'm serious; you've got to write a book."

After returning home, you would think my immediate response would be to sit down and begin writing. I wish that were the case. I wish I had been that immediate. But God again had to remind me to write. I received a phone call the very next week from a close friend living in Boston. Within our normal course of discussion, she asked me this pointed question: "Sue, when are you going to write a book?"

I have to admit that I'd been kicking and screaming internally. I'd put on all the brakes before God . . . but I could no longer avoid God's quiet providence. In my vast attempts to find things to do, my husband finally peered into my life with these simple words of advice: "Sue, you've been running too long. What if God is providing you this season of quiet so that you can write?" Nothing like a good, swift kick in the you-know-what! But he was right, and it was about time that I admitted it.

Throughout Scripture, God provides examples of His being silent . . . completely absent . . . as if He'd hung up the phone and was not answering prayer. When the Egyptians were persecuting the Israelites, God was busy forming a nation. When the Jews were sentenced to death, the king was enamored by Esther's beauty. When Ruth just happened to be picking up leftover oats in a field, Boaz, her kinsmen redeemer, took notice. When Daniel was thrown into the Lion's Den, the lions were not hungry. And the list could go on and on and on . . . in the lives of the pages of Scripture as well as throughout church history.

I believe God can and will profoundly speak to us in His silence if we will only listen.

Lord, I confess I didn't want to be that girl who ran away from Your quiet providence.

Like me, have you been avoiding God or running the opposite way? Do you avoid quiet times because you are afraid of what the Holy Spirit may say?

Write your response to God today:

O God, do not remain silent; do not turn a deaf ear, do not stand aloof, O God.

—Psalm 83:1

IS GOD REALLY GOOD?

Week 1: Day 3

Are you wondering when we will get to the mention of Eve's name in Scripture? If you are anything like me, you are tempted to jump ahead to get to the good stuff. I've been known to skim through the first few chapters of books to get to the juicy part of the story. I've even been found guilty of prematurely reading the last chapter of a book to find out how it ends. Of course, by doing so, I spoil it for myself. I deny myself the pleasure of anticipation and the thrill of adventure that could have captivated me. Let's not be guilty of that today. Let's allow the Holy Spirit to speak to us and inspire us today through His Word.

Read the following verses: Genesis 1:4, 10, 12, 17–18, 21, 25, 27 and 31. How does God describe His own creation? Write verse 31a in the space below:

I think most of us would agree that God's creation is good when we are thinking about the great outdoors. We established on day 1 that it is pretty breathtaking to take it all in. Merriam-Webster Dictionary uses such words as *suitable, fit, attractive, of noticeable size or considerable,* and *commendable* to describe the word *good*.[8] I would agree with all of those definitions in terms of God's creation, but I wonder how many of us paid close attention to verse 27. Please write this verse in the space below:

I don't know if you realized that in verse 31, when God was looking around at all that He had made, He summed it all up by saying, "Yep, it's all good." He gave Himself a pretty good pat on the back—and rightly so; after all, He is God. Yet I have to wonder if we would all come up with the same conclusion. Sure, it is easy for us to look at the stars in the heavens and the birds of the air and the fish of the sea and all the living creatures and come to the same summation—that God is good, and so is the work of His hands. But what about when we start taking a look at the

---

8   "Good." Def. 1 and 2. *Merriam Webster Online,* Merriam Webster, n.d. Accessed August 5, 2013. http://www.merriam-webster.com/dictionary/good.

human beings that He created in His own image? What about when we step outside our front doors and take a good look at our neighbors, family members, coworkers, spouses, kids, "so-called" friends, and yes, even exes. What would we say about them? Would we agree with God's conclusion that they, as representatives of His creation, were "very good"?

Now, with a little more insight, what words would you *honestly* use to describe God's creation?

I bet all of us have wrestled a time or two with believing that God's creation is truly good. Sin has entered the world and taken a toll, and in many ways it has perverted and marred the perceived goodness of this world. We will discuss that topic more next week. However, even despite the wickedness that has invaded this world, nowhere in Scripture will we see that God's creation is called evil, or bad. Yes, it has been affected by sin, but it is still good. I know that may seem like an oxymoron. I can think of a few of God's creations in my life right now about which I would honestly like to stand back and tell God, "I'm not amused by that one. Can you move *that* creation out of my way? Did you really have to plop that one right down in the middle of my life and my lil' ol' world?"

But what does Scripture have to say about my wrong attitude? Read Ecclesiastes 11:5. Can I always make sense of this world? Why or why not?

Read Acts 17:26. Do I determine when and where I live?

Read Hebrews 4:12. Is God still active today? Does He know what I'm thinking?

Read Mark 10:18. Who alone is good?

Read Romans 8:28. Will everything work out for my good?

These verses may be difficult for us to read, let alone swallow. It is difficult to believe that despite our current seasons of pain and affliction, our difficulties and trials, God is in control. And then, not only is He in control, but He is also good. We can theoretically say, "God is good," but believing it and living it is a whole new ball game.

Do you really believe that God is good? Why or why not?

That, sisters, may be a difficult pill for us to swallow. Not only do we like being in control—we also like to have the last say about how this is all going to work out for our good. But what we fail to recognize is this: we want to play God. In fact, to put it bluntly, we want to be our own gods. We want to call the shots and make sure that everything that happens makes sense to us. We want to determine not only where we live, but also *who* crosses our path and *when*. We want to control how others treat our family and us. We want everything to work out perfectly, *how*, *when*, and *where* we planned it. We want to believe we have some say in *what* our life will become. We want to know the *who*, *what*, *when*, *where*, and *how*. And when things start to crumble, and our worlds start slipping, we step back and ask, "Where are you, God? Because I don't like what is happening here, and it certainly is not good."

Maybe it all boils down to the fact that we don't really understand that word *good*. We are unable to see and understand what is truly good for us. We may not even be able to see how this thing, this current situation, could possibly work out for good. But, then again, we don't have to. That is not our job. It is reserved specifically for God. He is the one with the pressure on His back to make sure that all the pieces will come together in perfect harmony, that the timing will be just right, and that everyone will be accounted for. Maybe it's time that we quit trying to play God, and let Him be our God. But will you let Him?

Lord, I didn't want to be that girl who was unable to call You good.

Do you believe that God is truly good? Will you fully trust Him with your problems, your difficulties, your cares, and your concerns? Will you let Him be your God?

What did God speak to you today?

Give thanks to the Lord, for he is good; his love endures forever.

—Psalm 107:1

WHERE WILL MY REST COME FROM?

Week 1: Day 4

In the United States, most of us cannot escape the fact that we live in a fast-paced, multitasking culture. Why, with two teenagers in the house, I can barely sit down for a family dinner without interruptions from the phone ringing, text messages dinging, or "Words with Friends" distracting. We are certainly a society on the move. It has become our norm to be running here and there, keeping our calendars maxed out to capacity. It is funny that our level of importance has come to be measured by how full our calendars are. Our line of reasoning goes something like this: if you are busy, well then, you must be important and therefore content. A common response to the question, "How are you doing?" is no longer "I'm fine," but rather "I'm so busy" (which therefore triggers the assumption that I must also be "just fine"). Our busyness has become our identities and intertwined with our self-worth.

I keep my kids busy . . . therefore, I must be a good mom. I'm busy at work . . . therefore, I am a good provider. I'm busy socially . . . therefore, I am a good friend. I'm busy at church . . . therefore, I am a good Christian.

Can you see how this line of logic can create a problem with your identity? Explain your answer.

Have you ever noticed busyness in your own life? List a recent example.

If we are not careful, we will find our identities in what we do rather than in who we are in Christ. We can become so busy "doing" that we no longer know our "beings." Many times I have been known to create something to do when I actually had nothing I had to do. I'll be honest: I like to be busy. My husband calls me the "Master of Project Creating." I find satisfaction in having a to-do list. My self-approval ratings soar when I feel like I'm actually accomplishing something. However, if I'm not careful, I can quickly become captive to my own activity. I can become so busy that I lose sight of proper priorities. What principle did God instruct us to follow? Read Genesis 2:2–3.

During the creation account, we are introduced to a principle of rest. After six days of working and creating this world, God took time to rest. Most theologians would agree that God is so almighty and powerful that He did not physically need to rest. Psalm 147:5 states, "Great is our Lord and mighty in power." In Isaiah 40:28, we are told, "He will not grow tired or weary." God did not need a day to recuperate His strength or to take a break from His work. Certainly His creativity did not need time to rejuvenate. He simply stopped creating to teach us a principle of rest. This principle must actually be important to God because it is also repeated in the Ten Commandments. Read Exodus 20:8–11.

In both of these texts, we are reminded to "remember the Sabbath day," because I think we have the tendency to forget. Fill in the blanks from verse 11:

> For in six days the Lord made the heavens and earth, the sea, and all that is in them, but he _____ on the seventh day. Therefore the Lord blessed the Sabbath day and made it _____.

The word *holy* means "to be set apart." We are instructed to set aside one day as a Sabbath day. The formula is pretty simple: work six days, rest for one. Exodus 20:10 specifically instructs us to set aside a Sabbath day, or day of rest, "to the Lord your God." In other words, we are to set aside one day to keep our focus and attention on God. But too often, we have set aside a Sabbath day to catch up on our errands, get ahead on our work week, enjoy some football, flip through a magazine, watch our kid's sporting events, and a plethora of other hobbies and recreational activities that we enjoy. Many of us, if we are honest with ourselves, enjoy these activities much more than direct interaction with God. We merely check our church attendance off our to-do lists in the hope that the qualification for holy Sabbath keeping has been honored. But if we are far more interested in what we have going on after church than the encounter we could have with God at church, then I'm sorry, we have somehow missed the mark.

Read 1 John 5:3. What are God's commandments *not* to be?

If we find that we do not look forward to spending time with God, either through reading and meditating on God's Word, worshiping in song, communicating to Him through prayer, or fellowshipping with other believers, then something is askew. It may be time to reevaluate the matters of importance in our heart. Setting aside a Sabbath day should not be considered drudgery, but rather a time to reconnect with our Lord. It also should not become a legalistic holiday, as it became for some in the New Testament (see Matthew 12:1–12). When our hearts are right before the Lord, we will find the Sabbath day to be an incredible gift from God.

Read Isaiah 58:13–14. Where will our delight come from?

I find it interesting that in Genesis 2:3 and Exodus 20:11, God both "blessed" and "hallowed" a day. What do you think that means?

If God has instructed us to set aside a day as "holy" and then also issued a blessing on it, then it must be for our own good. I don't know if you are old enough to remember the movie *Field of Dreams*, but there was a famous one-liner from it that said, "If you build it, they will come." In essence, this is what God is trying to tell us as well. If you build a Sabbath day into your schedule, blessings will come. In other words, if you revere God as holy, you will find the strength of your labor comes from God, not from yourself. Your strength, your labor, and the work of your hands are all a gift of God's grace, not of yourself. The reverse is also true: as you bless God for all that He has done for you, you will find your eyes taken away from the things of this world and redirected to God. What other "blessings" can you identify from setting aside a Sabbath day?

It's not as if God decided to rest on the seventh day because He physically needed rest. That's crazy. After all, He is God and is the source of our strength. He rested on the Sabbath day as a reminder for us to reflect on all that He has done, to rejoice in His goodness, and to revere Him as God. Read Deuteronomy 5:15. Why were the Israelites instructed to keep a Sabbath?

The entire point of a Sabbath day is to point, or redirect, our attention back to God. We often busy ourselves to the point where we no longer have time for God. I can vividly recall a Sunday afternoon when my husband was sitting on the couch, watching football. I seemed overwhelmed and focused on all the chores that needed to be done around the house. I can remember stomping my feet heavily as I marched right in front of my husband with a basket overflowing with laundry while inwardly crying out, "Can't you see how busy I am? Why can you afford the luxury of watching football while I do all these mundane tasks around the house?" I recall being pretty upset with him at the moment. Seeing that I was upset, my husband asked me to leave the chores behind and come sit by him and watch some football. I told him that I didn't want to watch football. I wasn't interested in that particular game. He quietly turned off the television and said, "I could care less about the game. I just want to be with you."

I can envision our Lord and Savior saying the same thing to us now as He watches our frantic pace down here as we become wrapped up in all that we have to do. Oh, the things of this world that seem so important to us right now that just *have* to be done today. Are they really that important for eternity? Are they valued more highly than spending time with God?

Lord, I didn't want to be that girl who was too busy for You.

Pour out your heart before the Lord today:

Yes, my soul, find rest in God alone; my hope comes from him.

—Psalm 62:5

CLAY IN THE POTTER'S HANDS

Week 1: Day 5

We've almost completed the first week of our study, and it has been such a joy to have you along for the ride. I pray that you are discovering more about yourself and identifying some common pitfalls that keep you from being entirely sold-out for God. Please begin today by reading Genesis 2:4–5.

Our text today begins in verse 4 with "the account of the heavens and earth" as Scripture proceeds to explain the record of sin entering this world. It is here in this verse that we see God's name recorded as both Lord and God combined together for the first time. The Hebrew word for Lord is *YHWH, pronounced Yahweh Jehovah* in English, and it is the personal and covenant name of God. It means that God is life—our Provider, Sustainer, and Sovereign Creator of all things. YHWH was the divine name of God to the Jews, and they never pronounced it. His name was held in the highest honor and respect, and certainly, reverence. One who thought little of God had little to think about. One of the Hebrew words for God is *Elohim*, meaning Mighty Creator or Strong One. The very first reference to God is found in Genesis 1:1, "In the beginning, God . . ." It basically tells us that God is who He says He is and is able to do what He says He can do. If God is able to create the heavens, the stars, the mountains, the seas, and the entire universe, He can also take care of me! Throughout Scripture, we will find these names for God used, and when they are used together, they are clearly indicating that God is the one and only God.

God is identifying Himself to Adam not only as God but also as Lord. So many times we will readily call God "God" without even recognizing Him as our Lord. It is easy for us to claim that there is a God and to shout it from the rooftops. Many of us have been reared in the church and can quickly spout out Bible story after story. But Scripture gives us a clear warning in James 2:19. Write it below:

What does it mean to make God your Lord?

The word *Lord* means "a ruler by hereditary right or preeminence to whom service and obedience are due."[9] We often invite God into our home, which is evident through the books found on our shelves, the crosses hung on our walls, and even the prayers that are said before meals. But to be Lord means not only that He is an invited guest to our home, but also He is the master of our home. The thought of allowing a guest in my home that kind of authority seems a bit scary at first. I can already envision my next guests kicking me out of my own bed, calling the shots in my kitchen, and calling dibs on the remote control. But if we want to live lives of obedience to God's Word, then that is exactly what we are called to do. We must not only call Him *God*, but also make Him our *Lord*.

What is one area in your life that needs to be put under the authority of the one and only God? Are you willing to turn it over to Him as Lord?

God created the heavens and the earth and then formed man from the dust of the ground and breathed into his nostrils the breath of life. It was at that moment that man became a living being. The Hebrew word for the verb *formed* denotes God's intentionality in taking His time to create man with great accuracy and exactness. This verb commonly refers to the work of a potter who fashions his work out of clay. Like clay in the potter's hands, God has crafted each one of us uniquely and individually. We are the work of His hands. We are His masterpiece.

Please read Isaiah 45:9–12. What warnings are written to us here?

Have you ever questioned God, asking Him, "Why?" Was it an appropriate response to your circumstances?

Our natural tendency is to ask God, "Why?" But in all honesty, a better response would be "Why not?" When we try to take control of a situation or begin telling God what to do, we have put ourselves in the driver's seat. In those times, we are telling God what to do rather than relinquishing control completely to Him. I frequently have this kind of knee-jerk reaction myself. When the situations in my life start pressing in and making life a bit hard, it is easy for me to react with angry fists toward God. Naturally, I don't want my life to be difficult. It's certainly not easy to relinquish control of my life to God. I have struggled in this area greatly, and I have watched many others struggle as well. Some have come through on the other side of hardship broken, yet

9   "Lord." Def. 1a. *Merriam Webster Online*, Merriam Webster, n.d.. Accessed August 5, 2013. http://www. merriam-webster.com/dictionary/lord.

better. They end up much more humble, gentle, and kind. Others, unfortunately, have become embittered, resentful, and angry—never getting over the hurdles that have been put in their paths. They are forever and ever holding a grudge.

Have you ever felt anger toward God when things did not turn out as you expected? Why do you think you reacted this way?

I would love to hear the responses to this question. Hopefully you have allowed the Holy Spirit to speak to you. I know there may be many reasons for our reaction of anger toward God. I would like to address what may be at the root of it all. First, it reveals my selfishness. I no longer have control of my situation, and I see it as an infringement on my personal freedom or rights. I no longer get to do the things I want to do when I want to do them. Or I may face disappointment when my life doesn't turn out as I expected. For example, I currently have a friend who is in a fight for his life against brain cancer. It has demanded much of his family financially, emotionally, and physically. He has had to quit working due to the physical constraints now placed on his life. His wife is his full-time caretaker, and a tremendous amount of pressure has been placed on her. She has to "hold down the fort," so to speak. Most responsibilities for the care of her husband and their son now fall solely on her. Just the thought of this makes me feel mad . . . because it is hard. My friend cannot spend her time the way she chooses. She has very little free time to indulge in selfish endeavors. Not to mention that it is incredibly difficult to watch a loved one suffer. She has daily had to surrender to God. However, this husband and wife will testify that they are thankful for their current trial because they have come to know God more.

Second, a response of anger toward God is rooted in pride. Our pride has been stepped on when we see our world of control begin to crumble. We don't like the way this makes us feel. It is very unsettling, at first, to not be in control. It is our natural inclination to live without God. Our pride would choose for us to remain in power, rather than to live lives dependent on God. Once again, we want to be the Creator, not the creatures, and live lives of self-sufficiency. Somewhere along the road, we have bought into the notion that the maturity of a Christian is marked by a life of perfection. It is my pride that gets in the way of me admitting, "Hey, I need help here." Read what Scripture has to say in Revelation 3:17 about finding sufficiency in ourselves. Do you think self-sufficiency is pleasing to God after reading this verse? Why or why not?

I believe we have all felt this way a time or two. It is a constant battle for us to live a life in full submission to the Master Potter. Our discontentment with God may be due to our own selfish desires. We all long for something. It is our human nature. Everyone has desires, dreams, hopes, and wants. And our day-to-day happiness varies in direct proportion to what we deem most important. For example, if you desire the praise of others, then any criticism you receive can be devastating. If you desire beauty, then the sight of wrinkles or cellulite can be extremely depressing. If you desire financial comfort, then any fluctuation in your 401(k) or bank balance can send you hurling. If you desire perfect health and long life, then any slight deterioration can send you searching for answers (and doctor visits). If you desire acceptance, then you will bend over backwards to be a people pleaser, resulting in feelings of guilt and agony over your chameleonlike personality. Our contentment is only full, or complete, when that which we value most is obtained.

May we all learn from the apostle Paul: "I am not saying this because I am in need, for I have learned to be content whatever the circumstances" (Philippians 4:11).

What we value and how we perceive ourselves can be described as our self-image. A simple definition of a person's self-image is her answer to this question: "What do you believe people think about you?" If what we value most matches the view we have of ourselves, we will feel content and, may I say, happy. However, if it does not, we will end up with poor self-esteem.

That makes me wonder . . . what do you perceive people think about you?

Our honest appraisal to this question should result in a deep inner reflection as to what drives and motivates us. What do we value most? Does an extra pound on the scale ruin the day? Does a pat on the back result in great jubilation? Does a raise at work give us extreme satisfaction? Does a lil' criticism deflate our tires?

Our self-image and happiness are tied directly together and fluctuate in direct proportion to what we value as important. All of us, whether we realize it or not, are in pursuit of our own happiness. The means by which we believe happiness is achieved will vary from person to person. The pursuit of happiness is even noted in the Declaration of Independence as one of the unalienable rights or sovereign rights of human beings. John Locke, in *An Essay Concerning Human Understanding*, wrote, "The highest perfection of intellectual nature lies in a careful and constant pursuit of true and solid happiness."[10]

In our pursuit of our own happiness, we will eventually wind up feeling frustrated, disillusioned, angry, empty, guilty, and so much more. This unsatisfying pursuit of happiness with a worldly value system has never succeeded. It doesn't work because the focus is on _____ (fill in the blank with your own name).

---

[10]   John Locke, *An Essay Concerning Human Understanding* (New York: Penguin, 1997), 244.

Jesus combats this self-love with an entirely different view. It doesn't make sense to us. It certainly doesn't come naturally to us. Write Mark 12:31 below.

Lord, I didn't want to be that girl who pursued my own desires above You.

Write your confession to the Lord here:

"Go down to the potter's house, and there I will give you my message." So I went down to the potter's house, and I saw him working at the wheel. But the pot he was shaping from the clay was marred in his hands; so the potter formed it into another pot, shaping it as seemed best to him. Then the word of the Lord came to me. He said, "Can I not do with you, Israel, as this potter does?" declares the Lord. "Like clay in the hand of the potter, so are you in my hand, Israel.

—Jeremiah 18:2–6

Week 2: God's Perfect Plan

Day 1—The Beauty of Boundaries

Day 2—The Wedding Planner

Day 3—I've Made a Mess of Me

Day 4—God Has Purpose in Marriage

Day 5—The Mystery of Marriage

The Beauty of Boundaries

Week 2: Day 1

It is early November, and the anticipation for the approaching holidays is definitely buzzing. Why, you can't even walk into the grocery store without noticing all the Christmas trees and decorations galore. And yet I wonder, where have all the Thanksgiving turkeys gone? You see, I am especially excited about Thanksgiving this year since I have been designated by both sides of our family to be the "hostess with the mostest." And I would certainly hate to see Thanksgiving not get its fair share. Thanksgiving has been a special occasion in my family that is steeped richly with tradition; it's a time when rain or shine, in sickness or in health, in good times and bad, we mark our calendars and set it in stone to be together as one big "almost happy" family. Sure, we will stuff our faces with the typical holiday fare and watch some football as well. But I can guarantee you that the biggest rivalry in my household will not be one that flashes on the television screen.

The competition sometimes gets fierce, and the battle of the wits rages on, as a notorious annual tradition of card playing begins. The turkey and stuffing will be cleared from the dining room table to make room for youngsters and elders alike. It's not so much what the game is, but rather who will win bragging rights in the end. And so the game begins.

However, without fail, whether it is a simple game of crazy eights or farkle or hearts, a challenge of the rules will ensue. I don't know if a year has ever gone by without someone being caught cheating or bending the rules, at least just a tad. Rules will be debated, argued, fought over, challenged, and not always abided by. Emotions may get heated, but in the end, everyone agrees that we can't wait to do this again sometime soon. It makes me wonder if anyone has ever considered that it wouldn't be much of a game without a few rules.

Please read Genesis 2:4–17.

Where did God place Adam (verse 8)?

In verse 9, the trees are described as these two things:

Why did God place Adam in the garden of Eden (verse 15)?

What is the one rule that God gave Adam (verse 17)?

One thing is very clear after reading Genesis 1 and 2—God likes boundaries. We see God creating the world with order: dividing light from dark, morning from evening, the waters from dry land. And then we see in Genesis 2:17 that God further extends a boundary upon Adam by commanding him not to eat from the tree of knowledge of good and evil.

Do you believe that boundaries are good for you? Why or why not?

If I were to ask my kids that same question, I can almost guarantee that they would say they do not like boundaries; they would cite their mandate as, "Rules are made to be broken." As a parent, I am well aware that if I don't want my kids to touch something, I'm better off telling them to put their dirty paws all over it than to tell them, "Don't touch it!" It's just our innate nature. If we are told that we can't have something, then we want it all the more. Yet, here in Scripture, we see God tell Adam that he is free to eat from all of these trees in the garden, except for one. You've been given all of these. You have more than enough. Look at all that I have provided for you . . . but don't touch that one.

One thing that we don't readily recognize about boundaries is that they provide us great freedom. They give us the freedom of choice. We can choose to stay within their limitations or we can choose to venture outside, and it is within this freedom of choice that we come in contact with God's amazing love. Walk with me a second through the following thought process.

Do we all struggle with sin? Read Romans 3:23, Romans 7:15, and 1 John 1:8.

Whose will are we following when we sin? Read 2 Timothy 2:25–26.

Are we able "not to sin"? Read Galatians 5:16.

As believers living under the influence of the Holy Spirit, are we controlled by sin? Explain your answer. (Read Romans 6:14.)

What is our motivation to *not* sin? Read Philippians 3:12.

It may seem upsetting to you that even a sinless man, Adam, was able to sin. *How do I even stand a chance then?* you may ask. You don't. Not really—at least not on your own merit. We will all sin. We will all choose to walk outside of God's boundaries. And we all will need a Savior. The good news, however, is that God can overcome our resistance. John 10:27 tells us, "My sheep listen to my voice; I know them, and they follow me." There have been times when I have heard the Holy Spirit speak and yet still have deliberately chosen not to listen. One recent example occurred just last night, when my husband chose to drive a route different from the path I recommended. Of course we quickly found ourselves in a traffic jam at rush hour and were thirty minutes late to our appointment. I could not let it go. I felt compelled to remind him of his idiocy in not listening to me and even encouraged our children to join me. I did so despite the fact that the Holy Spirit was jumping inside me, as on a trampoline. But I ignored this still, small voice and did not bite my tongue. I wanted to make sure that I got the last word in and allowed it to simmer.

Thankfully, for my sake, we can learn from our mistakes and past misbehavior. We serve a God who graciously gives us grace and patiently teaches us. Despite our wanderings, He continues to guide the way.

Read John 6:44–45. How does this make you feel?

We tend to see boundaries in a negative light, restricting us from the things we want to do. But in reality, just the opposite is true. Boundaries provide us with extraordinary freedom. By following God's commandments in Scripture, we are afforded incredible leisure in that we don't have to come up with the rules. The weight is taken off of our backs. Let me provide you with an example:

When I am throwing a party, there is an incredible amount of work that needs to be done. I have to decide on, first of all, the reason for the party. Then, I have to make the complicated decisions of an invitation list, taking into consideration my budget, whom to invite (in the hope that no feelings will be hurt), and when I can fit a party into my busy schedule. I also have to determine the menu, remembering food allergies and dietary restrictions of my guests. Furthermore, I have to decide what we are going to do at this party. And, of course, there also must be decorations and party favors. And when it is all said and done, I have to clean up after the party. Some of you may say, "It's not even worth it" and have prematurely decided to never throw a party again, and I think I would have to agree. It sure is a whole lot easier to simply be the guest at a party!

Well, guess what? We are the guests at God's party. He has done all the work on our behalf. Read Matthew 11:29. What are we promised in this verse?

Boundaries not only provide us with tremendous freedom but also protection and safety. My home backs up to a greenbelt, and we get so excited to see the wildlife that exists right out our back door. We frequently see deer, and just a month ago, to our utmost surprise, our son caught a fox. We have seen raccoon prints and the remains of armadillos and possums. It is such a thrill and adventure to explore the great outdoors.

However, just six months ago, my neighbor's little dog ventured beyond the back fence, and within a moment, a coyote ferociously snatched him up. The entire family watched the tragedy unfold right before their eyes, but they were too late. There was nothing they could do to save their dog. If only he had stayed within the boundaries of the back fence. If only he hadn't been lured out. I've learned that coyotes can be very cunning. The coyote came right up to the back fence and wagged his tail, as if he wanted to play. The family could see the coyote and quickly began calling the dog's name, but he didn't listen. The little dog fell for the old trick and squeezed his way between the fence railings.

Our enemy, Satan, can be very cunning too. And despite what some will say, he is real. He is active. How can we prevent the attacks of the Enemy? Read 1 Peter 5:8.

Continue to stay plugged into Scripture and in constant communion with God through your prayers. Then, you will be able to fight off the Enemy!

I am so thankful for all that the Lord has done on my behalf . . . and feel inclined just to end today by praising Him. For despite my sinfulness, He forgave me. Despite my waywardness, He provided a way of escape for me.

Lord, I didn't want to be that girl who ignored your boundaries.

Write your reasons for praise below:

It is for freedom that Christ has set us free. Stand firm, then, and do not let yourselves be burdened again by a yoke of slavery.

—Galatians 5:1

THE WEDDING PLANNER

Week 2: Day 2

Finally, the moment we have all been waiting for! The first wedding is about to begin! I know that there are some die-hard romantics out there. The stage has been set, the flowers have been ordered, and the musicians are lined in place. Can you imagine God Himself being your wedding planner? This certainly is an event we don't want to miss! And not only is God Himself identified as the first wedding coordinator, but He has also selected the prime destination wedding location . . . the garden of Eden. Go ahead . . . I know you can't wait! Read today's text, Genesis 2:18–25.

In Genesis 1, we are given a specific account of God's creation. Then in Genesis 2, we see Moses circle back to give us more details about the events that unfolded. I am so thankful that a man was interested in the details! God's creation of man and woman was certainly worth some more explaining! There are some important aspects about the marriage union that I don't think any of us want to miss out on . . . and whether you're single, divorced, widowed or married, God has something to share with you today.

Many of us grow up dreaming about our wedding day. We look forward to falling in love and living happily ever after. We have idealized (and possibly even idolized) the concept of marriage. We've read princess stories since the time we were little. We've fantasized about the hero coming to save the day. We've had our hearts pitter-patter and our palms turn sweaty when our dream man walks our way. There is nothing quite like falling in love. I guess that's why women will buy bridal magazines even when they're not engaged.

The average wedding takes 120–200 hours to plan. Countless hours will be spent preparing for your perfect day. There are so many details to be considered, so many tasks to be done, for this is the day you have been longing for. Fantasize or reminisce with me for a while. Imagine it is your wedding day, the perfect day. The guests are ready. The groom is nervous. Your time to walk down the aisle is quickly approaching. It will be your day to be in the spotlight. All eyes will be on you as you shine as the center of attention. Your wedding gown has been chosen, your nails have been done, and there is not a hair out of place. And for once in your life, as you make your way down the aisle, you feel beautiful. Absolutely beautiful.

Reread Genesis 1:27–28. Whose image are we created in? _____

How does that make you feel? _____

If only we could remain in that moment, that perfect bridal moment where we feel accepted and loved beyond measure. But once the wedding day has elapsed, or possibly never begun, we too quickly forget that we really are beautiful. We may no longer feel special. We certainly have lost that loving feeling, the glow has dissipated, and discontentment with how we look settles in.

First and foremost, I want you to recognize that you were created in God's image. Let that sink in for a bit. God uniquely and individually and creatively handcrafted you. There is no one else exactly like you. You are the only one in this world who can be you. Not only are you created in God's image, but let's not forget, God also said that His creation was good. Despite the forearms that wave right back at you, the wrinkles that never disappear, and the forever growing belly bulge, I want you for a moment to put aside all the things that you don't like about yourself. It is a universal dilemma that women face. We are never quite content in our own skin. I have met my fair share of incredibly gorgeous women throughout my life, and yet I can honestly say that I don't know a single woman who is completely pleased with her body. Even women I think are knockouts, strikingly gorgeous, and able to turn any man's head, are not completely satisfied with how they look. We all have an opinion about how we look and have predetermined whether or not we measure up. So then, do we really believe that we are beautiful? Are we able to take God for His Word and believe that He did a good job creating us?

Let me ask you, what is your definition of beauty?

As you watch movies or television or flip through a magazine, who in your eyes is beautiful? What about these individuals do you find beautiful? (Go ahead—be honest; God already knows what you think anyway).

Read Psalm 139:13–16. Have you ever thought about how much care God took in making you "you"? How does this make you feel?

Read Ecclesiastes 3:11–14. How many things has God made beautiful?

Despite what you've been told or conjured up in your head, sister in Christ, you are beautiful. You do matter, and God views you as a masterpiece. His masterpiece.

Read Song of Solomon 1:6. Do you think King Solomon's gal was content with her beauty? Why or why not?

"Beauty" defined in our own eyes is an age-old dilemma. For in this passage, we see the girl of Solomon's dreams lament over the dark color of her skin because it reflects the fact that she is a working gal. Ethnicity is not the issue here; rather, the issue is that she has to work outside in the fields doing the work of men. Her skin has become tan and darkened by the sun. Because of her preconceived idea or notion of beauty, she then comes to the conclusion that she is not beautiful, and certainly not worthy to be married to a king.

What we consider and accept as "beautiful" is counterfeit for the real thing. Just like the love of Solomon's life, we easily point out our flaws and refuse to look at the uniqueness or individuality of our beings. Josh McDowell, in his book *Seeing Yourself as God Sees You*, says, "To some degree, our sense of identity has been shaped by how we appear—or think we appear—to others. We have subconsciously come to believe that beautiful people are more highly valued, and since everyone wants to be highly valued, we strive to be beautiful people."[11]

When we fall for the trap of comparison, there is only "has" or "has not," and neither is a win-win situation. We either end up unjustly elevating ourselves above others around us, falsely thinking that we are better than we really are, or, on the flip side, we feel we don't measure up. We feel that we are not talented enough, pretty enough, smart enough, rich enough . . . you get my point. When we are lured into a worldly value system, we will never be good enough. We become a "has not," and what we are left with is feelings of rejection and defeat.

But how does God view us? What matters most to Him? Read I Samuel 16:6–7.

If you could see yourself through God's eyes, He would exclaim to you, "You are beautiful!" Are you willing to accept that your eyes have been tainted by our current culture? Are you willing to challenge the way you see yourself and begin to look at yourself through another lens? The lens of Scripture provides an entirely different point of view.

Lord, I didn't want to be that girl who refused to accept my beauty.

---

[11]   Josh McDowell, *See Yourself as God Sees You* (Chicago: Tyndale, 1999), 9.

Do you spend more time making yourself pretty on the inside or the outside? Close today with an honest evaluation before the Lord.

Charm is deceptive, and beauty is fleeting; but a woman who fears the Lord is to be praised.

—Proverbs 31:30

I'VE MADE A MESS OF ME

Week 2: Day 3

Yesterday we focused the majority of our discussion on one key verse, Genesis 1:27. Begin today by rereading it and reflecting on what you learned. In review of yesterday, I want to reiterate that we have been made in the image of God. The first step is *believing* we are truly made in God's image, and the next step is to start *accepting* it and *acting* on it. But what does that really mean? How do we get there? There are particular traits that we have that reflect characteristics of God, although one could argue that those traits are hardly recognizable in us because we have been so marred by sin.

Is your life the reflection of God that you want it to be? _____

Well, maybe my life reflects God while I'm sleeping, but I can't even make it throughout a day without sinning. Let's be honest with ourselves; I think we could all say, "I've made a mess of me." And although we've been created in God's image, our lives fail in comparison to the Lord God Almighty because of our sin. The book of Genesis is just the beginning of God's redemptive story. Beginning here and throughout Scripture, we will see that humankind, male and female alike, was created to bring God glory (Isaiah 43:7). But our own sinfulness has gotten in the way of our reflecting God's image perfectly. Read Ephesians 4:17–24.

In what ways should our lives reflect the image of God (verse 24)?

Due to our sinfulness, we have gotten into a boatload of trouble. I think it is important to point out that neither male nor female can escape God's judgment seat. We stand *equal* in our desperate need of a Savior. There is no reason to go back to elementary school and argue that girls are better than boys or vice versa: we all have sinned and come short of the glory of God (Romans 3:23). There is no one righteous; no, not one (Romans 3:10).

Read Ephesians 2:1–10. How is salvation obtained?

For it is by grace, through faith, that we are saved. It is not by ourselves. It is a gift from God. You and I were created by God to be a part of His grand story. He created male and female uniquely and individually to point us to Christ as part of His redemptive plan.

Write out Ephesians 2:10.

I want to make it clear before we go on today, that in order for our text in Ephesians 4 to make any sense to you, you must be a believer in Christ Jesus. You must believe that He is your Lord and Savior and attend His school of theology. It is only by the power of Jesus Christ that we can have a breakthrough from the waywardness, futility, and blindness of our old "pre-Jesus" selves. Ephesians 4:17 tells us that we should no longer "live in the futility of our thinking"—in other words, in our minds. Our lives are not meant to be futile. Our lives are to be filled with purpose.

I have been reminded today of how powerful our minds can be over us. Out of the blue today, I started pondering what would happen to my kids and me if my husband were to suddenly die. I got so wrapped up in that thought that, unfortunately, it consumed most of my morning. My mind got so carried away. I had his funeral planned out, including arrangements of who would preach and who would sing. I even went so far as to plan what photos I would display at the ceremony. I thought about my financial situation and determined that I would have to go back to work (since currently I am a stay-at-home mother). I even decided that we would most likely have to move because the financial burden of our current mortgage would be too much for my limited budget. Now I confess all of this to you because I want to point out that my thinking today has been absolutely ludicrous and ridiculous! My husband's health is totally fine. He is fit and healthy, and I can't remember the last time he had any medical concerns. He doesn't even have the sniffles . . . and why I wasted so much of my day focusing on this fear is beyond me.

Can you relate to me? Have you done the same? Have you made your fear appear real? Go ahead and share below.

FEAR can be an acronym for "false evidence appearing real." Our minds can do a great job of convincing us that what is happening to someone else is going to happen to us. We can quickly take someone else's tragedy and make it our own. That is why it is imperative that we relearn how to think. Ephesians 4:20 reminds us that we need to go back to the basics of what we have learned.

Let's take a quick look at what we've been taught. Write out Ephesians 4:22–24:

Put off your old self! It is time for a wardrobe change. Paul is instructing us to put off our former ways of life, to put off our old selves, which were corrupted with their deceitful desires. To gain insight into what Paul is saying, look also at verse 25. We are instructed to put off falsehood and speak truthfully. To put it bluntly, we are instructed to stop lying.

On *The Today Show* this morning, the magazine *Parenting* reported that 85 percent of moms lie to their kids to get out of social obligations, and 29 percent of moms had lied to their spouses in the past week.[12] You may find the following article fascinating:

> "Motherhood and lying—they go together as naturally as motherhood and apple pie. Of course, you know we didn't really bake that apple pie ourselves, right? Yeah, we bought it at the supermarket, threw out the plastic packaging and pretended it was homemade when we brought it to the bake sale.
>
> We all know honesty is best, especially when it comes to setting a good example for our children. But a survey of 26,000 moms by TODAY Moms and Parenting. com found that a third admit to lying about their parenting practices.
>
> And that doesn't count the lies we tell others, like the half of moms who say they've sent a sick child to school or day care (a lie of omission, if nothing else). And how about the whoppers we tell our kids? If you keep making that face, it'll freeze that way . . . Santa is totally watching you right now!"[13]

I have watched lying become an epidemic lately, even in the lives of professing Christians. I've seen lies easily roll off our tongues in order to avoid complicated and confusing situations and, at other times, to ease us back into control of a situation. Lying can certainly be used to manipulate others in order to get what we want.

How have you seen lying to be hurtful and harmful?

I'm afraid that a "little white lie" isn't so little in the eyes of God. We can become so clothed in the coat of lying that it becomes natural for us. If we are not careful, lying can become addictive and habitual. In an article titled "The Truth about Deception," a "compulsive liar is defined as someone who lies out of habit. Lying is their normal and reflexive way of responding to questions.

---

[12]   "How often do moms really lie?" *The Today Show.* NBC. Season 61, episode 0111. January 11, 2012. Television. *www.tv.com/shows/the-today-show/january-11-2012-1742358.*

[13]   "How often do moms really lie?" *Today Moms.* Last updated January 11, 2012. *The Today Show: www.moms. today.msnbc.msn.com* (January 13, 2012).

Compulsive liars bend the truth about everything, large and small. For a compulsive liar, telling the truth is very awkward and uncomfortable while lying feels right."[14]

We can find additional insight into the meaning of "old self" in Colossians 3:8–9. We not only are to "put off" lying but also the practices that go along with it, such as anger and malice. These may be underlying problems that need to be addressed in order for our problem of lying to be resolved. These emotions, attitudes, and patterns are signs of our "old self" and need to be *put off*.

Put on your new self! Paul continues in Ephesians 4:24, instructing us "to put on the new self." The traits, or characteristics, that should be displayed in our new selves are further explained in Colossians 3:12. List them below:

But that begs the question, how in the world do we get from verse 22, our old selves, and become our new selves, as discussed in verse 24? If we attempt to do it ourselves, we will wind up confined in legalism rather than fully experiencing God's grace. What do you think the key is?

I believe the answer is given in verse 23: "to be made new in the attitude of our minds." It is not something we do or earn on our merit, but it is the work of Christ within us. In order for our minds to be renewed, we must continually saturate ourselves in God's Word and begin applying it to our lives.

Read the following passages of Scripture and answer the following questions:

2 Corinthians 4:16–18. Why do we not look to things of this world?

Colossians 3:2–3. What has happened to our old selves? Where are our lives hidden?

Ephesians 1:18. Why are we encouraged to read Scripture?

---

14   "What is the Difference Between a Sociopath, a Compulsive, a Pathological, a Chronic, and a Habitual Liar?" *Truth About Deception*. Web, n.d. *www.truthaboutdeception.com/lying-and-deception/confronting-a-partner/ compulsive-lying/types-of-liars.html* (August 7, 2013).

The answer is pretty simple . . . the more we read about God, the more we understand about God. The more we understand about God, the more our lives will be changed and transformed by the renewal of our minds. God wants us to see things from His perspective, not ours. When we fully grasp God's everlasting love for us and fully place our trust in Him, our lives begin reflecting the image of God, in true righteousness and holiness.

Lord, I didn't want to be the girl who made a mess of me.

Ask God to renew your mind today and give you a bigger glimpse of Him:

And I pray that you, being rooted and established in love, may have power, together with all the Lord's holy people, to grasp how wide and long and high and deep is the love of Christ, and to know this love that surpasses knowledge—that you may be filled to the measure of all the fullness of God.

—Ephesians 4:17–19

GOD HAS PURPOSE IN MARRIAGE

Week 2: Day 4

Today we are going to talk about marriage, and before you skip over this subject matter entirely, as some of you may be tempted to do, I want to encourage you to stay the course. Yes, I'll forewarn you—today may be a bit difficult. Marriage can be a difficult subject. But it is also an urgent matter that we should not avoid. You may be struggling with just the concept of marriage, as you've been waiting and waiting for your special wedding day to come, and it seems it never will. You may be married, but if you are completely honest with yourself, you might wish you could "untie" that wedding knot and have a "redo." In your current marriage, you feel stuck. You are struggling. Marriage has not exactly turned out like the picture you had envisioned in your head. Then there are some who think, "My marriage is fine, just fine. I don't understand why I need any help to 'better my marriage.' We are fine. We are comfortable. Nothing too bad—and yet nothing too good, either." You feel content with the status quo. You are okay with just getting by. But maybe, praise God, you have a great marriage, and you can't even imagine it getting any better. You live sacrificially by serving each other on a regular basis. You feel blessed beyond measure. But what if even you could have a better marriage, one that is fulfilling and satisfying beyond your wildest imagination?

Now that is a challenge! But I think you are up for it. I challenge you to take your socks off today and look afresh at this whole idea of marriage because I believe that God intended for our marriages to do just that: knock our socks off! God's perspective on marriage is so vastly different from our own. However, in the sexually uninhibited, highly entertained, excitement-seeking culture that we live in, we may have never really seen marriage from God's point of view before.

Begin with reading Genesis 2:18–25. Why do you think marriages struggle? (And, if you really want to make it personal, why has your own marriage struggled?)

First and foremost, we must all understand the basic principle that God designed the institution of marriage. I hope that's not a complete shocker to anyone. But maybe from your vantage point, this concept of a "godly marriage" makes absolutely no sense right now. It is no surprise to anyone that many marriages struggle. In fact, I heard a statistic the other day that marriage in America is at an all-time low and is expected to fall below the 50 percent marker sometime next year. In other words, there will be more people not married than married in the United States. Married people for the first time in American history will be in the minority. The idea of marriage has been so tainted in our current culture that many have decided to avoid it altogether. They have chosen, rather, to live together without ever confessing the words, "I do." Some have forgotten the sacredness of marriage and committed adultery. Others have tried out the marriage vows for a while, only to decide later that it really did not suit them. They've decided that the "till death do us part" seemed unbearable to them. Let's face it, divorce runs rampant, even among professing Christians. However, this was not God's intent. And once again, due to our own sinfulness, it is difficult for us to see God's intentions in marriage.

Marriage was intended to be a God-ordained, covenant relationship between a man and a woman. Marriage is a "God thing"—and yes, a very good thing too. And for some of us today, it may take a while to unwrap our preconceived notions regarding marriage and put aside our hurts and battle wounds and fess up that we do not know everything there is to know about marriage. Marriage is a struggle for us because we look at it through our tainted lenses rather than try to see it from a godly point of view.

Read Genesis 2:18. Who is it that determined that man should not live alone?

God, from the onset, from the very beginning, determines as part of His creation to create man and woman for the purpose of marriage. I think it is important to notice that *before the Fall*, God Himself, not human beings, decides that it is not good for man to be alone. As the animals are paraded before Adam, it quickly becomes evident that none of them will do as a "helper suitable for him." It is, therefore, God Himself who designs and handcrafts a "helper fit for him" (ESV) . . . and that is his wife.

As a woman, have you ever considered this definition of your role as a wife? How does this change your perspective about marriage and why you were created?

I want to point out that as women, we were created to be helpmates to our spouses. I don't know if many of us realize the godly role given to women in marriage. It's definitely not a popular definition in our current American culture and may even send chills down your spine.

What do you think God meant by the phrase "helper suitable for him"?

This concept of being our husbands' helpers can be somewhat confusing. This doesn't mean that you can't work or volunteer at your child's school or be actively involved in activities outside the home. It is just a shift in our focus. Will we believe what God created us for and then act accordingly with how we live our lives? If you are married, do you think you are fulfilling the description of a "helper suitable for him" in your own marriage? Do you trust that the God of the universe who created you really and truly knows what will ultimately fulfill you? Share how you are living this role day-to-day (and if you are brave enough, ask your husband how you are doing):

Coby and I met our junior year of college and began dating shortly afterwards. We married a year after graduation. We thought we knew everything. But to our surprise, we struggled significantly in the first few years of our marriage. I believe it is only by the grace of God that we are still married today. When I was first married, I did not understand the concept of being my husband's helper, and therefore, I lived very independently from him. I wanted to be the one in charge in our marriage and selfishly wanted to have control of my time, my finances, my career, and sadly to say, even my own body. I thought I had the right to determine how I spent my time, regardless of my husband's input, concerns, or needs. If I wanted to go out with my girlfriends, I would just do it. If I wanted to work late, I would simply call and let him know. If I wanted to buy something, I would use "my money" to do so. If I didn't feel like having sex, I would tell him I was too tired or pretend to already be asleep before he came into the bedroom. Our marriage quickly spiraled downhill, and we became like two ships just passing in the night. We both lived our lives very separately, with very little regard to biblical concepts of marriage. Looking back now, I can say that those were the worst years of our marriage, and it wasn't until we both decided to live sacrificially toward each other that things began to turn around. God's Word is so counterintuitive to us. It doesn't necessarily make any sense to us. But after twenty-two years of marriage (and some really great years lately!), I can testify that God knows what He is talking about, and His precepts work!

My responses toward my husband have changed drastically over the years—and for the better. For example, before making any plans with my friends or filling up the family calendar, I check with my husband first. I make sure that everything in our relationship is "in-check" and "in-balance." As a wife and mother, I can set the emotional barometer in our home. If I am stressed out and tired, how easily that is passed on to my husband and kids!

A godly wife is one who is an encouragement and companion to her spouse. A godly wife will also make her husband a priority—not before God, but certainly above her work, family, and friends. She is not controlling or manipulative in her submissive role. Rather, by dying to herself and loving her husband unconditionally, she will discover that she can make her husband feel like a man.

It breaks my heart when a woman walks away from her marriage with the idea that "I'm just not cut out for this," because honey, yes indeed, you were cut out for this. You were made by the Master Creator for this role, and God has put considerable thought and deliberation into handcrafting you for your mate. God is very intentional and loves planning every detail of your life. As Isaiah says, "Lord, you are my God; I will exalt you and praise your name, for in perfect faithfulness you have done wonderful things, *things planned long ago*" (Isaiah 25:1, emphasis added).

Maybe a better reaction would be to evaluate how well you are showing respect to your spouse: Do you spend more time lifting him up or cutting him down? Do you make it a priority to spend time with him alone? Do you allow your husband to be the spiritual leader in your home? Do you regularly pray for him? Do you show him random acts of kindness or words of appreciation? Do you spend time doing things that he likes to do?

Evaluating *our* responsibilities and roles in a marriage may be the perfect way to begin making changes in order to have a marriage that honors and glorifies God. If your hair is standing up on the back of your head right now, don't worry; I get it and understand. I am right there with you. I would much rather be the one being helped than the helper! I would much rather be the one calling the shots, too. But when I fall into that mindset, I no longer am doing what God calls me to do—to be the helper. Even though it absolutely makes no sense to me, even though it goes against what seems so natural to me . . . it is when I take that step of faith and actually start doing it that this whole marriage thing starts to work. On those really tough days (when you don't feel like it), remember Christ's example to us in Philippians 2:8. What will it take for us to serve our spouses?

A little humility will go a long way! Remember you were made for this. And yes, I believe you can be the woman God created you to be!

In verse 21, we see God take a rib from Adam in order to "form woman." Follow on down to verse 22, where we see God bringing Eve to Adam. God chose Eve for Adam; he handpicked her, so to say. It is God who made the first marriage proposal. There is something incredibly exciting about a man's proposal to his girl. When a man gets down on one knee and proposes to a woman, our hearts begin to flutter. Our thoughts are not "Oh yeah, I finally caught him" or "He's hooked." We're not talking about being a fisher of man, here. What really is going on is that we want to make a declaration to the world that he, our man, *wants* us. Why do you think we run around showing everyone in sight (including people we don't even know on the awkward elevator ride) our engagement rings? We are thrilled beyond measure because our man has *picked* us. Yes, he *loves* us. He has *chosen* us. And that's what we see going on here. We see an omnipotent, sovereign, loving God choosing Eve. We see God in essence saying, "Yes, Eve, I have chosen you, handpicked you, to marry Adam."

God is the first father to give away a bride in marriage. It is also God that performs the first marriage ceremony. This whole idea of marriage is obviously God's—not ours. Our text today ends with verses 24 and 25, where the "two become one flesh." Clearly, God ordained marriage and was intentional in creating this relationship. He takes two totally separate individuals, a man and a woman, and unites them as one flesh. Becoming one flesh, this unexplainable and unifying experience that occurs during sexual intercourse, is something only God can do. To view sex from this perspective . . . from the perspective that it is God in the spotlight, not the husband nor the wife nor the pastor or priest nor the parents nor the friend that "set you up" on your first date . . . but God. Only God. It is God who created this wonder of becoming one flesh that the world cannot understand and therefore so easily takes for granted by casually entering into sex. To put it bluntly, God created sex.

I have repeatedly heard the testimonies of many who wish they would have remained sexually inactive, or pure, until marriage. They wish they had waited for their spouses. They wish they would have understood this concept of "becoming one flesh" more clearly because now when they have intercourse with their spouses they cannot seem to push away the images, or flashbacks, from previous sexual encounters. It is those images that pervade their minds while they are in bed with their spouses. If you find yourself in this situation today, I would encourage you to begin preparing yourself for sex with your spouse with prayer. Maybe the two of you can join in prayer together. Ask God to protect your mind from thoughts of previous relationships and to focus your mind on Him. Ask God to reveal Himself to you during sexual intercourse with your spouse and for you to see the significance of the marriage union.

In summary, today we have learned the following:

God designed marriage.

As a woman, I have a specific role as a "helper" in my marriage.

It is God who joins together "two as one flesh."

Stay tuned for tomorrow, when we will see the mystery of marriage revealed. Let's close today by taking a self-evaluation of exactly how are we doing in our roles as wives. This is not a time to point fingers at your husband for all the things he could do better. (*Oh, if he would do this, then I would start doing that.*) Nor is it a time to compare your husband to "Mr. Universe," the perfect husband that can do no wrong, the man who has the perfect body, the perfect job, the perfect personality, and is the perfect lover, the perfect parent and the perfect friend. No, this is a time for an honest self-evaluation. Regardless of how I feel or what time of month it is, do I believe that God designed me? Regardless of how I'm being treated, will I honor God by being obedient as a "helper" to my spouse? Regardless of my past, will I trust God's grace in joining us together as one? Even if I'm not married right now, do I believe that God has a plan for my life . . . that He has formed a plan for my life long ago?

> *Lord, I didn't want to be that girl with a messy marriage.*

Write your response to God here:

I wonder how different our lives would be if we started believing and living that His Word is true.

> *God is not human, that he should lie, not a human being, that he should change his mind. Does he speak and then not act? Does he promise and not fulfill?*

> —Numbers 23:19

The Mystery of Marriage

Week 2: Day 5

But why then? Why this whole elaborate marriage thing? Why did God have to do things this way? What is His purpose for marriage?

Everything written in Scripture is to point us toward Christ. St. Augustine made the statement, "Our hearts are restless until we find our rest in Thee." God has pre-wired us, so to say, with a hole or vacuum in our souls designated specifically for Him. He has created us with this void that can only be filled with Him, and that is why we have this innate desire to be in and have relationships. Do you realize that God desires to be in and have a relationship with you? God has chosen you (just as He chose Eve for Adam). I don't know about you—but that sends goose bumps right down my spine. Write out Psalm 149:4 below:

I want to stop for a moment and ask you to pray before reading our Scripture text for the day. Please pray that you will have an open mind and be freed from any negative misconceptions about marriage. Please pray for the Holy Spirit to speak to you today.

Flip over to the New Testament where this great mystery of marriage is further explained. Read Ephesians 5:21–33.

In one word, what is God's directive to men? _____

In one word, what is God's directive to women? _____

Now write out verses 31 and 32 below:

There are clearly three beings involved in this marriage thing: man, woman, and Christ. This profound mystery, the mystery of marriage, is further explained as a reflection of the covenant relationship that Christ has with the church. In other words, *marriage was created to be a reflection of our relationship with Christ.* I think one of the most fundamental truths to wrap our arms around regarding marriage is that it was meant to bring God glory.

To bring God glory means to make His name known. He is worthy of our utmost adoration and praise, and our lives are to be a reflection of Him. We were then, in essence, created to *display* His glory so that He might be known and praised.

So, if marriage was designed to bring God glory, how is it all to work? Let's take a moment to break down these three individual roles:

The Role of the Wife

"Submit to your own husbands as you do to the Lord." (Ephesians 5:22)

This is such a difficult subject to approach because since the fall of Adam and Eve and the entrance of sin into this world, the "ideal" marriage no longer exists. We all have seen marriages flopping around like fish sucking for air because the roles of husband and wife have been misunderstood or misused. In women, we have seen their dominance reign supreme, manipulation and control kick in, and flat out insubordination. We have seen men misuse their authority with physical and verbal abuse. In others, we have seen complete indifference, or a failure to lead. It is difficult for us to grasp how God intended marriage to operate. That's why it is imperative for us to take a fresh look at marriage through God's eyes. We are commanded to submit to our husbands *as we do to the Lord.* What do you think that means?

We must recognize that Paul is instructing us on order in the home. Submission means "to place in order under." The Greek word for *submit* is *hupotasso. Hupo* means "under" and *tasso* means, "to place under or in an orderly fashion."[15] Imagine you are in a terrible storm with hail, wind, and rain beating down on you. Suddenly God throws you an umbrella. You quickly put it up and hand the umbrella to your husband, finding shelter under his arm. He is much taller than you and can protect you from the incoming wind and rain. As long as you stay under his arm, which is under the umbrella, you will stay warm and safe. But if you decide to venture out from his protection, you will once again find yourself being beaten down by the storm. This is how

---

[15]   "Hupotasso." *Bible Study Tools Online,* Bible Study Tools, n.d. Accessed September 3, 2013. http://www. biblestudytools.com/lexicons/greek/nas/hupotasso.html

marriage works: Jesus is the umbrella (the ultimate protection), your husband is the spiritual head of your home, and you can remain safe under your husband's arm. I have learned that there is incredible freedom in submission. As a wife and mother, I can find great relief in not being the spiritual head. When there is a big decision to be made or I don't know what to do, I can go to my husband for the answers. I can find rest in the fact that if he does not know what to do, he will go to the Lord to ask direction. I cannot tell you how many times my husband has provided insight into a situation where I did not see things clearly because my emotions were in mass hysteria.

I know that not everyone is fortunate to be married to a Christian spouse. So, how does the idea of "spiritual headship" apply in your home? Submission is the act of the wife to honor and respect her husband's leadership, as long as it complies with Scripture. A wife should not follow her husband into sin. We, as women, still have a responsibility to God. He is still the head. That being said, we should still respectfully allow our husbands the right to lead. For many years in my marriage, I took on the role of leading in our home. I made all our plans for the weekend, I decided what activities our kids would be involved in, and I scheduled all our family commitments. I took it upon myself to lead the family devotions and to make sure everyone was ready to go to church and had said their bedtime prayers. I decided I would take on this role and responsibility without anyone even assigning me this task. I sort of just owned it. It was mine. And to be honest with you, it became a burden. I would get frustrated when my kids didn't want to do the activities I had decided on. I became mad when my husband was still asleep in bed on a Sunday morning when I thought he should be helping me get everyone ready for church. I was irritated that he did not want to play by my rules. A Christian friend finally peered into my world and told me, "You are not letting Coby lead. Stop doing his job." And so slowly, I let go of the reigns. I began asking my husband what he wanted to do on the weekends. I asked him what activities he thought our kids should be involved in. I let him set his alarm to wake up on Sunday and be the one to wake the kids up in order to go to church. I slowly began letting him make some decisions. Yes, I'll admit it was really awkward at first. It was extremely difficult for me in the beginning. I was so used to being my family's Holy Spirit. I was accustomed to being the one in charge. But now that I no longer wear the pants in my family, I am *free*! There is amazing freedom in letting your husband lead! I had no idea what I was missing out on. I have seen such joy in our family now that we have aligned our lives in accordance with God's order of command.

Are there still times when I feel I know better than my husband? Yes! Each of those times is one more opportunity to learn to "die to myself." Are there times when my husband makes a mistake and I want to rub it in? Absolutely! Those are the times I must remind myself that I make mistakes too and practice humility. Take a moment to ask God to reveal if there are any areas in your marriage that need to be submitted to your spouse. Jot down what God reveals to you here:

The Role of the Husband

"Love your wife as Christ loved the church and gave Himself up for her." (Ephesians 5:25)

I think this advice came as a bit of a surprise to the Jewish men of Christ's time. Women were almost thought of as property, being passed with a dowry from their parents to their spouses. Although submission of the wife to the husband was included in Hebraic law, there was no mention of a man's responsibility to his wife. Shocking, I agree. The original Greek word for love is *agapoa*, meaning "to esteem, love, indicating a direction of the will and finding one's joy in something or someone."[16] Please pay careful attention to the definition declaring love as a "direction of the will." Love is not merely a feeling or an emotion. There are times when you will have to make a decisive choice to love your mate, regardless of how you are feeling, and work at your marriage. I have watched many marriages fail, and one of the most common expressions that I hear is, "I never really loved her"—or "him," since I've equally heard this reasoning from a woman. Falling in love may come easily, but staying in love will take some elbow grease and commitment.

Let's take a look at some biblical principals from Ephesians 5:

1. "Husbands, love your wives, just as Christ loved the church and gave himself up for her" (Ephesians 5:25). Men are to sacrificially love their wives. The paradox is quickly twisted from leadership to servanthood. A husband leads by serving. This is exactly what is spoken in Luke 22:26, where Jesus says, "Let the leader become as one who serves." The husband is to provide a safe environment in his home, not with control and abuse, but rather with humility and love, constantly looking out for the needs of his wife. My husband will tell you that a lightbulb went off in his head when he finally got this concept. He realized that he receives greater joy from serving than from selfishly doing what he wants to do.

2. ". . . to make her holy, cleansing her by the washing of water through the word" (Ephesians 5:26). Under Jewish customs, the bride has a ceremonial bath called "Mikveh" just prior to her wedding. The ritual bath symbolizes being washed from sin so that the wife can enter into her marriage with purity. May we be reminded again that God's primary purpose in marriage is to be glorified, and our earthly marriages give us a visual illustration of our relationship with God. God loved us so much that He sent His son, Jesus, to become a man (John 3:16). Jesus, becoming like man, became a servant, submitting to the will of His Father, so that through His death on the cross we could be made clean. This act of cleansing is referred to as "sanctification," a lifelong work of transforming us into the image of Christ. As the Bible tells us, "And so Jesus also suffered . . . to make the people holy through his own blood" (Hebrews 13:12).

---

[16] Zodhiates Th.D., Spiros. "Strong's G25." *The Complete Word Dictionary: New Testament* (Westminister: AMG, 1998).

Without a doubt, God wants to make us holy and uses marriage as part of this sanctifying work. In our marriages, our sin surfaces quickly. We frequently are more ugly with our spouse than with complete strangers. But in a loving relationship, and with the confrontation of God's Word and the Holy Spirit, there is also restoration. For God's ultimate goal is revealed in Ephesians 5:27. How does God want us to be presented as His bride?

3. "In this same way, husbands ought to love their wives as their own bodies. He who loves his wife loves himself" (Ephesians 5:28). The whole premise of this verse is that we should be as concerned for others' happiness as we are for our own. We are to have this unconditional and unselfish love for others. When we love while expecting nothing in return, that is true love. It is assumed that we all have "self-love" in looking out for ourselves. Most of our days are spent thinking about ourselves. What do *I* have to do today? How does this situation affect *me*? What do others think about *me*? We pay a great deal of time throughout the day thinking just about ourselves. So Christ's command here to husbands is to love their wives with the same amount of love that they have for themselves. The already apparent self-love and adoration that they have for themselves is to be the measuring rod for which they love their wives. (But wives, let's not forget that we too have been given a similar command in Mark 12:31: "Love your neighbor as yourself.")

The Role of Christ

"And the two will become one flesh." (Ephesians 5:31)

And now the mystery of marriage is revealed so that we can clearly see that the purpose of marriage is to provide us with the imagery of Christ and the church. John Piper refers to marriage as a "living drama of how Christ and the church relate to each other."[17]

This triune relationship between husband, wife, and Christ is also exemplified to us in the Trinity: the Father, Son, and Holy Spirit. The persons in the Trinity are constantly and sacrificially putting each other before themselves, loving unconditionally, and as an end result, God is unceasingly happy and glorified. It is as if they are in a beautiful, choreographed dance. Can you remember the days of your courtship, those days when a moment apart seemed like eternity? When you would do absolutely anything for your boyfriend? When you absolutely adored him, and he felt the same about you? Those days were absolute bliss! C.S. Lewis writes, "What does it all matter? It matters more than anything else in the world. The whole dance, or drama, or pattern of this

---

[17]   Piper, John. "Husbands Who Love Like Christ and the Wives Who Submit to Them," *desiringGod*. Last updated June 11, 1989. *http://www.desiringgod.org/resource-library/sermons/husbands-who-love-like-christ-and-the-wives-who-submit-to-them* (September 3, 2013).

three-Personal life is to be played out in each one of us."[18] Whether you are married or not, Jesus is asking you to come join Him in the dance.

I love the idea of our relationship with Christ being a dance. It is a flowing relationship where everyone is mutually giving of himself or herself. Timothy Keller writes, "A self-centered life is a stationary life; it's static, not dynamic. A self-centered person wants to be the center around which everything else orbits . . . Self-centeredness makes everything else a means to an end."[19] But a self-sacrificial life, a life of putting others before ourselves, turns our lives into a beautiful dance.

Lord, I didn't want to be that girl without a partner to dance with.

Whether you are married or single today, I want to invite you to join Jesus in the dance. Write your answer to His invitation today:

However, each one of you also must love his wife as he loves himself, and the wife must respect her husband.

—Ephesians 5:33

---

18   C.S. Lewis, *Mere Christianity* (1952; Harper Collins: 2001), 176.
19   Timothy Keller. *King's Cross* (New York: Penguin, 2011), 8.

Week 3: A Call to Relationship

Day 1—The Bride of Christ

Day 2—High Maintenance

Day 3—Covenant Keeper

Day 4—Cheers

Day 5—Set Apart

HIS BETROTHED

Week 3: Day 1

What exactly does it mean to be the "bride of Christ"? If you've grown up in church, you probably already know that in Scripture "we," the church, are referred to as the bride of Christ and that Jesus is our Bridegroom. If you are new to studying Scripture, and this is your first Bible study, then that may sound a bit freaky to you right now. The thought of you being Jesus' bride may sound a bit outlandish. After all, we are talking about Jesus, a supernatural being, and we are also referring to Scripture, not some sci-fi movie where a human marries an alien. I bet Eve didn't truly get it either. I bet she had no idea that her betrothal to Adam carried such significance. I'm sure she had no insight that there was a much deeper, weightier meaning to being a bride. Surely she never fathomed that her name would be recorded in Scripture, or that she was a part of a much grander story, the redemptive story of Jesus Christ. But my curiosity got the best of me yesterday as I realized that I might not even fully comprehend what it means to be the bride of Christ. For if I did, would it change my life?

What does it mean to you to be the "bride of Christ"?

As written in Ephesians, "'For this reason a man will leave his father and mother and be united to his wife, and the two will become one flesh.' This is a profound mystery—but I am talking about Christ and the church" (5:31–32).

This week we are going to take an in-depth look at the analogies between a traditional Jewish wedding and our marriage relationship to Jesus, the ultimate Bridegroom. The similarities between a Jewish wedding and our relationship with Christ are fascinating! I pray that the length and depth and height and width of God's great love for us will be revealed in our study this week.

The Betrothal

The Jewish marriage process is deliberate and well thought out. It is also incredibly lengthy and formal—no "shot gun" weddings in Jewish tradition. Under Jewish customs in Jesus' day, the groom's father would choose his son's mate. This betrothal could take place at any point in time—when the future mates were mere children all the way up to a year before the wedding day. It would not be uncommon for the husband and wife to meet for the first time on their wedding day.

Read Jeremiah 1:5. How long ago did the Father choose you?

Have you ever thought that the God of the universe has chosen *you* as a mate for His Son, Jesus Christ? Before you were even created, God had predestined that you would be a part of His family. God gazed upon you and chose you for Himself—and you did not have to do a thing to earn His favor. He did not choose you because of how you looked. He did not choose you because of your family heritage. He did not choose you because of your accomplishments or talents. He did not choose you because of your wealth (or lack thereof). He did not choose you because you chose Him. No, He freely chose to choose you!

Read 1 Corinthians 1:26–30. What is God's purpose in choosing?

One of my favorite things about the church is how different we are—all different shapes, sizes, and ages. I love that there are people who will make me laugh when I so desperately need to laugh. I love that there are those who are much wiser than I who freely give out godly counsel. I love that there are those with "childlike faith" who can teach me so much about God with their questions. I love those who just "lay it all out there," vulnerably admitting their sin and struggles, so that I no longer feel all alone. I love those who speak truth into my life . . . as well as those who give encouragement. I am thankful for our differences. We are so different, yet so alike. We are so different in our upbringings, our culture, our families, our looks, our bank accounts, our marital status, our academic education, our successes, our failures, and our talents . . . and yet we have one thing alike. We all have discovered our need for a Savior. We all have realized that we are nothing without Him.

Just for grins, what do you like about your church?

In 1 Corinthians 1:26, Paul instructs us to "Consider your calling!" In other words, we are to think about how we came to Christianity. Have you ever stopped and asked yourself, "Why am

I a Christian?" Have you ever considered it is because God chose you to betroth? There are a lot of misconceptions out there regarding how one becomes a Christian. Many will say that they were born into Christianity. Their parents were Christians, their grandparents were Christians, and therefore, they've come to the conclusion that they automatically are Christians too. They believe it is by birthright that they are Christians, or possibly it is by infant baptism that they are Christians. Both of these conclusions are incorrect.

Then there are some who will say that they are saved because of what they have done. Maybe their salvation is not so much because of their accomplishments or great wealth, but all things considered, they have been "good" people. I mean, they have really tried hard to be good. They haven't done anything terribly bad, such as commit murder or anything. They try to be good neighbors and be considerate of others. Surely a good God would not condemn them to die. But this is incorrect as well. Read Ephesians 2:8–9.

How would you answer the question, "How do you know you are a Christian?"

I like Wayne Grudem's answer to this question. "The answer should be because God in eternity past decided to set his love on me. But why did he decide to set his love on me? Not for anything good in me, but simply because he decided to love me. There is no more ultimate reason than that. It humbles us before God to think in this way. It makes us realize that we have no claim on God's grace whatsoever. Our salvation is totally due to grace alone."[20]

What should be our reaction to God's choosing us?

Assurance of Salvation

Simply knowing that we did not choose God, but rather that He chose us, should give us peace of mind that we do not have to worry about losing our salvation. I know that I can change my mind several times a day. Thankfully, God is not like that. God is the same yesterday, today, and forever (Hebrews 13:8), and we can rest assured that He is not going to change His mind. If you struggle with the thought of losing your salvation, I would encourage you to memorize these Scriptures: "What do you think? If a man owns a hundred sheep, and one of them wanders away, will he not leave the ninety-nine on the hills and go to look for the one that wandered off?" (Matthew 18:12). "I give them eternal life, and they shall never perish; no one will snatch them out of my hand" (John 10:28).

---

20   Wayne Grudem. *Bible Doctrine* (Grand Rapids: Zondervan, 1999), 292.

Exultation and Praise

I can vividly recall when the realization that the "God of the universe chose me" finally registered deep within me. I was so overwhelmed with intense gratitude. I know we have all come from varied backgrounds, but I know deeply from what I have been saved. Watching all the dysfunction in my extended family is just one way that this realization has hit home for me. I humbly realize that this could have been me. It so easily could have been me.

By our not taking any credit for our salvation, all the glory is transferred to God. It diminishes our pride from saying, "I'm so smart that I chose God" or "I'm better than you, because I figured out my salvation." These arguments quickly fall to the wayside, because we realize that it had nothing to do with us. Our salvation is all God. The apostle Paul also recognized that salvation is ultimately up to God. He wrote, "We always thank God for all of you and continually mention you in our prayers . . . For we know, brothers loved by God, that he has chosen you" (1 Thessalonians 1:2, 4). He also wrote, "He predestined us to be adopted as his sons through Jesus Christ, in accordance with his pleasure and will— to the praise of his glorious grace, which he has freely given us in the One he loves" (Ephesians 1:5–6).

Desire to Evangelize

We are not the only ones God has chosen for salvation, for there are many. This should be such an encouragement for us to continue to evangelize and tell others about Him . . . because we know we will have some success in doing so. There are still some people who have never heard and still others who have heard and not yet yielded.

My nine-year-old son loves to fish. He would literally fish every day if possible. However, for the past few months, he hasn't caught a thing. Not only has he not caught a thing, but also he hasn't even gotten a bite. He has tried fishing at different times of day. He has switched around his bait, and still nothing. He has convinced himself that there are absolutely no fish in Lake Austin (even though I've been told it is one of the best fishing lakes in Texas). He has begged us to drive him to a different lake with fish. And yet, as his parent, I know that there are fish out there. I know that he will eventually catch one. He should not give up the fight.

That's what kept the apostle Paul going. He knew that in order to be a "fisher of men," he could not give up the fight. Despite the setbacks, the persecution, and the rejection, he would continue on. He would continue to tell his story of salvation. He knew it was his responsibility to tell—not his responsibility to save (nor convict): "Therefore I endure everything for the sake of the elect, that they too may obtain the salvation that is in Christ Jesus, with eternal glory" (2 Timothy 2:10).

Read Ephesians 1:3-4. And finally, as God's chosen, what have we been given?

Lord, I didn't want to be that girl who took credit for what you've done.

Praise the Lord today for your salvation:

Praise be to the God and Father of our Lord Jesus Christ, who has blessed us in the heavenly realms with every spiritual blessing in Christ. For he chose us in him before the creation of the world to be holy and blameless in his sight.

—Ephesians 1:3–4

Hallelujah and Amen!

HIGH MAINTENANCE

Week 3: Day 2

You can set me down in a mall just about anywhere, and I can get a kick out of just some good ol' people watching. I find people absolutely fascinating—especially women (which is probably part of the reason I am so drawn to women's ministry). Although I would not consider myself a shopaholic, I do enjoy my occasional spending spree at the mall. I may allow myself the pleasure of buying something at a couple of stores. But what so often amazes me is how there are some women who will be carrying a plethora of bags. You can barely see their heads poking through. To me, it looks like they purchased something at every single store in the mall.

I recall one of my favorite "shopping stories." We had just moved to Austin, and my oldest daughter was still in the "assessment" stage of the girls at her new school. She was getting to know them and trying to figure out where she would fit in. She came home astonished after one of her new acquaintances shared that she had bought twenty-seven pairs of shoes over the weekend. That's right, twenty-seven pairs of shoes—and all for her, I presume. My daughter's response was, "Who in the world needs twenty-seven pairs of new shoes?" Although the purchase of twenty-seven pairs of shoes at one time sounds a bit extravagant, I'll be honest—it sounds downright fun, too. I later realized that my shoe count in my closet boasts well more than that number. Of course, they are not all brand spanking new, and I could easily justify why I need every single pair of them. Nonetheless, it is a bit convicting. I realized that I had a lot in common with my daughter's newfound friend.

At first glance, I would have categorized my daughter's friend as "high maintenance," which means, "Requiring a lot of attention. When describing a person, high-maintenance usually means that the individual is emotionally needy or prone to over-dramatizing a situation to gain attention."[21] But then, after my realization that I shared a lot in common with this high school girl, I didn't particularly like this terminology anymore. What the Holy Spirit had revealed to me is that not only in regards to shoes, but in many areas of my life, the shoe of "high maintenance" fits me quite well.

---

[21] A Gianotto, "High Maintenance", *Urban Dictionary*. Last Updated November 3, 2002. *http://www. urbandictionary.com/define.php?term=high%20maintenance* (August 13, 2013).

Just out of curiousity, why do you think that high school girl bought twenty-seven pairs of shoes (not cheap shoes, either, because all twenty-seven pairs came from Neiman Marcus)?

She saw something she wanted and didn't think she could live without it. She thought the purchase of those shoes would buy her happiness, fill her void. She told herself she could not possibly live without that pair of shoes. She justified her purchase that she "had to have them" to complete an outfit. She convinced herself that not just one pair of shoes would do . . . she just had to have more. Maybe she even thought that those shoes would heal an emotional wound, or help her become more popular, or make her feel better about herself. Or maybe she didn't think at all.

That's when the realization of how much I was just like that girl hit me. How many times I had convinced myself that I just had to have something, whether it be a new outfit, a new pair of shoes, a new house, a new car . . . and the list goes on and on. When the newness wore off, I just wanted something else, or more. I realized what a creature of discontentment I am. This hole, or more like vacuum, within me constantly needs to be refilled. It is never satisfied. It is non-ending. More. Give me more.

Have you ever been lured into buying your piece of the pie, thinking this is it; this is what I need . . . only to find out that the satisfaction faded quickly? The buyer's high was only temporary. Write of a recent experience here:

We seek comfort. We are living creatures who want and desire comfort and readily justify why we deserve it. There are so many things that get in my way of fully seeking after God because of my desire for comfort. I like having fun. I love going out to dinner and to the movies. I crave chocolate chip cookies. I carve out time to go to lunch with friends. I even enjoy a good workout. None of these things in and of themselves are wrong. I believe that God wants us to enjoy things here on this earth. He has created the world for our pleasure. However, my desire for comfort, my pursuit for contentment, gets in the way when it takes precedence over my pursuit of God. If I'm filling my day seeking things of this world to bring me joy, then I will never be satisfied.

I seek things other than God because I don't get it. I don't understand that they will never satisfy. I don't realize how quickly my discontentment will return, how I will always want more, and in doing so, I fail to recognize the gift I already have.

Something always comes to fill the empty places. And when I give thanks for the seemingly microscopic, I make a place for God to grow within me.

That's it. That's the answer: being thankful. When I take my eyes off of what I already have, I become ungrateful. At a much deeper level, I take my eyes off of God, because I don't realize the price that has already been paid for me. I become unthankful. I fail to remember the gravity of the debt that was paid for my salvation and me . . . and in doing so, I cheapen the grace that has already been afforded me. I become a high maintenance girl, seeking to have my unmet desires fulfilled through things other than God. Maybe it's because I've forgotten about the price that was paid for me. Let's turn our attention for the remainder of today toward what it cost to purchase a bride according to ancient Jewish customs.

Three Components of the Bride Price

The Mohar

The wedding arrangements would not be completed until the two respective fathers agreed upon the bride price. The father of the groom would pay the bride price, or *mohar*, to the bride's father. The mohar reflected the value of the bride to the groom. Marriage wasn't considered an incidental occurrence between two families, but rather the beginning of a long-term relationship, or alliance, between them. One family would give away their precious daughter in return for a highly valuable and esteemed gift. The bride price was considered a reimbursement to the bride's family for raising her, as well as payment for the loss of their daughter and her contribution to the household chores. The mohar was typically paid with gold or silver, or other fine jewels, and possibly even with the exchange of cattle. It also was customary for this payment to be made with acts of service or labor by the groom. Read Genesis 29:16–18 to see a portrayal of mohar when Jacob is willing to work for the love of his life, Rachel.

Our heavenly Father, God, has also paid a mohar for us. What is the mohar that was paid for us? Read John 3:16 and I John 5:11.

Read 1 Corinthians 6:20. What should be our proper response to the mohar paid for us?

The Mattan

In addition to the mohar, the groom would give the bride a gift as an expression of his love, called the *mattan*. Although the setting certainly wasn't perfect in this marriage proposal, you can get a glimpse of the Jewish customs from Genesis 34:8–12. The mattan was a gift of deep affection that the groom had for his future wife.

Jesus Christ, our groom, has paid the most expensive mattan ever imaginable. He was willing to pay such a high price because of His unending, unconditional love for us. Read John 15:13 and Acts 20:28.

What was the price of the mattan given to you?

As a result of the price that was paid on your behalf, what have you been given? Read Romans 6:23 and 1 John 5:11.

The Shiluhim

We also see a gift given by the father of the bride to his daughter, called the *shiluhim*. The shiluhim was basically a dowry, or portion of his inheritance, to help his daughter begin her new married life.

Likewise, God has given us such a gift to help us begin our new lives in Christ. What is the name of this gift? Read Acts 2:38.

Three gifts were exchanged and yet, interestingly, the bride didn't pay a thing. She had no gift to give. Nothing was required of her. Nothing is required of you. Not even a pair of shoes.

Lord, I didn't want to be that girl who grew unappreciative of the price You paid for me.

Spend time today thanking God for the bride price that was paid.

Salvation is found in no one else, for there is no other name under heaven given to mankind by which we must be saved.

—Acts 4:12

COVENANT KEEPER

Week Three: Day Three

To have and to hold, from this day forward, for better, for worse, for richer, for poorer, in sickness or in health, to love and to cherish till death do us part. And hereto I pledge you my faithfulness.

Vows. Wedding vows. We've heard those words before. But what do those words really mean—especially in our current self-satisfying, pleasure-seeking, and thrill-riding world, where divorce papers stack higher than marriage licenses? Are they merely just words? Or do they actually have some depth, some meaning? Too often we have seen the wedding vows broken, leaving us doubting their sincerity. Why are they so often broken? Deep in our hearts, we want to believe. We want to trust. And yet, so many times, we fail. I admit that I too have failed.

What do you think the wedding vows mean?

Certainly the wedding vows are a public confession of a legal arrangement that we have termed *marriage*. However, I would contend that they are meant to be much more than that. We are stating that we will not jump ship when the going gets tough, but rather that we will have a level of stick-to-itiveness. Not only is a level of legality involved, but also we are declaring that we will put our spouses' needs and wants before our own. Ouch! That's when the going gets especially rough. I would confess that I am happily married—or at least, most of the time—and could also make a pretty good case that I have kept my marriage vows. With my mouth I will say that I have remained faithful; however, I'm afraid that my heart may have made an occasional blunder.

If I had to rewrite my vows, they may realistically sound something more like this: "I promise to complain throughout sickness, unless you make me chicken noodle soup, drive carpool for the day, and let me just lie in bed uninterrupted. I promise I will take for granted our good health and fail to fully recognize all our blessings. I will mumble over measly manna, always wanting our bank account to have more. I'll worry sick and be anxious about everything—especially when we can't pay the mortgage. But don't worry; I will never ever leave me. I will promise to put myself first in the majority of situations. Oh yes, I do. I do."

For Better or for Worse

You've heard the saying that the "grass is greener on the other side of the fence." I think that we often apply that saying to marriage. When I was single, I always had a desire to be married, with the conception that marriage would make me happy. But shortly after marriage, that preconception was blown to pieces because I came to the realization that the grass really wasn't greener on this side of the fence. Marriage was not created to make me happy. Instead, it would take a whole lot of work. It is only now, after many life experiences, that I can say that through the worse times in my marriage, I've been made a whole lot better. It is through those times that I have been molded and shaped like clay to become a better reflection of Christ. It is only God who can transform us into the image He created us to be: "Yet, O Lord, You are our Father. We are the clay, you are the potter; we are all the work of your hand" (Isaiah 64:8).

Think of a difficult experience that refined you and molded you to be more Christlike. Write about that experience here. (I like to call these times "rearview mirror" moments. They are moments that seem excruciatingly difficult at the time, but in proper perspective later on down the road, we can say that those times were so good for us.)

For Richer or Poorer

Have I ever complained when the debts piled higher than our combined paychecks? Have I been upset when I saw new golf clubs sitting in our garage? Have I thought I knew best how to budget our income? Have my wants weighed heavier than his? Has my security system been emotionally unraveled with each unsuspecting difficulty? Share your thoughts:

I confess right now that I, too, am a vow breaker. We've had fights when we are weary and tired. We've battled through debt piled high. Why, we've even blown up at each other in the middle of the supermarket arguing over which brand of peanut butter to buy. I, being the cheap one in the household, wanted to save a buck or two and buy generic. My husband, on the other hand, recognizing that we would never eat peanut butter that tastes like plastic, opted for purchasing

Jif. Yes, I had to learn the hard way why "choosy mothers always chose Jif." We didn't speak to each other the rest of the night.

In Sickness and in Health

Does that mean I will not complain when my husband is sick, lying in bed, and wanting me to wait on him hand and foot? Does that really mean that I should be thankful at these times? Once again, will I have to wait up all night with a sick child? Is it not my husband's turn for such duties? Does that mean I will be a cheerful caretaker when terminal illness uproots our daily routine? What do these words really mean?

To Love and to Cherish until Death Do Us Part

What I have so often failed to recognize is that the traditional wedding vows include the words "I promise to love and to cherish until death do *us* part." I want to point out that the words *love and cherish* are verbs, and verbs require action. They require me to do something for someone else, regardless of how I may feel or the response I may get in return. My end of the bargain is to uphold my husband at *all* times (even though I would rather complain about him in the midst of my girlfriends).

I hereby pronounce that I don't believe the problem lies in the vows themselves, but rather in the vow keepers, or should I say, breakers.

The Covenant

The Jewish marriage covenant is called a *ketubah.* The ketubah covenant is a contract, or binding agreement, between the bridegroom and the bride. Traditionally, it would be presented to the bride in the presence of her father. This contract would declare what he, the bridegroom, would be willing to provide for his bride—much like our wedding vows today—as well as document the bride price he was willing to pay. Furthermore, the ketubah was much like a will. It included provisions for the bride-to-be by naming her as the heir of his estate, should he die.

We see the equivalent of the ketubah in the act of God giving Scripture to the Israelites after Moses had received the Torah on the Mount of Olives. Read Exodus 24:7.

What was given to the Israelites?

What did the Israelites say they would do?

You may have heard the saying that slow obedience is called one thing . . . disobedience. I have come across so many Christians (including myself) who like to pick and choose which parts of the Bible they are going to believe and obey. As if we have a choice. We treat the Bible in the same way we treat a menu. We sit down and may even read it thoroughly, weighing all our options. At the end of the day, we make a decision on what we want to order. We tell our server exactly what we want and how we want it cooked—even down to the minute detail of having our salad dressing on the side. We frequently read our Bibles with the same mindset. We pick and choose. *Oh, I like that verse, and I'm going to memorize that one and stick it on my mirror.* I may even go the extra mile and share it with a close friend. But there are other ones, such as denying myself and picking up my cross and following after Him, that I don't necessarily like the sound of. I don't want to do that today because I've already picked out my agenda. I've already chosen the way I want to live. There are so many verses in the Bible that I don't like the sound of because they are hard and do not come naturally or easily. What are we to do with those verses? What is our covenant vow?

I remember now: *for better, for worse, for richer, for poorer, in sickness and in health, to love and to cherish, till death do us part.* I remember now that I don't get to pick and choose. The Scripture, our covenant, was given to us in entirety. And when I took the vow, I also made a commitment that I would obey. In entirety.

Write out the latter part of Exodus 24:7 . . . but make it personal. Replace the *we* with *I*.

Is the Holy Spirit speaking to you today? Have you been slow to obey in a particular area of your life? Or maybe it's not even been slow obedience; it's been flatout deliberate disobedience. Close with me today by reflecting on the words from the Christian hymn "Come Thou Fount of Every Blessing"[22]:

> Come Thou Fount of every blessing; Tune my heart to sing Thy grace; Streams of mercy, never ceasing, call for songs of loudest praise. Teach me some melodious sonnet, sung by flaming tongues above. Praise the mount! I'm fixed upon it, Mount of God's unchanging love.

> Here I raise my Ebenezer; hither by Thy help I'm come; and I hope, by Thy good pleasure, safely to arrive at home. Jesus sought me when a stranger, wandering

---

22   Robinson, Robert. "Come, Thou Fount of Every Blessing." 1757. Hal Leonard - Digital Sheet Music (HX.17484).

from the fold of God; He, to rescue me from danger, interposed His precious blood.

O to grace how great a debtor daily I'm constrained to be! Let that grace now like a fetter bind my wandering heart to Thee. Prone to wander, Lord, I feel it, prone to leave the God I love; here's my heart, O take and seal it; seal it for Thy courts above.

Lord, I didn't want to be that girl who would be a vow breaker.

Confess your wanderings:

What do you think? If a man owns a hundred sheep, and one of them wanders away, will he not leave the ninety-nine on the hills and go to look for the one that wandered off? And if he finds it, I tell you the truth, he is happier about that one sheep than about the ninety-nine that did not wander off.

—Matthew 18:12–13

CHEERS

Week 3: Day 4

When the bridegroom approached the home of his future bride, he would carry three things with him. We've already discussed two of these items in our previous lessons: a large sum of money, or bride price, and the betrothal contract. But the third item may actually surprise you, especially if you've grown up under a strict Christian code of ethics that suggested, "I don't drink, and I don't chew, and I don't go with boys who do." We're about to see Jesus massively destruct that rule. So, if you are an ardent rule-follower, you better hang on for our wild ride. Following along with Jewish custom, we see that the third item that the bridegroom would carry is a skin of wine. Once the father had approved of the marriage, the young girl would be called in, and they would all drink wine together. This was considered a celebratory communion.

But what was the significance of the wine? Throughout Scripture, we see numerous mentions of wine (235 to be exact). However, I want to turn our attention to one in particular. Please read John 2:1–11.

This story is very familiar to many of us who grew up attending Sunday school. So today, I would like to put this story in context in the hope that we will comprehend the greater significance of Jesus' first miracle. You see, up to this point, Jesus had not really made a public proclamation of His ministry. He had been baptized by John the Baptist in the preceding chapter and picked up a few disciples too. However, there is no mention of Jesus' publicly announcing His mission up to this point. So I find it curious that His very first miracle was turning water into wine. We don't see a lot of bells and whistles to draw attention to Him. In fact, Jesus is sort of a "behind the scenes" guy. No speech is made. He doesn't boast about His grandiose miracle wine. But why? Let's take a closer look.

Jesus is attending a wedding feast when something goes terribly awry. They run out of wine. This should not have come as too much of a surprise, because the typical wedding feast would last up to seven days. There must have been some heavy drinkers in the crowd. However, in that day and age, there was a wine steward who was hired to ensure that this type of catastrophe would not occur. Running out of wine was a complete embarrassment to the groom and his family. Leave it to a woman to be paying attention to the details. In verses 3 and 4, we see Jesus' mother, Mary, was the first to bring this disaster to Jesus' attention.

Mary had pondered many things in her heart. She was keeping track and chronicling all the events that had occurred in Jesus' life. She knew Jesus was the Messiah, and she also believed that He could rectify the current situation. She truly believed that He was who He said He was. At first glance, you may think that Mary was putting Jesus to the test or that she was ready for Him to take center stage. However, we see that Jesus' response was surprising. What did He say to her?

I've never met a bride-to-be who is not obsessively preoccupied with her wedding. When I was single, I would often daydream about what my wedding day would entail. When (if ever) would I get married? When would I meet the man of my dreams? What would he look like? What would my dress look like? Where would my wedding be? What colors would I choose for the bridesmaids to wear? What about the reception? And of course, what about the honeymoon? I had a lot of thoughts and anxiety about that! At this particular moment, when we see Mary approaching Jesus, we see that He is caught off guard. Many commentators believe that Jesus was caught in deep thought about His upcoming wedding day. Every other wedding is just a taste, a glimpse, of the one that is to come. The metaphor of the wedding feast is to point us deeper still. Revelation 19:9 says, "Blessed are those who are invited to the marriage supper of the Lamb." Let's not forget that we are the bride, and Jesus is the Bridegroom. We will one day enjoy uninterrupted joy and intimacy with our Bridegroom. However, Jesus cannot take His mind off of what it will cost to get His bride there. While we are consumed with thoughts of our honeymoon, Jesus is consumed with death. At this moment, Jesus reveals what He came to do. He came to give His blood for our wine. In other words, He is our wine! In the midst of great celebration and joy, Jesus is sipping the coming sorrow so that in the midst of our temporary sorrow (our sorrow here on earth), we might sip of the coming joy.

Jesus fully recognizes that in order for His wedding day to come, He must die for His bride. Our eternal joy is only made possible by the suffering of Jesus. This is the crux of the gospel. That even though we are spiritually ugly, wicked, unkind, selfish, mean, calloused, pious, unlovable, and low . . . God still lavishes His love upon us by sending His son as our groom. I don't know if you can fully grasp this . . . Jesus is your groom!

Jesus then takes six large jars that were typically used for ceremonial washing and told the servants to fill them with water. I love the symbolism in this small act! When we partake in communion, when we drink from the cup and partake of the wine, we are then washed clean by the blood of Christ. Only His blood makes us clean! In essence what Jesus is telling us is this—we are no longer bound by the law and the ritual acts of purification. There is nothing that we can do to make ourselves right before God. But by drinking from His cup, we have been set free. Write the warning for us found in 1 Corinthians 7:23.

We are told in John 2:6 that each of these stone water jars held between twenty and thirty gallons. Applying simple mathematics, that equates to between 120 and 180 gallons of wine in total. This wasn't cheap wine in a box, either. The master of ceremonies notices that the best wine, which is normally served first, has been saved for the end.

Nothing is too small for God. Jesus could have easily ignored His mother's request and done nothing. But having compassion for the master of ceremonies, He permitted the party to go on. He saved this man from complete embarrassment and the unemployment line. I believe that Jesus wanted the party to go on! He wants us to enjoy life here on earth. There is nothing wrong with having a good time (within the boundaries of Scripture). It's okay to have fun! The Bible frequently associates wine with blessing and joy. Read the following verses and note the references to wine: Joel 3:18, Amos 9:13, and Isaiah 25:6–8.

Throughout this story, we are being pointed to the final feast that is yet to come. We are filled with just a glimpse of what that glorious feast will entail. There will be no shortage of food and wine. While we are still here on earth, we are being invited to "come"—to come participate in life with Him and to drink from His cup. "Taste and see that the Lord is good" (Psalm 34:8a).

What promise are we given in Jeremiah 29:13? How are we to seek God?

When we seek God with all our hearts, our eyes will be opened to the wonderful things found in His Word (Psalm 119:18). Take in the beauty and splendor of God. Go ahead and drink from his cup. Luke 24:30–31 says, "When he was at the table with them, he took bread, gave thanks, broke it and began to give it to them. Then their eyes were opened and they recognized him." Let's make a renewed commitment today to seek Him with all our hearts. I don't want to miss out on all the wonderful things found in His Word, do you? I don't want to miss out on a life spent with Him.

Jesus gives us an amazing example of Communion, commonly known as the Last Supper. In closing, read this text and imagine yourself as a participant at the table.

Matthew 26:26–28 says, "While they were eating, Jesus took bread, and when he had given thanks, he broke it and gave it to his disciples, saying, 'Take and eat; this is my body.' Then he took a cup, and when he had given thanks, he gave it to them, saying, 'Drink from it, all of you. This is my blood of the covenant, which is poured out for many for the forgiveness of sins.'"

When I think about partaking in real communion with Jesus Christ, my Lord and Savior, the One and only, Holy God in the flesh, I cannot help but tremble. Let's be honest; real communion is scary. It takes your breath away. You are being asked to come and join Jesus in holy matrimony. To live in union with Him. He is giving an invitation to you when He says, "Come." It seems overwhelming and daunting. It's as if you've won the lottery! Your name has been selected. Then reality sets in, and not only do you realize that you've won the lottery, but there are also some choices that need to be made in how you spend your winnings. Yes, you have won—but now how will your winnings change the way you live?

If Jesus is truly your lottery, then how has He affected the way you live?

Walter Brueggemann says it like this: "The shock of such a partner destabilizes us too much. The risk is too great, the discomfort so demanding. We much prefer to settle for a less demanding, less overwhelming meeting. Yet we are haunted by the awareness that only this overwhelming meeting gives life."[23]

David Platt puts it even more bluntly, "To everyone wanting a safe, untroubled, comfortable life free from danger, stay away from Jesus."[24]

But let me add one more comment: to live life without Christ is a choice not to live. Think about it. Now go out and live! Go out and live for Christ, and enjoy the wild ride! Now, I'll drink to that!

Lord, I didn't want to be that girl who missed out on communion with You.

Ask the Lord to speak to you personally today and to teach you how to live.

Remain in me, as I also remain in you.

—John 15:4

---

23   Walter Bruggemann, *Finally Comes the Poet* (Minneapolis: Fortress, 1989), 45.
24   David Platt, *Radical* (Colorado Springs: Multnomah, 2010), 167.

SET APART

Week 3: Day 5

Once the bridegroom paid the purchase price, the marriage covenant was thereby established, and the young man and woman were regarded as husband and wife. From that moment on, the bride was declared consecrated or sanctified, set apart exclusively for her bridegroom.

At this point, the bridegroom would leave to prepare their future dwelling place. The wedding vow would not be consummated (meaning, no hot and heavy sex) until a later time, a time when the bridegroom would return for his bride. In the meantime, the bride would wait. And wait. And wait.

We've all heard the saying that "absence makes the heart grow fonder." This certainly can be the case. However, more of the norm is that "absence makes the heart wander." I imagine this time of waiting was extremely difficult, and can I add that it was *long*? Waiting for something that we are highly anticipating makes time stand still. I swear the clock stops ticking. We live in a day and age when we want everything instantaneously, and our expectations have quickened with every update in technology. We want our fast food faster and our lines shorter. No one likes to wait. This time away from her bridegroom was intended to make the bride anxious, or excited, for the return of her man. There was supposed to be this feeling of anticipation for her bridegroom. This feeling of "I can't wait for his return!" Hang on to your horses, because we will dive more into that topic next week.

Today, I want to focus our attention on what the bride was to do while she waited. I had the luxury, if you could call it that, of waiting today in a doctor's office. I realized that it didn't take very long for me to become very fidgety. I had quickly flipped through every magazine in sight, none of which I was particularly interested in reading in the first place. I also had read and answered every single email waiting in my inbox. I tried playing a mindless game on my iPhone, and I thought about listening to some iTunes to help with the jitters. But the heavy anticipation of what could possibly lie ahead kept me, to say it simply, waiting. After all, who can really engage in reading or playing games when you are waiting to see the doctor! You see, I had a ski accident last week while enjoying spring break vacation with my family. There was a ski jump in the terrain park that I had finally gotten up enough courage to try the day before. I took the jump really slow on my initial attempt, probably leaving the ground by only an inch or so. I knew I could do

71

better, and my husband's last words to me went something like this, "Let me see you catch some method air." (In case you are wondering what "method air" is, it is a snowboarding term that my brother-in-law indoctrinated me on, meaning "some wicked cool trick.") I really felt that I was up for the challenge. As a novice skier, I decided to take the jump with some speed this time around. I skied straight toward the jump. Apparently, I had plenty of speed and never heard my husband screaming at the top of the mountain, "No, no!" Needless to say, I completely cleared the down-sloped landing (where you are supposed to land). When I should have started my descent, I was still ascending. This was so much the case that my fall was approximated around ten to twelve feet. That's equivalent to getting a running start and jumping off a one-story building. (No doubt, my blondness really does run through and through.) Fast-forward a week, and I find myself awaiting an MRI to see what is going on to cause the swelling and pain around my knee.

Clearly I wasn't adequately prepared for that ski jump that day. Although I've skied many a time, I tend to suit myself quite well by staying on the blue runs. This day was different, though. I had convinced myself that I could do that jump. Why, even my kids were doing it . . . why couldn't I? My problem, however, did not lie in the steepness of the slope or my own personal athleticism. The problem lay in my lack of knowledge and training. I was completely unprepared. In fact, I'd go as far as to say that I was arrogant in thinking that I could catch some gnarly air.

The time the bride spent away from her groom was to be a time for her to prepare herself (body, soul, and mind) for the task that lay ahead of her as a married woman. It was a time for her to get ready, to train herself in the duties of womanhood. Analogous with the Jewish bride being declared to be sanctified or set apart exclusively for her groom once the marriage covenant was established, the church has been declared to be sanctified or set apart exclusively for Christ. The word *sanctification* certainly doesn't come up in our day-to-day conversation very frequently. However, it is a term that we should be familiar with and come to grips with. *Sanctification* comes from two Latin words: *sanctus*[25], which means *"holy,"* and *ficare*, which means *"make."*[26] Throughout Scripture, we will find many references to the work of sanctification. Let's go ahead and get familiar with a few.

Please read 1 Corinthians 1:2. What are we called to be?

Read 1 Corinthians 6:9–11. Pay particular attention to verse 11. What three things have happened to us?

Once we have accepted Jesus Christ as our Lord and Savior and asked for the forgiveness of sins, we are forgiven. Our sins have been washed away. Psalm 103:12 tells us, "As far as the east is from the west, so far has He removed our transgressions from us." Furthermore, we have been

---

[25]   "Sanctus." Latin Def. *Dictionary.com*, Random House Dictionary, n.d. Accessed September 11, 2013. http://dictionary.reference.com/browse/Sanctus

[26]   "-ficare." Latin Suffix Def. *myEtymology.com*. Etymologia, 2008. Accessed September 11, 2013. http://www.myetymology.com/latin/-ficare.html

set apart and sanctified, which we will dive further into in just a second. We are also told that we are justified. We are able to have right standing before God because of the redemptive work that Jesus Christ did on our behalf. All three of these things are possible in the name of Jesus Christ and by the Holy Spirit. Hang with me here to get this point: when you get married, you take your spouse's last name. As a believer, you have been given a new name as well. You are now named after Christ. You are a Christ follower, a disciple of Jesus.

Write out 2 Corinthians 5:17.

Please also write out 1 Peter 2:9.

Throughout Scripture, God was in the habit of giving people new names. Some notable examples are changing Abram to Abraham, Sarai to Sarah, and Jacob to Israel. In the New Testament, we see Saul of Tarsus become Paul and Simon-Cephas become Peter. I love how God gave these people new lives and new identities. For example, Simon-Cephas was an obstinate, impulsive, easily angered, argumentative, and prideful man. Then Jesus comes along and renames him (see Matthew 18). Our obstinate Simon-Cephas is renamed Peter, meaning *rock*. We might have only seen the man who tried to walk on water but failed, who refused to have his feet washed by Jesus, who rebuked Jesus, who cut off the soldier's ear with a sword, who deserted his best friend during his death, and who infamously denied Christ three times. Well, guess whom Jesus saw? He saw a pillar for the church. He saw the man who would bring three thousand souls to Christ on the Day of Pentecost. He saw the man who would someday write Scripture. He saw the man who would courageously give his life as a martyr for Christ. Jesus sees our potential, not our past. Take a moment and praise God for that!

We can't just stop there. We can't just take our new name and not act on it. We can't behave the same ol' way. No, we have to change. It will take some effort on our parts. We will need to inform our employers of our name change and also the IRS. Our social security cards and passports and driver's licenses all need some updating. Not only do we need to make a formal and legal name change, but we also need to start acting like it. If a married person continues on in her "singleness," let me tell you something: there will quickly be some marital discord. If you still behave like a single, dating around and hanging out at the bars, then no one will even be able to recognize that you are married. Imagine, if you are married, if you still talked as if you were single and flirted with cute guys. Or what if you acted like you were single and tried to get dates? Maybe even at home with your new spouse you continued on in this regard, watching your favorite TV shows, talking incessantly on the phone with your friends, working out on a whim . . . paying no attention and having no regard for your new spouse, or your new name. I may not be a marriage counselor, but still I would like to ask the question, "And how is that working out for you?"

Unfortunately, many of us treat our mate, Jesus, in that same way. We have forsaken our first love and completely forgotten about our new name. We have gone back to doing what we like and making choices for how we spend our time. We have fallen back into our old habits and rhythms, taking little consideration of what Jesus would have us do. We rarely talk to Him, let alone spend any quality time with Him. What about listening to Him? Have we forsaken that altogether?

James 1:22 says this: "Do not merely listen to the word, and so deceive yourselves. Do what it says." To be "set apart" and sanctified does not mean to sit idly. It means to be obedient. Real faith is demonstrative. It means to be intentional and deliberate in how we spend our time. I've spent nearly a lifetime watching Christians sit idly watching the world go by, growing numb to the lostness around them. They have been regulars in filling up the church pews. Besides helping the janitorial staff dust the pews, they've done little else to make a difference for the kingdom of God. They have Sunday church attendance down pat. But take a look at how they spend their time the remainder of their 164 hours in a week, and you probably would not be too surprised. They spend more time watching their favorite television shows than reading their Bibles. They spend more time talking on the phone than they spend in prayer. They use more time sitting in traffic than at the feet of Jesus, listening. They spend more time exercising than doing or seeking the will of God. They spend more time in their holy huddle than in reaching the world. (Ouch, that last one might hurt.)

If the Holy Spirit is starting to prick a little bit in your heart today, that is a good thing. I'm right there with you . . . I can feel it too. I have substituted my own agenda and preferences and idols for Jesus far more than I am comfortable admitting. Conviction can be a good thing if it results in change. Scripture is given to us to not only penetrate, but also to activate. Reflecting back on 1 Corinthians 6:11, it is the Holy Spirit that spurs in us to change. When the Holy Spirit does His job, He convicts and compels us to action. Please read James 2:17. For what is faith without works? Without change?

According to the *Word Biblical Commentary*, the Greek verb forms in this verse could be restated like this, "If a person *keeps on saying* he or she has faith, but *keeps on having* no works," (emphasis added)[27] then the person may not be saved.[28] Our actions are evidence of our salvation. If we are not motivated to do good works out of compassion and love for our Savior, it may be a result of our own callousness, or growing numb.

Read Ephesians 4:19. What has been lost? _____

It is the words of the last line, "a continual lust for more," that really strike me. *Pause*. It is that incessant desire for more and more that continuously gets me in trouble. It is the truth that I

---

[27]   Ralph P. Martin, *Word Biblical Commentary*, vol. 48 (Nashville: Thomas Nelson, 1988), 80.

[28]   Beth Moore, *James: Mercy Triumphs* (Nashville: LifeWay Press, 2011), 101.

frequently desire things other than God. It is those few little things that cause my downward spiral, the things in my daily life that I use to replace God. They are my self-indulgences. Yes, it is a slow fade. I say no to God a few times, and before I know it, it becomes easier and easier to say no. Whatever becomes common to us quickly becomes *invisible* to us. We become insensitive to our own sins as we become more comfortable with them. Like a pair of favorite old jeans, we just like 'em. This verse describes this type of eroding away as callousness. Calluses form due to excessive use of a particular body part, whether it is a foot, hand, finger, etc. Once a callus has formed, the feeling on that body part is gone.

When our sin becomes commonplace in our lives, we are no longer able to see it. We become immune to its numbing effects, and furthermore, we become immune to the nudging of the Holy Spirit. We tend to think of those who are "continually lusting for more" as the non-contributors in our society. Images of drug addicts and alcoholics may quickly come to your mind. We don't tend to think of addicts as people who wear suits and ties, live in the suburbs, coach our children, teach our Sunday school classes, run successful businesses, or push baby strollers. But the truth is, they are. We all are. The addict you know best is the one wearing your own clothes. The honest truth is we all are prone to addictions. We all are easily caught up in our latest business venture, one more glass of wine, a lottery ticket, our kids, the corporate ladder, the latest diet . . . sex, power, fame. We want more . . . we *continually lust for more*. It is a continuous battle to fight the fight against more!

The addictions of this world are so appealing, so anesthetizing. An addiction can be anything in your life that you are unwilling or possibly even unable to give up. It is that something in your life that you cannot live without. The rich young ruler wouldn't give it up (Matthew 19:22). Agrippa wouldn't give it up (Acts 26:28). Judas wouldn't give it up (John 12:4–6). The Pharisees wouldn't give it up (John 9:24–29). Countless others in this world, believers and unbelievers alike, won't give it up either.

My good news for the day—I don't need surgery. The MRI revealed that my meniscus looks fine and that there are no bone fractures. The swelling around my knee is due to a partial tear in the medial collateral ligament. It's nothing that wearing a knee brace for six weeks can't repair! For that, I am rejoicing! If only all of me wasn't in desperate need of repair. I am confronted with the truth today, that my "continual lusting for more" will require the need of a surgeon, a very gifted and masterful surgeon. For my heart is in continual need of repair.

Be honest with yourself today. Is there an area of your life that "continually lusts for more"? An area that is never satisfied? An area that you can't imagine living without? Are you able to say the words of the psalmist, David, "I seek you with all my heart; do not let me stray from your commands" (Psalm 119:10)?

I've always loved the words from Casting Crowns' song, "Slow Fade."[29] I think they encapsulate our conversation from today quite well.

Be careful, little eyes, what you see.
It's the second glance that ties your hands as darkness pulls the strings.
Be careful, little feet, where you go, for it's the little feet behind you that are sure to follow.

It's a slow fade when you give yourself away.
It's a slow fade when black and white have turned to gray.
Thoughts invade, choices are made, a price will be paid when you give yourself away.
People never crumble in a day.
It's a slow fade; it's a slow fade.

Be careful, little ears, what you hear.
When flattery leads to compromise, the end is always near.
Be careful, little lips, what you say, for empty words and promises lead broken hearts astray.
The journey from your mind to your hands is shorter than you're thinking.
Be careful if you think you stand; you just might be sinking.
It's a slow fade . . . People never crumble in a day

Lord, I didn't want to be that girl with an addiction!

Thank you, God, for giving me a remedy:

You, dear children, are from God and have overcome them, because the one who is in you is greater than the one who is in the world.

—1 John 4:4

---

29   Hall, Mark. *Slow Fade*. Casting Crowns, 2008. Digital Download.

WEEK 4: GETTING GROUNDED

Day 1—The Wait

Day 2—Reality Check

Day 3—Great Fanfare

Day 4—Change Is Comin'

Day 5—Spring-Cleaning

THE WAIT

Week 4: Day 1

The young groom will quote the words from John 14:1–3 prior to his departure. Let's begin our study for today with that text. Remember, the young groom is about to depart from his new bride and go away for some time to prepare a room for them. Typically, this would mean adding on a room to his father's house and could take up to two years to be completed. He promises that when the construction is complete, he will return for her, and they will forever be together from that point forward. The chamber that is being built is referred to as a *chuppah*, or honeymoon bed.

Many nosy neighbors will begin asking the groom when he will be done. "How much longer?" they will ask. I'm sure that the bride is thinking the same. Oh, how quickly I am reminded of the many family road trips that we've had. Just minutes after getting on the road, one of my kids will quip, "How much longer?" As if I don't feel the same agony. But the irony of it all is that our journey has just begun. We have hours ahead of us before reaching our final destination.

Jesus, our Bridegroom, will not be hurried. He does not operate according to our time. But how often do I feel just like my kids on an insanely long road trip? They've not been given a road map, so all they can do is trust the driver behind the wheel. They cannot fully comprehend the length of the drive. The explanation of "an hour" means nothing to them. The best I can do is to quantify time with how many movies they will watch along the way. A drive to Houston is a two-movie drive, a drive to Dallas is more likely a three. But even that doesn't quite register. I still persistently receive the inevitable question of, "Are we there yet?"

Time is difficult to quantify. Our grade school teachers have done their best to lay ground rules for how to tell time, but no one can quite explain how there are situations during which time seems to be on speed dial, as if someone has magically turned the hands on the face of the clock. It's then that time disappears quickly, before you even know it. The treasured time you spend with a loved one or dear friend, the time you have before a difficult assignment or task is due, or the dear time that is run out with errands and last minute chores before it's "pickup" time at your child's school: no one can really explain what happens to that time. On the contrary, there's also the time that never seems to end. Some things never seem to come quickly enough. As much as we try to hurry things along, the hands on the clock don't seem to budge. They stand still, just as they do when you cannot fall asleep and you've counted all the sheep in your head. It's the same when you are waiting for the test results from your doctor's office or waiting for your body to heal and recover from an illness or injury. Oh yes, time can drag on.

What time are you in right now? Is time speeding by or slowing down?

Imagine attending a wedding where the bride and the bridegroom are from two contrastingly different "time" cultures. The bride's side of the family is always on time and errs on arriving early. You will find them sitting in the front row of every concert, being the first in line for the next "freebie" on Black Friday (that is, the shopping day after Thanksgiving, just in case you're not from a family like mine), and going to bed before nine so that they can rise at the crack of dawn. This family's motto is "the early bird gets the worm." On the other hand, the bridegroom's family is never in a hurry. They easily lose track of time or pay no mind to it to begin with. The school registrar has called them umpteen times to discuss their incessant number of tardies. They go to bed late and enjoy sleeping in. Their family motto goes something like this: "better late than never."

On the left side of the sanctuary, you will find hand-wringing and text messages flying. Worry is written on every face. On the right side, no one has even noticed a reason for concern. It hasn't even dawned on them that the wedding is running late. There is no sense of hurry. My point is this: timing is relative. Just out of curiosity, what side of the sanctuary would we find you sitting on?

To put everyone at ease, I want to make it clear that God's sense of timing will confound all of us. There will be times when we want Him to speed up and we cannot wait for His return. We think we can't wait to exit this planet earth because the pain and suffering seem too hard. There will be other times when we have completely taken our eyes off of Him, where we haven't thought about His coming back for us in months. We are having so much fun down here that we can't imagine life being much better than this.

A few months ago a pastor from my church, Halim Suh, preached a sermon entitled, "And Then They Will Fast" from Mark 2:18–22. Please read this text now. It is here that we see Jesus instructing His disciples to wait to fast until He has departed from them. Once again we see Jesus compare Himself to a bridegroom. Since the Jewish wedding is such a joyous occasion, it would not make any sense to deprive oneself of the wedding banquet. It would be unthinkable to fast during this time, because a fast was associated with sorrow. However, Jesus goes on to say that once the Bridegroom has been taken from them, fasting would be appropriate. We, in fact, should fast.

However, we rarely talk about fasting, even in our Christian circles. Surely you've heard more sermons on prayer and obedience and money management than you have on fasting. What exactly is fasting, anyway? Fasting is depriving yourself of food so that you can focus on the depravity of your own soul. Halim Suh says this in regards to fasting: "Fasting is a distinguishing factor of one who loves Jesus." I'm right here with you on this one . . . fasting is difficult, and my flesh doesn't like it. I don't like the feeling of being exceedingly hungry. I don't like depriving myself of food. But why are we to fast? We are to fast in obedience to God. The primary purpose of fasting is to express our longing for Christ's return. The Jews would fast because they were desperate for His return. The cry of the early church was "Oh, Lord, come! Oh, Lord, come back!"[30]

Just out of curiosity, when was the last time you fasted? What was your purpose for fasting? Did you fast for an urgent prayer need . . . or like so many women I know, did you fast out of response to a sermon you heard but internally thought, "Well, I did want to lose a few pounds"? Did that, therefore, become your primary reason for the fast?

The question posed during this convicting sermon was this: "Are you avoiding the practice of fasting because you are not longing for Jesus' return?" To put it another way, do you long for Christ's return? If you do, then you will fast. Jesus connects fasting with His second coming. Is your heart crying for His return? If not, are you brave enough to reflect within and ask why?

Growing up, I fantasized about being married. I would dream and imagine what my future husband would look like. By the time college came around, I began to date more frequently. I dated around like crazy, looking for the man of my dreams. That period of looking and waiting seemed like forever. There was a desire and longing in me to be married. I desired for someone I had not yet met. Then, my senior year in college, I was introduced to a guy named Coby. He wasn't like anyone else I had ever dated. I wanted to spend every waking moment with him. I could not wait until I would see him again. This feeling was more intense than any longing I had experienced before. We were engaged that summer and set our wedding date thirteen months away. Those thirteen months seemed like an eternity! Why? Because now I *knew* who my bridegroom was, and all I could think about was being with him, being his, and him being mine. This longing and desire was much stronger and deeper than I had experienced before I knew him.

We should feel this same kind of intensity in longing for the return of our Lord and Savior, Jesus Christ. We should be anxiously waiting for His return. However, we may not feel that way because we have become too comfortable here. We've made our mind up about things that we want to accomplish here on this earth: graduating from college, having children, earning a job promotion, watching our children grow up, and so on. Are there things in your life that you desire more than Christ's return? Let me word it like this: "Once I _____ (fill in the blank), then I'm okay with Christ coming back."

---

[30] Halim Suh, *And Then They Will Fast* (sermon), Austin Stone Community Church, March 4, 2012, audio recording. http://austinstone.org/sermons/item/and-then-they-will-fast.

Circle back with me to our initial text at the onset of today's lesson, John 14:1–3. Please write out John 14:1 in the space below:

Two opposing forces are at work here: faith and fear. Both faith and fear are an unshakable belief in an unseen future. Neither is merely emotional, but both are spiritual forces. The only difference between the two is that one believes God will come through for you—and the other believes that He won't. One believes that God will know what is best for you—and the other does not. One puts God in the driver's seat—and the other does not.

Can you think of any other contrasting statements between faith and fear?

It is impossible to be fully trusting God and to be filled with fear simultaneously. They cannot coexist. As is written in 2 Timothy 1:7, "For God did not give us a spirit of timidity, but a spirit of power, of love and of self-discipline."

The times in my life when I've been given over to fear are the times when I've taken control of my situation. I've tried to fix the problem, but it hasn't quite turned out as I thought it would, and then fear comes creeping in. Fear takes over when I rely on myself and find myself in a pickle because I don't see any way out. I can't come up with a solution. Things are not turning out as planned.

What about you? Have you ever been filled with fear?

When I finally surrender to Jesus and go to Him for help, seldom do things turn out as I expect. Some of life's curveballs have thrown me for a loop, but what I have received from God in return has been worth the ride. Jesus looks us square in the eye and poses the question, "Will you trust Me? Do you believe that what I have in store for you is better than anything that this world has to offer? Will you trust Me with your plans, your life, and your agenda? Will you trust Me with your children? Will you trust Me with your career? Will you trust Me when I say that I will return for you?" Oh, dear sister, will you trust Me?

There is an old illustration that brings the concepts of faith and fear into better focus. Imagine yourself near the beautiful and dangerous Niagara Falls. Suppose a circus performer has strung a rope across the falls with the intention of pushing a wheelbarrow to the other side. If he loses his balance, he will surely drown or be crushed in the churning waters below. Just before stepping on the rope, the stunt man turns to you and says, "Do you think I can accomplish this feat?"

You reply that his reputation has preceded him and that you fully believe that he has the ability to walk the tightrope. In other words, you believe he will succeed.

But then he says, "If you really believe that I can do it, how about getting in the wheelbarrow and crossing to the other side with me? How about going with me?" All of a sudden, it becomes an invitation of trust.

In the same way, God's reputation precedes Him. Sure, we believe that He parted the Red Sea and turned the water into wine. We believe that He is great and mighty. We believe that He is real. Yes, we have faith. Yet, when the invitation includes us—when we are asked to join Him on the journey and jump into the wheelbarrow, to let Him steer the way—we aren't quite so sure anymore. No longer is it just a matter of faith, but one step further—it is trust. Do we trust Him? Trust involves a level of risk, and risk involves a level of action.

We often want to hurry God along and, in our impatience, to take over the driver's seat. We want to be in control, but inevitably what we discover is that we cannot hurry God. There is a lesson to be learned in the waiting. The delays in my own life have always been filled with purpose.

It makes me sad that I have chosen to place things in priority over Christ. He has done so much for me, yet I find myself filling my day with stuff that I think is more important. I fill my day by thinking about all the stuff I want to do and accomplish, without once even considering that this could be the day Jesus returns. Would I be ready? What would He find me doing?

Lord, I didn't want to be that girl who continually lusted for things other than You.

Think about our lesson today. Are you ready for Christ's return? Are you living your life as if you believe He could come back today?

When everything is ready, I will come and get you, so that you will always be with me where I am.

—John 14:3, NLT

REALITY CHECK

Week 4: Day 2

To talk about this wedding stuff day after day may seem a bit boring to you. Or worse, it may seem as if you've just stepped into a reality TV show where you've married Jesus . . . it just seems a bit, well, weird. How do you pull this idea that Jesus is your mate into your everyday life scenario that is steeped full of laundry, taxi-driving the kids from here to there, making ends meet, and working nine to five? If you find yourself asking the question, "What does this all have to do with me?" I want to encourage you to keep up with the ride. The purpose of this Bible study is to encourage you to continue studying God's Word, making sense of it little by little, so that you will discover a great love affair with Jesus. We have a difficult Scripture waiting ahead for us tomorrow. Before we approach it, I want to make sure we are buckled in for the ride.

If you're anything like me, there is a time in your life when you will ask yourself the questions, "Well, what in the world is it that I am supposed to be doing?" "Why on earth am I even here?" "Am I living the life that God intended for me?" and "God, if You are up there, what is it that You want me to do?" Let's face it; even for those of us who've been reared in the church, living a life of purpose for Him is not always that easy to do.

There are two main reasons for that, I believe. For one, we may know what God wants us to do, but plainly and simply, we just don't want to do it. We'd rather live our lives in our own comfort zones and according to our own purposes. It sure does sound more controllable and palatable than following the will of God. And therefore, out of pure rebellion and with little hesitation, we rewrite Luke 9:23 to read, "Whoever wants to live a life of unending dissatisfaction must deny God, take up their own burdens, and follow their own selfish pursuits." I have to admit to you that I find myself falling into the same trap over and over again as well. We all have succumbed to this temptation, living our lives for ourselves rather than for God. But what Luke 9:23 actually says is this: "Then Jesus said to them all, 'Whoever wants to be my disciple must deny themselves and take up their cross daily and follow me.'"

It is so easy to go through this life making our own decisions and facing our personal circumstances and challenges without even considering God or what His response may be. We so easily forget to include Him in our everyday. And before long, we have traveled down this road called life, only calling on Him during life's greatest triumphs or overwhelming pitfalls. We call on ourselves to decide which way to turn, what car to buy, where to enroll our kids in school, what job and career path to pursue, where to attend church, where to live, who to marry, and so much more. And yet, I believe, God wants to be involved in our day-to-day. He is a God who is concerned about the details or minutia of our everyday lives.

On a scale of one to ten, rate your current prayer life with one meaning, "I barely utter a word to God" and ten meaning "I pray without ceasing" (1 Thessalonians 5:17).

One_____Ten

If we can learn to trust God with the little things, we will be more prepared to turn over to Him the big things too. It's so easy for us to get into the habit of living our lives without God. For some, including God in their lives means merely attending church occasionally. For others, it means being involved in countless church activities and being a regular attendee at Bible study. Still others will kick it up a notch and sing in the choir or teach a Sunday school class. Unfortunately, we can do all of those things and still be living lives without any communication (or only the bare minimum) with God. Our prayer life may simply consist of a quick prayer before a meal or a shotgun prayer before bed.

The funny thing is, God already knows the little things. He knows every thing there is to know about us. He knows what you will chose to wear tomorrow before you even take a step out of bed. He knows what you will have for breakfast. He knows what you are thinking about your friend, even though you may say something entirely different out loud. He knows how you feel—physically, spiritually, and emotionally. He gets you! He understands you! Why in the world we avoid talking to Him or don't give Him the time of day doesn't reconcile. It doesn't make any sense.

Read Psalm 139:1–18. After reading today's main text, describe in your own words what God knows about you.

The truth is that God knows everything about you and desires to have intimacy with you. The entire Scripture is pointing to a love story where the God of the universe sends His only Son to die on the cross for our sins, so that we can have a relationship with God. It doesn't take a psychologist to diagnose that a relationship cannot survive without communication.

Read John 17:3. What is our ultimate purpose in life?

God desires that we *know* Him and His Son, Jesus Christ. Not that we merely *know about* Him. For even the demons know who Jesus is and tremble at His name (James 2:19). But rather, our primary purpose is to intimately and deeply know Him by being in a relationship with Him. To be in a relationship with Him means to spend time with Him. Communication is a two-way street, a time of talking and also listening.

If I did all the talking when my kids arrived home from school and told them all about my day, never lending an ear to hear about their day, I would eventually know nothing about their friends, their likes and dislikes, their troubles, or their accomplishments. If I never let them get a word in edgewise but rather dominated the conversation, they would eventually tune me out (as if that isn't already a struggle for a parent of two teens). No, I have to bend over backwards to pay attention to what they are saying. I have a deep desire to know my children and stay connected with them. But if I'm not willing to give them the time of day, there will soon be a great disconnect.

God wants to have a conversation with us, and this conversation is a two-way street. I love the words of John 15:15: "I'm no longer calling you servants because servants don't understand what their master is thinking and planning. No, I've named you friends because I've let you in on everything I've heard from the Father" (MSG). I believe that Scripture is God's inerrant word, and it is certainly the primary way He communicates with us. He has given us the gift of the Holy Spirit to help illuminate the Scriptures so that we can make personal applications of His Word. Make no mistake: God does still speak today! Later in the book of John, the Bible tells us, "But when he, the Spirit of truth, comes, he will guide you into all the truth. He will not speak on his own; he will speak only what he hears, and he will tell you what is yet to come. He will glorify me because it is from me that he will receive what he will make known to you" (John 16:13–14).

The other reason that we settle for a mediocre Christian life is that we have come to a point where we have a difficult time discerning and hearing the voice of God. We may have the desire to do what God has called us to do and to go where He wants us to go. But, amid all the noise of our current culture, we have an extremely difficult time discerning God's voice. We may believe that we have heard a word from God, but before we know it, that word has been clouded out by self-doubt and difficulty. We begin to second-guess if it was really God who we heard in the first place. *Or was it purely circumstantial that I began to travel down this road that I thought God was pointing me on? Was it only an emotional, fleeting moment that led me here?*

First, we must acknowledge that God still speaks today. It is possible for Him to speak to us through His Word. He desires to have a relationship with us. Many times we read Scripture for the pure act of simply "reading," for the sake of gaining knowledge. We do not read expecting to hear anything in return. We fail to engage in God's Word and ask ourselves how it applies to us. Second, hearing from God takes time. It takes effort. It is something we learn over time.

My son began taking guitar lessons a few months ago and would easily become frustrated that he could not learn the musical notes. Reading music seemed like an impossibility to him, like climbing Mount Everest. He so desired to be able to sit down and play a song that the idea of learning a single note seemed insurmountable to him. Many times he wanted to give up. He desired to be a guitarist, but his fingers were stuck playing chopsticks. After much coaxing and countless encouragement, he stuck with it. It has been a few months, and he can now play all the notes on his guitar strings. In fact, he can play "Amazing Grace" and "When the Saints Come Marching In" by memory. What a difference a few months can make!

What's in it for you? A lot! The difference between sticking with God and grinding it out, so to say, versus giving up, is indescribable. There is an eternal world of difference! It will take time and practice to learn to hear God's voice, but it is something that can be learned. It is worth every minute you invest in it. A conversational walk with God is possible and, hopefully, will become a normal part of your life.

No matter where you fall on the scale of Christian maturity, there comes a time when you will be faced with serious doubt. We have so much more in common with Eve than we may readily admit. Eve experienced serious doubts about God and fell to temptation by the serpent. I believe doubt is the number one way that Satan robs our ability to hear the voice of God. Doubt quickly settles in and steals away from us our desire to do God's will. We begin asking ourselves, "God, was that really You? Is this what You wanted me to do? How come I all of a sudden feel all alone? If this is where You want me to be, then why in the world is it so hard?"

We have come to correlate God's will with an easy task at hand. And when the road is no longer easy but instead is confronted with difficulty and discomfort, we find ourselves longing to turn back and take matters into our own hands.

I want to urge you to continue on this journey with me. For if we will choose to live this life with reckless abandon for Him, we no doubt will experience Him like never before. For on one hand, in Matthew 11:30, God promises us that "my yoke is easy and my burden is light." But if that is the case, then why do so few of us chose to follow it wholeheartedly, without holding back and digging our heels in resistance? (I can see the skid-marks that my new boots are leaving now.) For on the other hand, Matthew 7:14 says, "But small is the gate and narrow the road that leads to life, and only a few find it."

Choosing to follow Him each and every day of our lives is certainly no simple matter. Learning to hear His voice isn't always easy, either. But I can guarantee you this: it certainly will lead you to live with no regrets as you cling to Him and find your soul deeply satisfied.

Lord, I didn't want to be that girl who thought she could survive without You.

The other day, I failed to spend time in prayer and reading God's Word. The next day came, and before I knew it, that day slipped by without me spending time with God again. How quickly a pattern was developing until I realized how arrogant I was to think I could survive a day without any time spent with God. In reference to spending time in the Word of God, John Piper once said, "If you rake, you get leaves. If you dig, you get diamonds."[31] Share your thoughts below:

But if serving the Lord seems undesirable to you, then choose for yourselves this day whom you will serve, whether the gods your ancestors served beyond the Euphrates, or the gods of the Amorites, in whose land you are living. But as for me and my household, we will serve the Lord.

—Joshua 24:15

---

[31]   John Piper, Future Grace (Sisters, Oregon: Multnomah Publishers, 1995), 387.

GREAT FANFARE

Week 4: Day 3

I remember seeing a classic Christian movie back in the eighties called, *A Thief in the Night*. It depicted the end times, and I can honestly tell you that it scared me to death as a teenager. It left me with plenty of questions and anxieties regarding the second coming of Christ. I can remember replaying scenes over and over again in my mind, wondering if I was going to be left behind . . . or would I be fortunate enough to be caught up in the rapture? Would Christ really come back for me? And when would He come? Would I be ready? Would I mistakenly get the mark of the beast ("666") across my forehead, or would I be brave enough to withstand? Boy, did I ever lose sleep over it! I even had nightmares about it. How would my family survive? Would we have to go through the tribulation? Would Jesus' second coming be pre-tribulation, mid-tribulation, or post-tribulation? What would the tribulation be like? Obviously, I had a lot of questions. And unfortunately, these questions led to a lot of fear!

What questions or concerns have you had about Jesus' second coming?

In ancient Jewish tradition, once the groom had finished preparing the chuppuh, he would return for his bride. Typically, the coming for the bride would take place during the night. The groom, best man, and other male escorts would leave the groom's father's house and conduct a torch light procession to the home of the bride. Although the bride was expecting her groom to come for her, she did not know the exact time of his coming. As a result, the groom's arrival would be preceded by a shout. This shout would forewarn the bride to be prepared for the coming of the groom. Similarly, in Matthew 25:6, Jesus said, "At midnight the cry rang out: 'Here's the bridegroom! Come out to meet him!'"

Jesus will come back for his bride with great fanfare as well. Look for the similarities in Matthew 24:29–31. What will be some of the signs that Christ is coming? (I'll get you started—the sun will be darkened.)

Today we will take an in-depth look at the signs of the end of the age. There are plenty of misconceptions about the second coming of Christ, and we surely cannot address all of them in a day. However, there is one I certainly do not want to ignore. I know so many Christians who do not even take a look at the Scriptures regarding Christ's return because they become so filled with fear. They gloss over the verses that discuss Christ's coming back for His bride. They think about all the things that they still want to accomplish or experience here on this earth. By ignoring these pertinent Scriptures, they erroneously think that they can somehow control Christ's return. Still others believe that ignorance is bliss. It is better to "just not know." This attitude, simply stated, is that it is "better to turn the head and not know." Well, I've been a blond for my entire life, and I've grown weary of the dumb blond jokes. This blond wants to know. This blond wants to know the truth, and I hope you have the courage to join me today as we dig into some deep spiritual truths.

First, I know we are not supposed to live in ignorance. God gave us the entire Scripture for our benefit, not our detriment. It has been given to us to study so that we may know Christ more intimately. In 2 Timothy 2:15, Scripture urges us, "Work hard so you can present yourself to God and receive his approval. Be a good worker, one who does not need to be ashamed and who correctly explains the word of truth" (NLT). Second, we cannot pick and choose what Scriptures we want to read and obey. Let's face it; Scripture can be distorted and taken out of context. I have watched some spiritually proud people use Scripture as a weapon to defend their sinful actions. If we are not careful with Scripture, we can mishandle it to get what we want.

Let's desire after the truth today—the whole truth. Please take a moment right now to pray for the Holy Spirit to illuminate God's Word for us today.

I can tell you one thing for sure, which I did not understand as a teen: we are to look forward with great anticipation for the second coming of Christ. It should not be something we fear but rather something we anxiously await and look forward to.

Turn with me to Mark 13. This chapter is commonly referred to as the Mount Olivet Discourse, which is just a fancy way of describing a discussion Jesus had with the disciples on the Mount of Olives. It was a couple of days before He would be crucified, and He was seated on the Mount of Olives, which overlooks Jerusalem. He was giving His disciples a "heads up" on what was going to take place in the next few hours as well as what was going to take place as the events of those next few days ushered in a new "age," a new season. I suggest that you lay your Bible open today to Mark 13 since we will be constantly glancing back and forth at it.

Read verse 1.

The temple in Jerusalem, Herod's temple, was an amazing piece of architecture made out of massive stones. The building was a sight to behold. Stones used to erect the walls were enormous, and the temple site area was equivalent to six football fields laid side by side. There was cause for the disciples' amazement. It was the heart of the Jewish faith and the center of Jewish heritage, politics, and society. It had also become highly corrupted. Jesus had just lambasted it by clearing the temple of the moneychangers in Mark 11. Picture Jesus and the disciples coming out of this magnificent structure. They are walking with Jesus when someone pipes up, "Wow, this is really amazing! Don't you think the temple is magnificent?"

Jesus, however, is not impressed. Look at His response in verse 2. Jesus is quick to respond that no matter how magnificent and huge the stones, they are not going to be strong enough in light of the winds that are about to blow. Look at the disciples' immediate response. Read verses 3 and 4.

The disciples' question is the same question that we all have in regard to the end times: "When?" "Will this be in my lifetime?" "What will be the signs that this season is coming?"

So many people get consumed with the same question the disciples were concerned with. Many people and many studies get so focused on the "when" that they totally miss the lesson that Jesus is trying to teach. Earlier I discussed the fallacy of ignoring the Scriptures discussing Christ's second return. I've also seen others fall for the trap of dedicating their lives to studying Christ's second return to the point where they become no earthly good. They spend so much time looking for the signs of Christ's return that they forget about everything else that Scripture commands. I've known of Christians who have stocked up their pantries and built underground rooms to prepare themselves for the tribulation. I've also watched others become consumed with the latest headlines and spend countless hours watching the news. They think that by being tuned into the current happenings, they can somehow predict Christ's return. There is something to be said for living in balance. Yes, we are to be prepared for Christ's return and live in expectancy for it. But no, it does not give us an excuse to quit living and obeying the Word of God. It is not our "get out of jail" card as in the game of Monopoly, where we can excuse ourselves from obediently following God's Word. We cannot stop living in this world. We are called to be in this world, just not consumed by it (Romans 12:2).

You notice, Jesus never really answers that question about when He will return. In fact, in verse 32, Jesus says, "But about that day or hour no one knows, not even the angels in heaven, nor the Son, but only the Father." Throughout history, there have been moments when people have thought, "This has to be it!"

We like to know the who, what, when, and where, but clearly from this Scripture, we are not going to know all the answers. Nonetheless, there will be some indicators to look out for. Please read verses 5 through 13 and write the sign of the end times next to it.

Verse 5: <u>worldwide winds</u>

Verse 6: _____

Verse 7–8a: _____

Verse 8b: _____

Verse 9–11: _____

Verse 12: _____

Verse 13:_____

Understand that what Jesus is describing is not what we refer to as "signs of the times," meaning signs that His return is coming at any moment. They are signs of what will be characteristic of the final age. If these were signs of the end, for all practical purposes, the end would be today.

You and I know that all of these things have been happening since immediately after His death and resurrection. That singular event ushered in the "church age," which is the final age on the calendar before the second coming of Christ.

There have been people proclaiming to be "Christ" for generations. Truth has been distorted since the wind of the Holy Spirit blew upon the church at Pentecost. In fact, I believe that since even Satan does not know when the end times will occur, he always has to have someone ready to step up into the role of the Antichrist. As you look back over history, you can surely see how this was true. Many could easily have thought that the Roman emperors, Hitler, Stalin, Chairman Mao, and others were the Antichrist. So many people reported that WWI was the end of time, that there could never be another war so devastating and global—until WWII. If I had been alive during the Holocaust, I would have been convinced that it was an absolute fulfillment of the end of time.

In verse 9, Scripture describes the disciples being handed over to governors and local councils. This actually happened in the years immediately following Jesus' departure. However, all of these things were not the end.

The temple was massive and fortified, but in AD 70, about thirty-seven years after Jesus spoke these words, the Roman army came in and totally destroyed that very temple. It is said that the reason that "no stone was left on another" was not as much a result of the toppling of the temple as it was the aftermath. When the temple was burned, the gold ran down into the cracks and crevices, so the temple was systematically dismantled to retrieve the gold.

As proof of how unreliable the stones are with regard to human wisdom, seventh-century Muslim craftsmen rebuilt a Muslim shrine on the temple mount. This magnificent, beautiful structure, called the Dome of the Rock, stands out on the Jerusalem landscape even today. Its purpose was to prove the superiority of the Islam faith to both the Christians, because of its elaborate construction, and to the Jews, because of its geographic location. It is built directly over what was traditionally thought of as the exact spot where Abraham built the altar to sacrifice Isaac, as well as the spot of the other two temples: Solomon's temple, which was destroyed when the Jews were taken into Babylonian captivity, and Herod's temple, which Jesus spoke of here.

According to Jesus' words in verses 14 through 23, there will someday be another temple in Jerusalem. According to Mark 13, as well as Matthew 24, Jesus warns about "the abomination of desolation" as spoken of by Daniel the prophet in Daniel 9. Jesus says that when we see this event, it is time to run for the hills. At this time, the Antichrist will do the following:

- defile the temple
- stop the daily sacrifice according to the Word of God
- go into the Holy of Holies and claim to be God

Scripture further says, "He will oppose and will exalt himself over everything that is called God or is worshiped, so that he sets himself up in God's temple, proclaiming himself to be God" (2 Thessalonians 2:4).

Many Bible scholars and Jews alike believe that there will be, at some point, a third temple in Jerusalem. The Jews refer to this as an "end time temple," and preparations have actually been made for this temple to be built in the next few years. They are well on their way. Many things have to happen first.

An organization called The Temple in Jerusalem is actively engaged in research and preparations for the redemption services in the new temple. Piece by piece, the third temple is underway. They have priestly garments, including the breastplate, musical instruments, and vessels of gold, copper, and silver. There is a new generation of Levite priests being trained for temple service and animal sacrifice. They already have the large cornerstones that have been anointed and cut according to Jewish law. Their plan is to start with the altar and then begin the building. Hundreds of thousands of dollars have been set aside for the project. There is much left to be done. The problem is that the temple mount is the most explosive and most contested piece of real estate in the world.

There are so many unknowns. We tend to interpret in light of what we have been taught and our present knowledge of history. Every generation thinks the end times are just around the corner. It is fascinating to read the prophecies and study eschatology, but it is also easy to get wrapped up in it all and lose sight of what Jesus was really trying to teach us.

Jesus is unconcerned with the magnificence of the temple's structure. He is concerned with the faithfulness and preparation of believers to meet the coming stresses of persecution, suffering, loss, and change. Listed throughout this passage are the things that we cannot rely on:

- institutional religious structures
- human-made legislation
- brilliantly engineered peace treaties
- political structures
- financial systems
- human relationships
- social status
- elaborate educational systems

Even the best that human beings can offer in terms of wisdom, engineering, creativity, and depth of intellect will not stand in the last days. The things of this world will pass away. But one thing will not pass away.

Read verse 31. What is it?

Bottom line: Jesus is concerned with individual faith. Who are you going to trust? Where will you turn? When your foundation begins to be rattled, what will you do? This passage teaches us how to react in the midst of change or overwhelming circumstances, during times when we can't figure everything out, when things do not make sense, and when we do not have all the answers. How will we react when our world is turned upside down? Who will we turn to in times of change?

It is so easy to put our trust in human-made things or even in ourselves rather than in God. Many will put their trust in their bank accounts. Some will put their trust in their talents or good looks. Some will put their trust in their education or intellect. Still others will put their trust in others. I wonder how many of us are putting all our trust in God? Are you? Explain your answer.

Just remember, the Bridegroom will make a lot of noise when He is on His way to retrieve His bride. There is a lot of commotion. He will come with great fanfare. Being startled in the middle of the night can shake you to the core. However, once you discover that all the ruckus being made is for you, that your Bridegroom is coming back for you, there no longer will be any fear involved. Your whole being will certainly shake, but not from fear. It will shake with excitement that your moment is finally here!

Lord, I didn't want to be that girl who was no earthly good.

Write today's confession here:

You are the light of the world—like a city on a hilltop that cannot be hidden.

—(Matthew 5:14, NLT)

CHANGE IS COMIN'

Week 4: Day 4

Our discussion yesterday was difficult and challenging, and I am so proud of you for sticking to it! God's Word is deep and complex, like a flawless diamond. Diamonds are one of the hardest natural substances on earth. When first unearthed, rough diamonds resemble gravel more than they do the rock that we marvel over in engagement and wedding rings. It takes the work of a professional diamond cutter to bring out the natural diversity and beauty in a diamond. As the diamonds are cut, little imperfections may be revealed. These internal imperfections determine a diamond's worth. Obviously, fewer imperfections equates to greater worth. A flawless diamond is considered to have no imperfections, even when magnified ten times. Some say there is no such thing as a flawless diamond. If the magnification process is continued, eventually a flaw will be revealed. To the contrary, God's Word is perfect and without flaw: "The kingdom of heaven is like treasure hidden in a field. When a man found it, he hid it again, and then in his joy went and sold all he had and bought that field" (Matthew 13:44).

Let's not stop short. Let's continue unpacking God's Word and unearthing its hidden jewels. There are tremendous treasures waiting for us in His Word.

I want to turn back to our text from yesterday, Mark 13. There is still so much for us to unearth in the final few verses of this chapter. I know God has a word for each of us today if we will just give Him the time to work in our hearts.

Begin today by rereading Mark 13:28–31. Remember where we are in our bridal story? The Bridegroom is coming with great fanfare, coming to retrieve His bride. I wonder if that sweet little thing understands how much her life is about to change. Being a Christian has a whole lot to do with change. Our natural flesh patterns will change. Our ways of doing things will change. Our purpose on this earth will change. Our perspective on what really matters will change. God desires for all of us to change and be transformed. Scripture says in 2 Corinthians 3:18, "And we, who with unveiled faces all reflect the Lord's glory, are being transformed into his likeness with ever-increasing glory, which comes from the Lord, who is the Spirit."

Thank You, Lord, for changing me!

Some of you have been Christians for a long time, while others of you have just begun your journey. I can reflect back on my life with incredible gratefulness and proclaim that I have been changed. I am so glad that God got a hold of my life. I'm so thankful that I'm not the same person I used to be.

Can you relate? Share a story of how you've been changed.

Change is part of God's natural plan. Look at verse 28. Plants go through seasons of change: winter, spring, summer, and fall. They go through times of dormancy, times of bloom, and times of harvest. Change is part of God's plan. There are also seasons in our personal lives. We change with time, from our toddler years through adolescence, our college years, being newly married, our midlife years, and our senior years. Yet, so many of us don't want to change. We don't want to grow up. We're hanging on so tightly to the last season that our hands are blistering and splintered. We don't want to let go. We don't want to trust God.

We have a hard time with change. We say we want change . . . yet when it finally arrives, we start clinging to what used to be. We don't want to move on. We like our security, the familiar, and the known. We want to stay in our comfort zones. Sure, we complain that what we really need is change, but then when it starts happening, we want to go back to how things used to be. Change may mean that we no longer have control, and then we start getting a lil' nervous.

Change seems to really shake us to our cores. We try to take matters into our own hands and manipulate our situations rather than handing them over to God. God recently led my family to move, and I'll openly and vulnerably admit that it was one of the toughest decisions that we (my husband and I) have ever made in our lives. We had lived in Houston, Texas, for over twenty years, our entire married life. We loved our church and our friends and had developed an amazing support system there. Our three kids were plugged in with amazing friendships as well. But then God started shaking things up in all areas of our lives. We no longer had rest in our souls and knew that God was calling us to move. *It was so hard to move!* I fought it with every ounce of my being. We tried to reason our way out of it. However, we've never experienced such a strong conviction and overwhelming wave of the Holy Spirit leading the way in our lives. Pieces of the puzzle began to perfectly work together, and eventually we realized that this was not us—this was God. There was something much greater going on. It only had a little bit to do with us, and a whole lot to do with God!

After experiencing an incredible sense of the Holy Spirit working and guiding us in our move, I was able to pack the last box in the moving truck and drive away. However, I'm not perfect. Just a few weeks into our moving journey, I felt like the Israelites screaming, "Take me back to Egypt." I just wanted to go home. My conversations with God sounded something like this: "I don't care if You're working here, God, or that I'm right where You want me to be, because this is so hard. I just want to go home!" Life can be so difficult! Oh, how I longed—no, ached—to go back to the familiar, to what seemed comfortable and like home. I wanted to go back to where I knew my way around and could pop in on a friend when I felt lonely. Oh, how I sometimes dislike the uncharted and the unknown!

Have you ever felt the same? Relate a time when you have you not liked a situation you were sitting in and begged God to take you back to where you used to be?

I've learned a valuable lesson through my move to Austin, Texas. Jesus always moves us forward, not backward. My move here was so, so hard, and yet, I can now say that it has been so, so good! It has been good in ways I never expected or imagined. His first command to the disciples was "Follow me," and yet, they had no idea where He was going. They thought they were going to assist Jesus in ushering in and establishing the grand and mighty kingdom of God. They thought they would sit on the left and right side of Him and rule the world. Little did they know that following Him would lead to a cross, to His death. Injustices and disappointments will happen along the way in life. One dead end may seem to lead to another—but even then, will you still follow?

I can't even imagine how the disciples must have felt as they saw their friend, their Lord and Savior, die up on that cross. They must have thought that everything they had banked on just went up in smoke. They had left everything to follow Him. They had left their families, their careers, and (as my daughter would phrase it) their lives. They had wholeheartedly poured their lives out. They were emptied, and for what? I wonder if they thought they had made the biggest mistake of their lives. I wonder if they had doubts.

Little did they know that the kingdom of God was being ushered in, Christianity was about to explode, and God was going to use them to do something big! Our ways are not God's ways. Our thoughts are not His. George MacDonald wrote in *The Princess and the Goblin*, "The one secret of life and development, is not to devise and plan . . . but to do every moment's duty aright . . . and let come—not what will, for there is no such thing—but what the eternal Thought wills for each of us, has intended in each of us from the first."[32]

As Christians, we are comfortable proclaiming the fact of God's greatness. We are bold to state before the world that God is all-powerful as Creator. We have confidence in our descriptions about God. All too often, however, our proclamations regard external truths we accept but do not allow to impact our lives. We profess assurance in God, but do we live the assurance we so adamantly profess? The world is not so interested in what we know about God. God cares more for how our faith plays out in action.

---

[32] George MacDonald, *The Princess and the Goblin* (London: Blackie and Son, 1888), 155-212.

We delight in repeating the psalmist's words: God is our refuge, our counsel, our delight, and security. In Yahweh's presence, there is fullness of joy! Such words and phrases are comforting, soothing us from distress and quieting the issues of the real world. We use the phrases as retreat, but how does their truth infect our faith with courage? How does it impact our service to God amid the daily grind and pressures of living? We live in a world of change, a world where we do not always know what is coming around the next corner.

The purpose of the Mount Olivet Discourse was to warn the disciples about the wind that was to blow, the change that was coming, and to tell them not to be deceived, to "stay awake!" Jesus says it over and over.

Finish reading Mark 13:32–37. Peruse the chapter again. How many times are we told to "watch" or "be on your guard"? _____

In these verses, Jesus knows He is leaving soon. He wants to make sure the beloved He is leaving behind will be ready, will be awake, will be on their guard, and will be able to withstand the storms and wind that are about to blow—both on that generation and those in the future. Please take a moment to read Matthew 25:1–13. It is a parable about ten virgins who set out to meet the bridegroom. Five were well prepared and ready, and five went with inadequate supplies. These ten virgins represent the visible church, all professing to be Christians. Yet, not all will be allowed entrance into the kingdom of heaven. The groom will not recognize all.

All ten of these virgins were given a job to do. It was their calling to welcome back the bridegroom with well-lit lamps fueled by oil. Their job was to shine and be lights. However, five of them were unprepared and only took their lamps. They carried no oil. They had no way to be lights. On the outside, they professed to be Christians. But on the inside, there was no substance. There was no light. How foolish they were to think that they could get by with merely their outward appearances. How foolish of them to think they could wait until the last minute to purchase their oil. Oh, how foolish still of them to think their oil could be borrowed.

Why didn't the well-prepared five share some of their oil with the others? (See verses 8 through 9.)

The reason these five wise virgins did not share their oil was not selfishness. No, it's because they knew the value of the oil. In other words, our personal salvation does not come from another person. It is impossible to borrow one's faith. We cannot take the easy road and say, "My parents' salvation will get me into the pearly gates," or "the salvation of my spouse will or that of my children." If we come from Christian roots or surround ourselves with other Christians, that doesn't buy us a ticket into heaven. Rather, these verses are explicitly telling us, "Do not take your salvation lightly." It's personal. It's a relationship between you and the Bridegroom. The responsibility falls on you.

Thoughts of anxiety, worry, and fear can easily overwhelm us in the midst of change if we do not keep our eyes focused on God. But we are instructed, "Don't worry" (Mark 13:11).

Shortly after graduating from college, I received a phone call that a dear friend of mine had been in a motorcycle accident. Rod loved to ride his motorcycle around the hilly terrain of Tulsa, Oklahoma. One evening, he apparently was going too fast down a hill and failed to notice that the yellow light had turned red. Simultaneously, a large semi-truck had pulled out and began its turn. Rod quickly hit his brakes and lost control of his bike. He slid underneath the tire of the moving truck. The rest is history. The funeral arrangements were already being made, and Rod would be buried in his hometown in Minnesota. Upon hearing the news, I did not hesitate. I made plans to attend the funeral.

This funeral was not like any I'd ever attended before. The little country church was packed. Every pew was bursting. College friends had traveled from afar to give their condolences to Rod's surviving sister and parents. However, the one thing that was so supernatural and unexplainable to me was the joy and the peace that Rodney's parents shared with every single guest that day. I will never forget it. Their peace imprinted on my soul. I think words can only partially explain the peace that they had. Instead of being a comfort to them, they were a comfort to me. They had smiles across their faces. They held me in a breathtaking bear hug that reached to my inner core. They just grabbed me up and would not let go. It was very noticeable that something was different about them. They had a peace that this world could not explain, a peace that surpasses all understanding—the kind of peace discussed in Philippians 4:7. Only, I wasn't just reading about it—I was seeing it played out in action in what had to be the most difficult moment of their lives! Their peace did not make any sense to me at the time. It was so counterintuitive.

It has taken me a long time to understand how Rod's parents could go through such an experience with such peace. One of my greatest fears as a parent has been to lose a child. I don't know how someone could keep on living after such a tragedy. Mark 13:11 sheds light on this, however, that "at the time," or as the King James Version says, "within the hour," the Holy Spirit will be there with you. We can live in fear about things that have never happened to us. We can become worked up about things that have never come to pass. We can wonder how we would ever get through something tragic. We can easily become consumed with anxiety and fear about things that are "not our time." We can become overwhelmed with our circumstances. But let me tell you this, because God's Word will not fade away and His promises are always true: when your time does come, when it is your "hour," He will meet you there.

Difficult circumstances, overwhelming situations, and periods of change are not things that we are to handle on our own. We are not to fear the end of the age. In our hour, the Holy Spirit will come upon us. I guarantee you that we are not to live in fear but rather to put our trust in the One who will never change. His Word will never change. He knows all the answers. Rather than getting freaked out by your circumstances, get to know the One who has it all figured out. When your world starts to crumble beneath you, put your feet on solid ground. Human wisdom may change, but God's Word will never pass away. He comes for His bride with great fanfare, trumpets, His servants, friends, and family. It is a joyful day when He comes to receive His bride for the wedding ceremony. There is music and dancing and rejoicing.

Lord, I didn't want to be that girl who refused change.

Ask the Lord if there is anything in your life that needs to change.

But those who hope in the Lord will renew their strength. They will soar on wings like eagles; they will run and not grow weary, they will walk and not be faint.

—Isaiah 40:31

SPRING-CLEANING

Week 4: Day 5

It is that time of year again when the weather begins to warm up and the flowers are beginning to bloom. I especially look forward to spring in the hills of Texas, as the bluebonnets begin to bud forth. Something about this time of year gets to me every time. I don't know if you would call it a natural motherly instinct or something that was instilled in me since childbirth. Maybe the sun is shining more brightly so that I can see the dust balls collecting in the corners of my pantry. Maybe it's that my dog ate a century-old Cheerio from beneath the couch cushions yesterday as I was digging around for some loose change in order to send my son on his class field trip. (There's no way I wanted to run to the gas station at the top of the hill at that time of night for change. I already had my pajamas on.) Yep, you guessed it: my home is well overdue for some good ol' spring-cleaning.

But here's the deal with spring-cleaning: no matter how hard I try, it seems the dust monsters creep back into my house instantaneously. I may enjoy the scent of that Pledge moment for just that, a moment. But quite honestly, I can never keep my house spic and span, regardless of whether I kick my three kids, dog, and husband out of the house for a while. Even that is not enough to maintain my home for the mother-in-law white-glove inspection.

After arrival at the bride's home, the groom would take his bride and her attendants back to his father's house for the official wedding ceremony. Prior to the ceremony, the bride would undergo some "intense spring-cleaning." The bride was expected to stand before her groom without spot or blemish. Therefore, prior to her wedding day, the bride would be immersed in a *mikveh*, a spiritual cleansing bath. It was extremely important that there be no physical signs of un-cleanliness. The act of mikveh involves three immersions and one blessing. The bride was to enter the bath completely nude, spread her arms and legs apart to ensure complete cleanliness, and immerse herself so that every strand of hair was underwater. Even her eyes were to remain open underwater so that every speck of dust could be removed.

Upon immersion, a common blessing would be repeated: "Praised are you, Adonai, God of all creation, who sanctifies us with your commandments and commanded us concerning immersion."

The act of mikveh has deeper spiritual meaning and comes from the traditional preparation of the high priest for the Day of Atonement, Yom Kippur. The high priest of Israel was only allowed to enter the temple's Holy of Holies on this day of the year. The temple consisted of three parts: the outer court, the inner court, and the Holy of Holies, the most holy place. To put this in better perspective, the Holy of Holies was surrounded by a thick veil, and inside was the Ark of the Covenant. The mercy seat served as the lid to the ark of the covenant, and the very Shekinah glory of God—in other words, the presence of God—rested above the mercy seat. Leviticus 16:2 says, "The LORD said to Moses: 'Tell your brother Aaron not to come whenever he chooses into the Most Holy Place behind the curtain in front of the atonement cover on the ark, or else he will die, because I appear in the cloud over the atonement cover.'" Imagine the fear of the Lord and trembling that must have accompanied the high priest as he entered the Holy of Holies to make a sacrifice not only for himself but also for the sins of the Israelites.

There was an enormous amount of detailed preparation that took place before the high priest would be allowed to enter the Holy of Holies. He was put into complete seclusion a week beforehand so that he would not accidentally eat or touch anything that was unclean. Clean food would be brought to him, and he would "get rid of" or "strip off" all moral filth and un-cleanliness by bathing himself. Much time would be devoted to prayer and reading God's Word to prepare his heart for entering the presence of God. Then, on Yom Kippur, he would again bathe from head to toe and dress himself in pure, unstained white linen. He would enter the Holy of Holies and offer an animal sacrifice to atone for his own sins. He would come back out and completely bathe himself again and dress again in clean white linens. Then, he would enter the Holy of Holies a second time to offer a sacrifice for the sins of the other priests. Again, he would come out and bathe from head to toe and dress himself in new, clean white linen. He would then enter the Holy of Holies a third time to atone for the sins of the people.

Now here's the real kicker: the high priest did all his bathing in public, behind a thin screen, as the Israelites watched closely and intently. They wanted to make sure that the priest followed every procedure exactly, because he was their representative before God. They wanted to ensure that he was as clean as a whistle—not a speck or flaw on his entire body. And as he entered the Holy of Holies, they were outside cheering him on.

Now, with that bearing heavily on your mind, please read our text for today found in Zechariah 3:1–7. Read these descriptive verses and explain what happened:

Zechariah sees a vision with the high priest, Joshua, standing in the very presence of God in the Holy of Holies. Although the order of cleanliness has been followed exactly according to the law,

Joshua's garments are filthy. One commentary states that his garments are covered in excrement. He is absolutely defiled.

How this ever could have happened astonishes Zechariah. There is no way the Israelites would have allowed the high priest to enter the Holy of Holies this way. God gives Zechariah a prophetic vision so that he can see us the way that God sees us. In spite of all our efforts to be pure, to be good, to be moral, to cleanse ourselves, God sees our hearts, and our hearts are full of filth.

Read James 1:19–21. What are we told to do?

When a friend was asked the question, "What is wrong with this world?" her humble response was, "I am." We are what is wrong with this world. We tend to take God's message and hang it around someone else's neck, but its first target is our own souls.

Despite all our cleansing and striving, we never are quite good enough. We're still wearing filthy rags. We can get so easily entangled in the rut of doing, doing, doing, even in Christian ministry, but the reality is that all our doing will never be enough.

But here's the really good news. In both Zechariah 3:3 and James 1:21, we are instructed to "take off your filthy rags." Then in Zechariah 3:4, God says, "See, I have taken away your sin, and I will put fine garments on you." Despite all the sacrifices and all the cleanliness laws, Zechariah comes to the realization that we never can get rid of our sin by ourselves. Years later, another high priest named Joshua shows up. His name is really Jesus, Yeshua, and Joshua—it's the same name in Aramaic, Greek, and Hebrew. This High Priest wears our filthy rags so that we do not have to. And in lieu of our filthy rags, we have been robed in white, pure, and clean fine linen.

Write out 2 Corinthians 5:21.

Lord, I didn't want to be that girl trying to clean her dirty rags.

We all guilty of trying to cleanse ourselves from a past sin or make ourselves feel better by our deeds. We have tried to clean ourselves up before entering into His presence, thinking that we cannot even talk to Him before we get all our ducks in a row. We've compared ourselves to those around us and thought, "Well, I'm better than her." But the truth is that even our best is not good enough. It is by grace, and grace alone, that we will enter into the Holy of Holies.

Lord, I didn't want to be that girl with a dirty house.

Write a response to God:

May God himself, the God of peace, sanctify you through and through. May your whole spirit, soul and body be kept blameless at the coming of our Lord Jesus Christ.

—1 Thessalonians 5:23

Week 5: Taking a Bite

REJOICE!

Week 5: Day 1

Let us rejoice and be glad and give him glory! For the wedding of the Lamb has come, and his bride has made herself ready. Fine linen, bright and clean, was given her to wear.

—Revelation 19:7–8

Finally, the wedding. The groom has come. The bride has been purified. The veil has been lifted. The wedding has been officiated. The guests have gathered. A Jewish wedding is a community affair, so many gather, but did you realize that only one person goes home with the bride? Today we will take a look at the groom's perspective.

Begin today by reading Psalm 45. Many commentators believe this Psalm was written about King Solomon and his bride. However, this text also provides a great illustration of the wedding between Jesus and us, His bride.

Verses 2 through 8 give us a detailed description of Jesus' attributes. Take the time to write down what these verses tell us about our groom.

Verse 2: _____

Verse 3: _____

Verse 4: _____

Verse 5: _____

Verse 6: _____

Verse 7: _____

Verse 8: _____

The remaining verses provide us with a description of the bride. We are clearly told that the king, the groom, will be enthralled by her beauty (see verse 11). The definition of *enthralled* means "to capture the fascinated attention of[33], to hold spellbound[34]." John wrote, "the marriage of the Lamb has come, and his wife has made herself ready" (Revelation 19:7). A few chapters later, John writes, "I saw new Jerusalem coming down from God in heaven. She was like a bride made beautiful for her husband" (Revelation 21:2). Girls, I don't know if you are letting this sink in, but Jesus is enthralled with your beauty. I don't know if you have fully realized your worth. I don't know if you fully comprehend that you are truly beautiful to Him. Yes, sister, I'm talking to you—you are beautiful, despite the belly bulge, the saggy skin, the puffy eyes. Yes, my dear friend, Jesus thinks you are beautiful. And isn't what Jesus thinks of you enough? Isn't what He has to say what really matters?

Last night I saw a story on *Nightline* about teenage girls and the destructiveness of airbrushed photos in magazines. It should come as no surprise that magazines have the luxury of removing blemishes and making their models even thinner with photo editing technology. Little do the magazine editors understand how this is affecting our teenage girls (and women too). These images are unobtainable. One girl's response to *Seventeen Magazine* was this: "I look at this magazine and it makes me feel bad about myself. I start not liking the way I look."

Lies. We've been told them all of our lives. We've so deceived ourselves. We've bought into the marketing trap that we need to look differently. We are not pretty enough. Recently I became friends with a woman who has had almost every part of her body redone. She has fake boobs, fake eyelashes, a spray tan, colored hair, a chin lift, and a belly tuck. When, honestly, is enough, enough? Plastic surgery and dermatological visits are so common that it begs the question, "Is there anything real in there?" Who ever lied to you and said that you were not good enough? That you have no value?

Harsh reaction, you may say. But I think it is a real epidemic in our society that we struggle with feelings that we don't belong or fit in or measure up. I've talked to so many women recently who feel unaccepted by their peers or, worse yet, by their husbands. They feel unloved. They feel inadequate. They feel unattractive. They feel as if they don't have it all together. They feel in over their heads as moms, caretaker, wives, teaches, doctors, accountants—plain and simple, as women. Our insecurities can certainly get the best of us. And before you bat an eye and make the disclaimer that you never share in this struggle, let me point out that the best cover for insecurity is perfectionism. You may think that self-doubt and insecurity look this way or that. Let's keep an open mind today and try to stay focused within. I've been around long enough to know that everyone in this world has struggled with this beast a time or two.

---

[33]   "Enthralled." Def. 1. *Oxford Pocket Dictionary of Current English,* 4th ed. New York: Oxford University Press, 2009.

[34]   "Enthralled." Def. 2. *Merriam-Webster's Collegiate Dictionary.* 11th ed. Springfield, MA: Merriam-Webster, 2003.

Dr. Gerald Stein wrote a blog about insecurities and says, "Insecure people often reveal their self-doubt without being aware of it."[35] A short list of behaviors from Dr. Stein may make the meaning more clear.

- Are you able to give and receive a compliment? The latter may be more difficult for someone struggling with insecurity.
- Can you maintain eye contact when in a conversation?
- Do you excessively apologize . . . even when there is no need to?
- Are you willing to share personal information? Or due to the fear of being judged, do you quickly stir the conversation another direction?
- Do you make light of yourself or difficult topics by cracking jokes at your own expense?
- Do you avoid the spotlight in social situations?
- Do you have trepidation about making a phone call?

The list goes on and on. My point is not to make you feel disheartened that you may struggle with insecurity more than you realized; my point is to make you realize that you are not alone in this struggle. We all struggle. Don't be deceived by appearances. There is not a single person who has everything. We are all in this ship with you—so scoot over, sister; let me grab an oar.

What has been your most recent struggle in regards to insecurity?

I've always told my girls that you can't always tell what is going on behind the scenes. I think the same can apply here. We need to be careful how we size up someone and also cautious in what we covet. I betcha there's not a girl out there who has perfected what she is pretending to be. Somewhere in the chasm of our minds, there has been a time when we did not measure up. Improving our appearances, losing some weight, buying new clothes, bolstering our bank accounts, excelling at athletics, and esteeming our educations are all ways we may heighten our self-worth. The moment our self-worth nears an obsession, we better watch out! The moment our minds become consumed with our diet plan, our exercise regimen, our mutual fund, our children's success, or our fountain of youth, we know we have a problem. No longer is self-improvement the issue; there's something deeper driving us. An injured soul is at the root. But are we willing to face the tough questions to figure out what the real cause is?

I have a confession. I like to weigh myself every day. If I gain a pound or two, I try to be more attentive to what I eat throughout the day. I like to keep my weight in check. There are days when the fluctuation in my weight has really gotten to me, and it's entirely affected my self-esteem. It's made me feel more insecure. But then I have to ask myself, has anything really changed? Does my

---

35 Dr. Gerald Stein, *"Sign of Insecurity: Behavior That Reveals a Lack of Confidence,"* Last updated July 15, 2012. *www.drgeraldstein.wordpress.com/2010/07/15/signs-of-insecurity-behavior-that-reveals-a-lack-of-confidence* (August 27, 2013).

husband love me less? No. Do my kids love me less? Absolutely not. They have no clue the scales have tipped in the wrong direction. Has it changed what my friends think of me? Of course not; they are not that shallow. And what about God? Are you kidding me? He loves me no matter what!

I've come to realize that sometimes my insecurity can stem simply from what number my scale reads each morning. It is rooted in my size. According to Beth Moore, most of us have a prominent false positive, meaning we focus on *one thing* that we think would make us more secure in *all things.*[36]

Let me name just a few prominent false positives: being married, owning a large home, being proud of children and/or their success, wearing nice clothes, having credentials or educational success, earning prestige in personal achievements, having a sizable bank account, possessing talents, and even being proud of where we live.

Think of a person who you think is secure. What does she have that in your mind makes her so? Is it an earthly possession, a certain relationship, or a something that I haven't even thought of? Just for grins, write it down here: _____

Whatever it may be, I bet we all have our "go to" thing, the one thing that takes priority over the rest, the one thing that we struggle with coveting. We dream, *if only I could have _____, then I would no longer struggle with what others think of me.* (Only we never say those words, because we're unwilling to admit it—even to ourselves. We've only thought them.) Maybe you've thought, *if only I had a new car* or *if only I were married* or *if only I had better health* or *if only I had _____.*" And even if we do obtain that thing, the sad truth is that our damaged souls start longing for something else. We're wrecks. We're all in need of healing.

Now that we are in this boat together, let me offer some hope. There is a cure. The cure is to start believing what God says about us to be true. Let's take it one step further—not only to believe it, but also to act upon it. Please read Psalm 45:13 again. If you have the NIV version, it says, "all glorious is the princess in her chamber." You may have missed out on what this verse is really saying. It's not talking about Princess Rapunzel sitting high and lofty in her palace chamber, ready to let down her hair. The NASB version says this, "The King's daughter is all glorious within." That, my sisters, is the key—to move our focus from the outside to the inside. This verse, dear sister, is referring to you.

Be honest: how much more time do you spend prettying up the outside of "you" versus the inside? Tough question, right? You may be wondering where to begin, where to start making this

---

[36]   Beth Moore, *So Long, Insecurity* (Carol Stream: Tyndale, 2010), 36.

transition in your life. I'm going to give you a homework assignment today: spend time thinking about where to begin making some lifestyle adjustments.

Read Matthew 22:37–40. Write out the two commandments we are given:

1. _____

2. _____

Now, for the remainder of today, think about how well you are doing these two things. Ask the Holy Spirit to reveal areas where you need to change. I find it interesting that both of these commandments shift the focus from us to others. Self-absorption and insecurity run hand in hand. The best way for us to avoid the fatal trap of this materialistic, narcissistic, superficial world is to begin giving, not receiving; to serve, not be served; and to die to ourselves, so that we may live. After all, isn't that what Jesus, our Bridegroom, did for us?

Lord, I didn't want to be that girl with insecurity!

Ask the Lord to reveal your areas of insecurity, and then ask Him to reveal how to change.

For whoever wants to save their life will lose it, but whoever loses their life for me will find it.

—Matthew 16:25

Holy Union

Week 5: Day 2

It's a drizzly, rainy day here, so I've had a lot of time to contemplate. I don't really feel like going outside. There's no sense in getting my hair frizzy. All that is to say that I hope you are ready to put your thinking cap on today. You see, I got to thinking: Why in the world do I write? What is it that motivates me? Why do I stay on course? I'm not on staff at a church. I've never even attended seminary. A publisher has not hired me. I'm just a busy, sometimes overwhelmed, mom. I have two teenage daughters and a ten-year-old son. I am married to a pediatric emergency room physician. My life is filled with taxi driving, piles of laundry, athletic events, band concerts, guitar lessons, homework assignments, and church activities. Add to that a splattering of gym workouts, homeroom mom responsibilities, and occasional social outings. And that's what I do. That's this thing called my life.

When it is all boiled down, I can never seem to quickly come up with an answer to "What do you do?" I get asked it all the time. We all do. And yet, I seem to draw a blank. I could easily draw on past accomplishments. I could rattle off a few rungs from my ladder. Funny thing is, not much of it seems to really matter. Even when my husband comes home from a busy day at work and pops the question, "What did you do today?" more often than not, I cannot come up with a viable response. At least not a response that I think he would want to hear. I've achieved basically nothing. I've not built Rome in a day. Only monotony seems to drive me.

And now the ball bounces to you—what do you do? No, I'm not looking for your career title or your current résumé. I'm not concerned with your family name or college degree. I'm not an employer trying to hire you. I'm not even concerned about your hobbies or interests. We can easily hide behind titles and accomplishments, degrees and pedigrees, body images, and bank accounts. I'm not looking for that answer today. I'm looking for something more. I'm looking for you to peer way inside. Why do you do what you do? Have you ever thought about what really motivates you? Seriously, what compels you to get through each day? What characterizes your life? Because whether you are intentional about it or not, you are pouring it out. It is being poured into something. Every day, you're twenty-four hours closer to being done with this thing called your "life."

I thought it might be interesting to put some pen to our thoughts. What are the top five things that motivate you?

1. _____

2. _____

3. _____

4. _____

5. _____

Then, one step further, why are you motivated? What is the underlying factor that drives you there?

As I said before, whether we realize it or not, we all are being driven by something. Most of us never take the time to back up and take the closer look. We pile more things onto our agendas and fill our schedules tightly so that we don't have to look, as looking can seem so futile. It may make us seem superficial. It definitely can make us seem bad. It may even hurt. The Indigo Girls once sang a song called "Closer to Fine." Realizing that looking for answers in this life can be confusing, they reached the conclusion that "the less I seek my source for some definitive, the closer I am to fine."[37] They ultimately decided that to know was not to know. Yes, I agree with the Indigo Girls that this life can be confusing. But no, that does not mean that there is no definitive. They missed it. They didn't look hard enough. As the Bible tells us, "If from there you seek the LORD your God, you will find him if you look for him with all your heart and with all your soul" (Deuteronomy 4:29).

If it brings you any consolation, we all have been driven by something other than God. Let's admit that we have misguided motivators. It may be that we are motivated to finish reading the book that we cannot put down. It may be that we get through the day so that we can have some "me" time vegging out on the couch. We may work hard so that our children can have better lives than we had. Maybe we are seeking some approval from a parent, and we are driven to go to an elite college, to put in the extra hours at work, or to get the next advancement, so that our parent will be proud of us. Or maybe we are seeking comfort. We seek out recreation and are motivated by our hobbies and time with friends. Maybe we want to live well. We overachieve so we can live in a great big house, send our kids to the best school in the city, and take incredible

---

[37]   Indigo Girls. "Closer to Fine." By Emily Saliers. *Indigo Girls.* Scott Litt, 1989, CD.

vacations, thinking the entire time that we are almost there—just one paycheck away from arriving at our final destination. But the joke is on us. We never arrive. Scripture warns, "Do not lay up for yourselves treasures upon the earth, where moth and rust corrupts, and where thieves break through and steal" (Matthew 6:19).

This world cannot satisfy. I tried to explain that to my son this evening at the dinner table. This past summer he begged and begged for a tree fort, and my kind husband spent hours with him in the grueling heat building him a three-level one. It took several months to accomplish this incredible architectural work of art. Fast-forward a few months, and our son barely climbs on it. Now he wants a lake in our backyard. He wants to be able to fish, and he keeps asking if we can move. (Mind you, we just moved into our home nine months ago.) How quickly we become unsatisfied. How often we have fallen for that old trick.

What Jesus is teaching us in Matthew 6 is that nothing in this world can satisfy. What I have discovered is that there is only one thing that truly satisfies. There is only one thing that brings me complete and utter joy. His name is Jesus. Write out Matthew 6:20 below:

According to John Eldredge, "Intimacy with God is the purpose of our lives. It's why God created us. Not simply to believe in him, though that is a good beginning. Not only to obey him, though that is a higher life still. God created us for intimate fellowship with himself, and in doing so he established the goal of our existence—to know him, love him, and live our lives in an intimate relationship with him."[38]

Was God lonely? No, absolutely not. Did God need us? No, He was completely fulfilled. He in no way should be considered needy. He did, however, create us in such a way that we need Him. We cannot be fulfilled or satisfied without Him, and the ultimate reason that we were even created was to bring God glory. This entire universe was created by Him and for Him. When talking about God's glory, John Piper says, "The aim is no other than the endless, ever-increasing joy of his people in his glory."[39]

Once the wedding ceremony was completed, the bride and groom would enter the bridal chamber for seven days. The best seller, *Fifty Shades of Grey* (no, I haven't read it and have no intention to do so, but I certainly have heard plenty about it), has nothing on Scripture. What was enjoyed (and yes, sex is to be enjoyed) was seven days of lovemaking. Song of Solomon gives a glimpse of this steamy pleasure. Don't believe me? "Let him kiss me with the kisses of his mouth—for your love is more delightful than wine . . . Take me away with you—let us hurry! Let the king bring me into his chambers" (Song of Solomon 1:2, 4).

---

[38] John Eldredge, *Walking with God* (Nashville: Thomas Nelson, 2008), 12.
[39] John Piper, *God's Passion for His Glory* (Wheaton: Crossway, 1998), 32.

At the end of the seven days, the groom's "friend" or "witness" waits at the chamber door. The guests have arrived and are waiting for the door to be opened and the wedding banquet to begin. When the groom is ready, he knocks from the inside of the door of the chamber, indicating that they are ready to make their public appearance before everyone. The friend opens the door, and the guests cheer.

We are given glimpses throughout Scripture that Christ is our Bridegroom and we are His bride. This is a mystical union. This is what truly satisfies. And yet we beg to know, what does this look like in our own lives?

This, my friends, is worship: to know God in such a way that we surrender our all to Him, humbly letting Him hold the reins. When we surrender, truly surrender, we let Him have complete control. We read in 1 Corinthians 6:20, "We were bought at a price. Therefore honor God with your bodies." What we do with our lives, what we do with the gifts and talents He has given us, is our gift back to Him. It's how we enter into this thing called holy union.

Well then, why do I write? It's what today's journey began with and also what it will end with. I write because it is what God the Creator has created me to do. He has created you with a purpose too. (See Psalm 57:2.) To further illustrate God's activity in my life, let me share with you an event that happened this morning. I took my car to the brake shop for repairs and entered into a casual conversation with the woman waiting in the "brake room" with me. Before long, she realized that I was a mother of three kids, and the words that struck me as funny were these: "How in the world can you have three kids? You are so tiny!" Why were those words so humorous, so intimate? If you recall our conversation from yesterday, I vulnerably shared my insecurity with the scale. I knew right away that it may have sounded like the woman's voice speaking, but something far greater was happening, and it was God. God was using that woman to speak to me and confirm what I needed to hear.

Your greatest joy will be in sacrificing yourself to Him. Intercourse of soul with God is found in offering thanksgiving for whatever comes your way, the good and the bad. Take the cup of Communion and repeat these familiar words, "Not my will, Lord, but Thine be done" (Luke 22:42).

Lord, I didn't want to be that girl who didn't use her gifts for Your glory.

Close today by reading the text found in 1 Corinthians 1:4–9. What are your spiritual gifts? Are you using your gifts for His glory?

God is faithful, who has called you into fellowship with his Son, Jesus Christ our Lord.

—1 Corinthians 1:9

The Naked Truth

Week 5: Day 3

I hope you are enjoying this study as much as I am. I have fallen more in love with our precious Lord and Savior through this study, and I am praying that the same will be true for you. I am already praying in advance for you—even though I may not know your name. I am so thankful for you and your dedication to study God's Word. His Word will not return void (Isaiah 55:11).

I had the best time yesterday hanging out with a couple of my favorite friends. We went walking around Town Lake here in Austin and did some crazy gabbing along the way. There's nothing like some time spent with good friends. They set the tone for the rest of my day. I was so blessed by them. Our conversation topics were all over the place, like grease on a frying pan. So it surprised me today when I flipped back to our text in Genesis (yes, for you type A, stay-on-track people out there, we are heading back to Genesis today) that one of our problem-solving conversations would actually tie in perfectly with our Scripture for today. Before we jump there, though, let me ask you something. Why do you think we see a growing trend in cosmetic plastic surgery, breast implants and the like, and tattoos today? Do you think they are wrong?

This certainly could be a divisive topic, so before you go pointing fingers, please read on. As my mother always said, whenever you point a finger, there are always four pointing right back at you. I've seen so much of the church alienated from the unchurched for reasons such as this. I've also watched as the "self-righteous" in the church separate themselves from the so-called "sinners." With that caveat, let's tarry a little longer.

So, are outward physical enhancements, so to speak, wrong? What does the Bible have to say about such things? I would not be surprised if someone in your group spouts out Leviticus 19:28: "Ye shall not make any cuttings in your flesh for the dead, nor print any marks upon you: I am the LORD." I can already hear the counterattack saying, "That's Old Testament teaching. That rule doesn't apply to us today. I live under the New Testament teaching found in Matthew 22:39 that clearly states to love your neighbor as yourself." If those verses are not enough to rattle your brain, take a look at a few more. What do these verses tell us about our outward appearance? Write a brief synopsis after each one.

Deuteronomy 22:5 _____

Deuteronomy 22:11 _____

Zephaniah 1:8 _____

1 Corinthians 11:14–15 _____

1 Timothy 2:9 _____

1 Peter 3:3 _____

Now, is any self-righteous person in the room still standing? If you took the position that breast implants, tattoos, and plastic surgery are wrong, what are you thinking about it now? Have you ever violated any of the commands of these scripture verses? You will have to throw me under the bus. I certainly fall into the category of being an abomination before the Lord. You could find me guilty for wearing men's clothing . . . afterall, I do like to wear shorts and jeans. I'll admit I've also braided my hair more than once or twice and been known to wear fine jewelry. And should I add that I also have pierced ears? Do I have a fighting chance?

I believe that we've all been found guilty in at least one of these areas. There is no one *that* righteous; no, not one! In fact, I'll even be so bold today to say that we've *all* wanted breast implants or something similar. No! You may say, "That is absolutely ludicrous! I would never do that or spend money on that." Go ahead and name your reasons. Then, come back on course, and stick it out with me today, and you'll find out why I make such a proclamation so boldly.

Are breast implants or tattoos wrong? Is a little nip and tuck wrong? I'm not going to be so bold as to go that far. The reason I will not is because there are different situations and circumstances that I am not privy to. This, however, I will say: I think the question that needs to be asked before going under the knife or needle in any situation is this: what is my heart's intent? What is at the heart of the matter? Why am I doing this? Am I doing it to bring glory to God or bring glory to myself?

We've all wrestled at one time or another with our identities. We try to hide behind something. We have tried to "fit in" with the crowd that we think is "in." We don't like to feel out of the loop. We don't want to be left out. We've all shared in that sinking feeling when everyone is chattering about a party or social event, and we never even received an invitation. To make matters worse, what about all the "inside jokes" that we never understood because we were not on the inside? We know what it feels like to be excluded. It makes me just want to bury my head in the sand and hide.

You are not the first. Nor will you be the last, I'm sure. The feeling of being unaccepted can be brutal, and I believe it is often the root problem behind why we go to such lengths to alter our physical appearances. With the stage now set, please read our text for today:

Our text today is like a tweet—short and brief. Please read Genesis 2:25.

Why do you think Adam and Eve felt no shame?

Now read Genesis 3:7. Why all of a sudden did they hide?

Let me set one thing straight: Adam and Eve did not hide because their eyes were suddenly opened to each other's ugliness. Certainly Adam did not gaze at Eve and gasp for a lack of beauty. No, they hid because they felt shame. In one sense, they experienced shame because they were no longer at peace with God. Due to their own sinfulness, they now had feelings of guilt and unworthiness. They not only had let God down, but they also had disappointed themselves. They could no longer be considered safe.

Second, not only did they break covenant with God, they also broke covenant with each other. Each of them came to the realization that neither of them could be trusted. They felt vulnerable and scared that their hearts were no longer protected from hurt. The bottom of their boat fell out, as both Adam and Eve had to come to terms with their sinfulness. They could not put their trust in themselves or each other. This gap became readily apparent to them. What *is* and what *should be* were not the same. It's the inward wrestling match that Paul describes in Romans 7:19: "For I do not do the good I want to do, but the evil I do not want to do—this I keep on doing."

With great vulnerability and the stark realization that the covenant with God was now broken, they made a feeble attempt to "fix it." Their attempt to fix the situation was to make clothing for themselves and present themselves in a new way. Adam knew that before he sinned, what was and what should be were the same. There wasn't inner turmoil. However, after he sinned, he wanted to step back to the time before sin. He wanted to go back and restore what was broken. After all, haven't we done the same thing? Have you ever tried to cover up a sin or to "fix it"?

The clothing that Adam and Eve made was inadequate to cover up their sinfulness. God, bestowing great mercy, provided a more adequate covering of animal skin, not to aid and abet the sinfulness of Adam and Eve, but rather to cover them with his great mercy. The garments of clothing were provided to be a constant reminder of the necessity of confession. The clothing did not conceal their sin, but rather served as a constant reminder that a sin offering, or covering, was necessary to make amends with God.

How often we try to hide our sin. We may offer up a few confessions during our Christian accountability group, knowing full well that if anyone could see the true ugliness that lies within us, they would be disgusted. I recently was so utterly appalled by my own inward battle with sin that I felt like vomiting it all before the Lord. I was holding onto anger. I was struggling with bitterness. How much time do we spend covering up our faults, sugarcoating our sin with excuses, rather than honestly admitting them before God? We evade, cover up, sugarcoat, excuse away, and chime right in with our sin.

Read Psalm 69:5. What does it say about our sin?

If God already knows our sin, then the only ones being deceived are us. We deceive ourselves into thinking that our sin doesn't really matter, that we won't get caught, that everyone else is doing it (and, therefore, it must be okay), that we'll do it only this once . . . and before we know it, we get caught in a cycle of sin. We get caught in this cycle, and it quickly consumes us. Sin, like yeast in batter, can spread quickly and no longer be easily removed and/or identified. If not dealt with, sin can become a way of life for us, and we can become immune to its effects.

Read 1 Corinthians 5:6–7. How are we to deal with our sin?

I love how this verse reminds us to return to "who we really are." We are children of God, we are new creatures, we are made new in Christ Jesus—our identities are no longer found in the name brands we wear, the people we are friends with, the emblems our cars are labeled with, the sports teams our children play with—no, our identities are in Christ. He truly is all we need. He should be all that matters. This world teaches us to place our identities in fame, power, and money. God's kingdom teaches us something quite to the contrary. His kingdom is based on servanthood, submission, and suffering. For example, as a Christian, if you lose your job, you know things may be tough financially for a while. You may be taught a lesson in suffering, humility, rejection, and possibly even poverty. It's at times like this that you may be taught where your real treasure is, where your identity lies. As a believer, you work, but your work does not identify or control you. Christ is your identity. Coming to the realization that the things of this world do not matter is actually very freeing. Christians are not controlled by promotions, status, recognition, and money. God's kingdom operates in reverse: where the first become last, and the last become first (Matthew 20:16).

Prior to our move to Austin, I overheard a mother giving my daughter advice. She told her that she should be excited about the move because she could change anything about herself that she didn't like. She commented that one time she moved and changed her name, and another time she moved, she changed her hair color. She tried to convince my daughter that she could do the same—that she could seize the moment and become a totally different person. Her condolences quickly backfired when my daughter replied that she liked who she was. She didn't want to change a thing (nor did she want to move)! I love my daughter's response!

When we are lined up and have found our identities in Christ, we won't want to change a thing. There is nothing like having peace with God. He is all we need!

Lord, I didn't want to be that girl who hid from you.

Take time today to confess things of this world that have stolen your godly identity. (Let me suggest a few: the car you drive, the purse you carry, success of your children, and/or the job you envy.)

See what kind of love the Father has given to us, that we should be called children of God; and so we are. The reason why the world does not know us is that it did not know him. Beloved, we are God's children now, and what we will be has not yet appeared; but we know that when he appears we shall be like him, because we shall see him as he is. And everyone who thus hopes in him purifies himself as he is pure.

—1 John 3:1–3, ESV

A CRAFTY CREATURE

Week 5: Day 3

We often envision Satan to be this guy dressed in a red leotard with pointy ears, carrying around a pitchfork. I'm not really sure where this image got its roots; maybe it was Cupid gone awry. Have you ever wondered who this guy named Satan is anyway? I think in our culture we tend to picture him often as we do God. We tend to think that he is far off, distant, and uninvolved. Unlike God, we credit him with creating havoc in this world, but we often fail to recognize him as a threat affecting our everyday choices and decisions. We tend to forget about him, blaming circumstances or others or even ourselves for the struggles we face. The Bible gives us a pretty good account of who Satan, our Enemy, really is. Let's begin today by reading Genesis 3:1–7. What word is used to describe Satan?

The dictionary defines *crafty* as "clever at achieving one's aims by indirect or deceitful methods."[40] We see that is certainly true from the get-go. How does Satan twist God's words right away in verse 1?

John 8:44 describes Satan this way: "When he lies, he speaks his native language, for he is a liar and the father of lies." I want to dig a little deeper and have us grow in our understanding of whom we are dealing with here. Please take the time to look up the following verses, and write a brief description of Satan after each one.

Matthew 13:19 _____

John 12:31 _____

Matthew 12:24 _____

---

40 "Crafty." Def. 1. *Oxford Pocket Dictionary of Current English,* 4th ed. New York: Oxford University Press, 2009.

2 Corinthians 4:4 _____

Ephesians 2:2 _____

Revelation 12:9 _____

This serpent that appears in the garden of Eden is the Devil, meaning "slanderer,"[41] also known as Satan, meaning "adversary".[42] He is not a fictional character who magically appears in horror films and Halloween costumes. He is alive and real and actively seeking whom he may devour. Scripture depicts him as a roaring lion, prowling around looking for his next meal (1 Peter 5:8). So, the serpent that first appears on the scene with Eve is already evil, a murderer, and a deceiver.

Where did he come from? Somewhere between Genesis 1:31, "God saw all that he made and it was very good" and our text today, Satan appears. Thankfully, some other texts in Scripture provide valuable insight. Look up Jude 1:6. Why were some angels cast from heaven?

Read also 2 Peter 2:4. Is it possible for angels to sin?

Most Bible scholars agree that there were a host of heavenly angels, including Satan, who were led in an insurrection against God. They desired to have power and authority over God rather than under God. In a rebellious attempt to overthrow God, Satan and the other angels caught in sin were cast from heaven. Satan continues to lead this rebellion today and bring many with him. He desires to be fully exalted to the position that only belongs to God.

If Satan is so powerful, should we feel defeated or be afraid? Absolutely not. Our God is greater. Our God is stronger. Write out the words from Psalm 2:11.

God is sovereign, even over the Enemy. "You, dear children, are from God and have overcome them [Satan and demonic forces], because the one who is in you is greater than the one who is in the world" (1 John 4:4). God is ultimately the one in control and calling the shots. Here are a few Scripture verses to serve as a reminder:

---

[41] *Strong's Exhaustive Concordance: New American Standard Bible.* Updated ed. La Habra: Lockman Foundation, 1995. "G1228.diabolos."
http://biblesuite.com/greek/1228.htm

[42] *Strong's Exhaustive Concordance: New American Standard Bible.* Updated ed. La Habra: Lockman Foundation, 1995. "H7854.satan." *http://biblesuite.com/hebrew/7854.htm*

- Jesus is the final authority over all creation. "He is the image of the invisible God, the firstborn over all creation. For by him all things were created: things in heaven and on earth, visible and invisible, whether thrones or powers or rulers or authorities; all things were created by him and for him. He is before all things, and in him all things hold together!" (Colossians 1:15–17).
- Mark 1:27 says, "He commands even the unclean spirits, and they obey Him."
- When Jesus conquered death on the cross, He disarmed the spiritual powers that may try to come against us. Because we are believers, Satan no longer has a claim on our lives: "When you were dead in your sins and in the uncircumcision of your sinful nature, God made you alive with Christ. He forgave us all our sins, having canceled the written code, with its regulations, that was against us and that stood opposed to us; he took it away, nailing it to the cross. And having disarmed the powers and authorities, he made a public spectacle of them, triumphing over them by the cross" (Colossians 2:13–15).
- The Enemy cannot touch a hair on your head without first getting permission from God. We see this in the life of Job when the Enemy sets out to destroy Job and his family. In Job 1:12, God says, "Very well, then, everything he has is in your power, but on the man himself do not lay a finger."
- Satan uses suffering to inflict pain on us and defeat us, but God uses suffering for our own good. Scripture tells us to "Resist him, standing firm in the faith, because you know that the family of believers throughout the world is undergoing the same kind of sufferings" (1 Peter 5:9). What the Enemy intended for evil, God turns upside down and uses it for good. That's why the apostle Peter wrote this in 1 Peter 4:13: "But rejoice inasmuch as you participate in the sufferings of Christ, so that you may be overjoyed when his glory is revealed."
- Life and death are in God's hand, not Satan's. "Your eyes saw my unformed body; all the days ordained for me were written in your book before one of them came to be" (Psalm 139:16). It is God who determines how many days we will live: "See now that I myself am he! There is no god besides me. I put to death and I bring to life, I have wounded and I will heal, and no one can deliver out of my hand" (Deuteronomy 32:39).
- No one can sift us out of God's hand. Not even Satan! Satan may be a master at deception, but he certainly cannot fool God. We can rest assured of our salvation (with the caveat that we truly are saved), knowing full well that the Enemy has no power over us. John 6:39 says, "And this is the will of him who sent me, that I shall lose none of all that he has given me, but raise them up at the last day."

We know we are children of God if we have a desire to do His will and not our own. Having the "assurance of salvation" does not give us a green light to go and live however we want, sinning abundantly. It doesn't mean we can live as we please, attend confession once a week, and then go right back to intentional sinning. Being children of God means that the Holy Spirit lives within us and convicts us of sin. This conviction then leads us to repentance and changed living. Do Christians continue to battle with sin? Yes, but sin will not have the final victory.

A perfect illustration of this is found in Scripture when Simon Peter, a disciple of Jesus, is tempted three times surrounding the time of Christ's death and crucifixion (see Mark 14:26–31). Jesus predicts, "Before the rooster crows twice, you yourself [Peter] will disown me three times." We see that Jesus is fully aware that Peter will be tempted and ultimately sin. Now, turn over to Luke 22:31–32 to see Luke's account of this story. No doubt, Satan is a great tempter. But can Satan act without God's permission? Write out Luke 22:31.

Who has to ask whom for permission? _____

In this same text, can you see how God turns the situation around for good? (Hint: look at verse 32.) Why does God allow this to happen?

It is God who has the upper hand and sets a boundary for Satan. God is sovereign over each of the Enemy's moves. One of the greatest transitions you will make in your Christian maturity is coming to the realization that God can turn suffering, pain, and difficulty for His ultimate good. You may not be able to make sense of the situation, but you should never lose sight of the fact that God is always up to something, and that something is always for your good.

Can you think of a time in your own life when God used a terrible situation ultimately for good? I can think of many in my own. My life is like an onion. God has peeled off many layers of selfishness, pride, discontentment, love of comfort, control, manipulation, and so much more to transform me into the image of Christ.

God often uses pain, difficulty, and suffering to change us. Can you think of a personal story to share?

What then is God waiting for? Why doesn't He just wipe Satan out *now*? God certainly has the ability to do so. I've often wondered what in the world He is waiting for, especially when this life becomes so hard. But then I must remind myself that God's ways are not my ways and His thoughts are not my thoughts (Isaiah 55:9). There is something much bigger and greater going on here.

First, let's not forget that one day God will defeat Satan eternally. Satan's days are numbered, and we will one day no longer have to deal with him. He will be thrown into a lake of fire to be tormented day and night, forever (Revelation 20:10). We have a reason to hope, because the battle will be won!

Second, we would not appreciate God's goodness if we didn't have an Enemy. Think about it for a moment: if all you knew was goodness and never had to deal with pain, suffering, struggles, and difficulty, you would not have a very good understanding of evil. The word *evil* does not have significance to you until you personally experience it. Reading about evil is nothing compared to actually living it. Once you experience it, you begin to grasp just how good "goodness" is. If there were no contrast, no comparison, then we would be missing out. We would not fully comprehend the extensiveness of God's goodness. Without a villain, the hero has no one to save. You would only know the tip of the iceberg, the "candy man" God. Of course that's what our flesh wants—we want the easy life—but that life only leads to a greater dependence on oneself. We would become saturated with our wants, our desires, and our unsatisfied selves. We've witnessed this scenario all around us: the child who always wants more; the "I want an Oompa-Lompa now" syndrome. If God parented us in that fashion, we would all become superficial, selfish brats!

Finally, God has a different perspective than we do. His timing is not like ours. Psalm 90:4 says, "For you, a thousand years are as a passing day, as brief as a few night hours." What seems like eternity for us here on earth is like a blink of an eye to God. He doesn't operate according to our timetable. He does give us some insight, though, for the long delay. Read 2 Peter 3:9. What is God waiting for?

In the end, Satan will be defeated, and God will receive the glory. That's what it is all about—giving God the glory. We see it repeated over and over and over again throughout the Scriptures. God will win, and He will be glorified. We can all shout the words that Jesus did after Lazarus was raised from the dead: "This sickness will not end in death. No, it is for God's glory so that God's Son may be glorified through it" (John 11:4). God is patiently waiting for more of us to know Him so that there will be a great crowd at the ultimate party.

Lord, I didn't want to be that girl who cratered to a crafty creature.

Think of ways the Enemy has deceived you recently. Write a response to God below:

Jesus gave his life for our sins, just as God our Father planned, in order to rescue us from this evil world in which we live.

—Galatians 1:4, NLT

LOST

Week 5: Day 5

This past weekend, my family invested in some rest and relaxation at my brother's house on Possum Kingdom Lake. Being a lover of the great outdoors, I always look forward to this trip with great anticipation. Besides the great water sports to enjoy on the lake, there are also plenty of hiking trails and incredible scenic outlooks. Waking up early on Saturday morning, I thought I would get a jump start on the day and go out for an easy jog on one of the nearby hiking trails. Being in somewhat familiar territory, I presumed the hike was roughly three miles and, therefore, did not take a cell phone, watch, or water. I anticipated being gone only about thirty minutes.

If you're not from Texas, then you may not understand this about Texas. It can go from a cool, breezy morning to a blazing summer sauna in lightning speed. I happened to be on the verge of utter disaster. You see, I jogged for roughly forty minutes and had an incredible conversation with God along the way. I thought I knew my way and was on my downward descent from my mountaintop trail. However, what I quickly discovered was that the trail brought me to an area I did not recognize. On top of that, the heat index was on a quick rise. From that point, I stumbled across a trail map only to realize I had absolutely no bearings. I knew my brother's street address, but unfortunately, it did not appear on the map. Even if I could get to a phone, the only phone number I have memorized is my husband's (sad, but true), and in this remote area, our cell phones did not work.

I envisioned that my husband had noticed I was missing and had sent a search team out for my rescue. Then I remembered he was out fishing with our son on my brother's dock, and him noticing my disappearance was almost impossible. I reminded myself that he was on fisherman's time—not search and rescue. That's when the sinking, gut-wrenching reality that I was lost, utterly lost, set in.

In the past, I would have panicked and probably cried my eyes out. However, since I've lived a little, I tried to hold my composure. (Needless to say, I wanted to cry. I just didn't allow myself to. I figured I'd let that breakdown occur a bit later.) So, there I was, lost in the wilderness. I hadn't seen a soul the entire morning. I felt so lost and alone, with the panic of helplessness knocking at my heart's door.

Now imagine yourself in Eve's shoes. She has just done the unthinkable. She has disobeyed the one, the only one, command she was given: "Do not touch the tree of knowledge of good and evil or thou shalt surely die." And yet, she blew it. She blew it not only for herself but also for the ages to come. She forsook God. Now she was lost. Completely lost. Alone. Oh, so bitterly alone. And for what? Did she really believe she could outsmart God? Had the snake betrayed her? Yes, oh yes, she believed him. She thought the snake was wise. How foolish! If only she could turn back time. Disappointment overwhelmed her. What a fool she had been. She had been given so much, and the Lord God, Maker of all, only kept one thing from her hand. She'd felt lust. She caved. She just had to have it. Not only did she have to have it, but also she persuaded her husband to follow suit. She felt distrust in herself. Distrust in Adam. Distrust in the snake. Thoughts invaded her mind. If she could not even trust herself, then could she even trust God? Doubt, fear, abandonment: all three came creeping in.

There have been so many times in this life when I've completely blown it, just like Eve! I've wanted to run and hide. I have felt as if I've let God down and that He could not possibly accept me again, let alone love me again. I certainly felt that I didn't deserve His forgiveness. Truth is, I haven't earned His grace. I'm guaranteed just to muck things up again. Our natural tendency is to run and hide—to run straight toward the forest with the intention of fixing ourselves before facing God again. We convince ourselves that surely a holy God would not accept a mess like us. We desperately try to get our lives in order. We follow the behavior modification rules of the church. However, we find that even those fail. Our efforts are futile. We may eventually end up looking pretty on the outside, but still we wrestle with dark thoughts within. We're never able to clean every nook and cranny of our own souls. Thankfully, we serve a very gracious and forgiving God.

Scripture is the best remedy for our broken souls when we've journeyed afar. Throughout my lifetime, I've devoted myself to numerous Bible studies and have read countless Christian books. I love studying God's Word and reading commentaries that can provide additional insight. However, speaking from personal experience, there is nothing that even comes close to healing my broken soul like God's Word. Nothing. Every book and Bible study that I've dived into always comes out underlined, earmarked, and with countless stars and circles by words that have personally spoken to me. I mark things that I want to remember. Time after time, the most underlines and stars in my books are where the author has quoted Scripture, God's very spoken Word. There's no better remedy for a broken soul. Scripture has the power to find a lost disciple. It may seem a bit time intensive at first to locate the various Scripture verses throughout the Bible. Please don't cave on this one. Your time will not be wasted. Expect God's Word to speak to you today. Jot down what each Scripture tells you about the character and attributes of God.

Psalm 18:2

Psalm 23:4

Psalm 34:18, Revelation 21:3–4

Psalm 136:1

Job 14:5

Ecclesiastes 3:11

Isaiah 40:28–31

Ephesians 2:4–5

Philippians 2:13

1 Peter 5:7

Which attribute spoke most to you and why?

I once heard a preacher say that the best advice he had ever been given is to "start each day spending time with God—and don't leave your room until you are happy with Him." If I would adhere to this incredible advice, there would be plenty of days when I would never make it out of my room. What a better place this world would be without my demented, weary, moody, selfish, prideful, and self-righteous self out for a stroll. Rather, to my own detriment and the detriment of hopeless others, I often find myself spending too much time at the wrong campsite. I leave my room not even thinking about God. My mind wanders, and I lose track of His perspective, His purpose, and His plans. I find myself focusing on my circumstances and difficulties and suffering rather than finding the blessing in it all. I set up camp with "me." I start my day thinking about what I want to do—not what God wants me to do. I think about what will bring me joy—not what I can do for others. I ask what I can get out of my situations, "What's in it for me?" rather than ask, "How I can give?" I so often start my day thinking about me, me, and me.

If I'm not careful, I can thrust myself quickly into a pit of despair. The art of comparison can rob me of all my joy. The captivity of activity can drive me. Pride can send me falling. Getting a heavy dosage of Scripture helps me survive my wilderness days. Nothing more than God's Word puts this wandering mind back on the right trail, the trail that leads me directly back to Him. I have found that there is only one trail map that can lead me safely back home.

Many have put this trail map aside, overridden with guilt. They've tried to read God's Word, and they started out with good intentions, but after a while, they gave up. Just as with their exercise program, old habits set in, excuses were made, or church legalism drove them away. If you currently find yourself spending too much time in this campsite, let me offer a few suggestions:

1. Expect to hear from God. Look intently into His Word to see what He is speaking to you. If you don't anticipate hearing from God, then when He does speak to you, you most likely won't recognize Him. (See Psalm 63:1.)

2. Don't rush God. Put other distractions aside, and find a place and time where you can focus your thoughts on Him. (See Habakkuk 2:20.)

3. Read a section of Scripture, and examine what the verses are saying. It's good to read an entire book of the Bible at a time to understand the context. Don't race through it, but actually think about the text. Read it repeatedly to understand the author's intent. Consider reading it aloud to help you pay attention. Remember that you are not just reading to gain information, you are reading to be in a relationship with Christ.

4. Reflect and remember. As the Holy Spirit pricks or prompts you, think about a particular verse or verses. Meditate on Scripture throughout your day. In other words, chew on it. How do these verses apply to you and to your current circumstances today? Dedicate time to Scripture memorization. (See Jeremiah 15:16 and Psalm 119:11.)

5. Obey. If you want to live an exciting Christian life and hear God's voice, then you must obey what He is teaching you. Theologian Dietrich Bonhoeffer wrote this in his book, *The Cost of Discipleship*: "Cheap grace is the grace we bestow on ourselves. Cheap grace is the preaching of forgiveness without requiring repentance, baptism without church discipline, communion without confession . . . Cheap grace is grace without discipleship, grace without a cross, grace without Jesus Christ, living and incarnate."[43] What God requires of us is costly grace—the kind of grace that has action behind its words.

6. Vary your plan. If you are used to always having your quiet time in a specific place, mix it up. Go outside. Go for a drive. If it's been months since you've heard from God, take time to just listen. Don't let your quiet time become robotic. It should be relationship driven, not boring and legalistic. If you are having a difficult time reading Scripture or praying, try spending time thanking God for who He is and what He has done. If you are a type A personality, spend a whole hour in Scripture memorization. Knock yourself out. Just don't forget to also apply it.

God's Word is living and active (Hebrews 4:12) and is pertinent for our everyday. Let's not forget to talk to Him. Let's not grow weary. May we all persevere to the end. Don't give up, my dear sister. As Oswald Chambers said, "We tend to use prayer as a last resort, but God wants it to be our first line of defense. We pray when there's nothing else we can do, but God wants us to

---

43 Dietrich Bonhoeffer, *The Cost of Discipleship* (New York: Touchstone, 1995), 47.

pray before we do anything at all. Most of us would prefer, however, to spend our time doing something that will get immediate results. We don't want to wait for God to resolve matters in His good time because His idea of 'good time' is seldom in sync with ours."[44]

I studied the trail map intensely and wished desperately I had paid more attention in geography class. Why was it so difficult to read a map, and why didn't my parents ever put me in a Girl Scout troop? Maybe then I would've been better skilled at reading a map and surviving the wild. It's no wonder my kids make so much fun of me for only reading my GPS from the "bird's eye" view. Needless to say, I decided to keep moving and attempt to find my way home. I knew that my brother lived near a campground and saw several such campgrounds noted on the map. I set out with high hopes of finding the right one.

Although I missed the mark on my first attempt, I persevered. Several hours later, I found my way home. Sad to say, my search and rescue team never left home base. They were enjoying a hot breakfast when I arrived. They didn't have a care in the world. Everyone was laughing and conversing around the dinner table.

Lord, I didn't want to be that girl who was lost in the wilderness without You.

Don't give up on God, my dear sister. He cares deeply for you no matter what state or condition your life may be in. Turn to Him. No, run safely into His arms. Write a response to Him today.

This I recall to my mind, Therefore I have hope. The Lord's loving-kindnesses indeed never cease, For His compassions never fail. They are new every morning; Great is Your faithfulness. "The Lord is my portion," says my soul, "Therefore I have hope in Him."

—Lamentations 3:21–24, NASB

---

[44] "Quote by Oswald Chambers," n.d. http://www.goodreads.com/quotes/166479-we-tend-to-use-prayer-as-a-last-resort-but (September 1, 2013).

WEEK 6: SWEET REUNION

DANGEROUS SECRETS

Week 6: Day 1

Let's be honest—we all love it when someone shares a secret with us. We like to feel included in the loop. Whether it be an upcoming surprise party or our best friend's good news of a long-awaited pregnancy, it just feels good to be included. To know that your friend has considered you worthy of her confidence is quite the pat on the back. She has chosen you to confide in above all others in what appears to be a noteworthy cause. It certainly makes you feel special. It gives you a sense of empowerment to know something no one else does. Yet I find it interesting that we feel so empowered, when in actuality the act of carrying a secret can weigh us down.

Secrets are certainly burdensome. Numerous studies have indicated that the weight of carrying a secret can cause damage to both our physical and emotional wellbeing. *Psychology Today* reports that, "High self-concealers tend to be stressed out and depressed and have low self esteem. They suffer frequent headaches and back pain. People with secret memories fall sick more often and are less content than people with skeleton-free closets. Not surprisingly, a high degree of self-concealment is a dominant feature of people with OCD."[45]

A high level of self-control is required to keep a secret; therefore, this deliberate concealment of information taxes one psychologically and physically.

Dr. Coburn H. Allen, a pediatric emergency physician at Dell Children's Hospital, says that one of the first courses of treatment for a person who has undergone a traumatic event (whether it be rape, a car accident, death of a family member, etc.) is to get the person to talk about it. Talk therapy is a vital first step in the patient's recovery process. Research shows that talk therapy extends the life of breast cancer patients and that the newly widowed reduce their odds of getting sick by talking out their grief.

Keeping our sin secret can likewise cause us much harm. It can cause us to withdraw from others and from God. It can affect our emotional well-being. It can even make us physically ill. The simple act of talking, getting things off our chests, can reap great rewards. Did you know

---

45   Alex Stone, "Fooling Houdini: Secret Secret, I've Got a Secret," *Psychology Today*. Last updated July 3, 2012. *http://www.psychologytoday.com/blog/fooling-houdini/201207/secret-secret-ive-got-secret* (September 1, 2013).

that Scripture advises us to do so and likewise tells of the health benefits involved? Read David's account in Psalm 32:3–4. Describe how he felt below:

If we know bearing our souls and sharing our secrets is good for us, what is holding us back? We would rather jeopardize our emotional and physical health than show our secret skeletons. But why? I'll tell you in one word—*fear*. We are deathly afraid that others will know we are not perfect. We fear that we will let others down. We fear that when the depravity of our souls is revealed, no one will want to be our friend. We fear our reputation will be jeopardized.

The fear we feel today, says Dr. Gordon Livingston, only makes us preoccupied with safety, but total safety is impossible because life "is intrinsically unsafe." It's so unsafe, in fact, that we're all going to die. We can exercise, eat all the "right" foods, give up our vices, follow doctor's orders to the letter, withdraw completely from society to avoid contagion, and we'll still die. It's inevitable. The best we can do, Livingston says, is to find "the courage required to confront adversity of all sorts."[46] Courageous behavior involves a combination of choice, risk, and a willingness to benefit others, and it ultimately gives life meaning.

Still, even with this insight, few of us are willing to take that risk.

Instead, secrets tax us like lies. They carry the same health and emotional implications for us. Mimi Beardsley, infamously known for her former affair with president John F. Kennedy, broke her silence after fifty years of anonymity. In her book *Once Upon a Secret: My Affair with President John F. Kennedy and Its Aftermath* she claims "she came to understand that shutting down one part of her life so completely had closed her off from so much more."[47]

Keeping secrets should be seen as a hindrance, not a help.

People will fail a polygraph test for keeping a secret as if they are telling a lie. This act of deception is nothing new. I realize that we've touched on these verses previously, so don't think I'm totally losing my mind. I feel the Holy Spirit tugging on some additional truths in there that I don't want to skim over. Turn with me today to Genesis, and read Adam and Eve's reaction to their own personal secret (Genesis 3:8–9). Once again, how did Adam and Eve react to their personal sin?

---

[46] Dr. Gordon Livingston, *The Thing You Think You Cannot Do: Thirty Truths About Fear and Courage* (Boston: Da Capo Press, 2012), xiii.

[47] Mimi Alford, *Once Upon a Secret: My Affair with President John F. Kennedy and Its Aftermath* (New York: Random House, 2012), book description.

We've already discussed that God knows our sin and that we are incapable of hiding from Him. The point I want to touch on today is slightly different and will take us one step deeper into understanding God's Word. Not only are we, as believers, to confess our sins to God, but also we are to confess our sins to each other.

Read James 5:16, and document the reason for confession. What is the ultimate goal?

We live in a narcissistic culture that encourages our attention to be focused on ourselves. We have been taught and are teaching our children that self-love is the remedy for true healthiness. The current flow of thinking is that one should focus on oneself in order to feel "empowered" and "loved." No one can love you like yourself. The words *self-admiration*, *self-expression*, and *self-absorption* become more than tolerable; they have become acceptable. Self-centeredness and self-indulgence are no longer an exception; they are the norm. We feed ourselves lines, such as "I deserve this" or "I don't care what others think; it's all about me." "Psychologists have been tracking narcissism through surveys of American college students since the late 1970s, and levels of it—often measured as a lack of empathy—have never been higher, according to Sara Konrath, an assistant professor at the University of Michigan's Research Center for Group Dynamics. "If you look at the levers in society, almost all of them are pushing us towards narcissism," she says. These levers go beyond Twitter feeds and Facebook pages, which offer endless opportunities for self-admiration. They also include advertising that tells consumers, "You're worth it," and reality TV shows that turn regular people against each other in a battle for celebrity."[48]

Our culture preaches that our focus should be on ourselves and that our empowerment comes from within. With the surge of Facebook, Twitter, and Instagram, we've concluded if we can't live the life we want to live in reality, at least we can live it virtually. Our reality is becoming intertwined with our virtual selves. We become preoccupied with living this so-called life that we want to live . . . or wish we could live. We spend countless hours presenting an unrealistic perfection. The harsh reality is, though, that it doesn't exist. Yet, we persist. If we can't be perfect, at least we will try. Right? We diet. We Botox. We work out endlessly. We whiten our teeth. We color our hair. We embellish our kids' stories. We name drop. We pluck our nose hairs (maybe I've gone a bit too far; sorry). We wear designer jeans and carry around designer purses. We pursue fame and fortune, and if that is not possible, we get as close to it as we can. We befriend as many people as possible on Facebook, Twitter, and Instagram, so that even if we don't feel as if we have any friends, at least we have the appearance of having tons of friends. We resign ourselves to the fact that we may not be happy, but at least we can have the appearance of being happy. Why do

---

[48]   Daniel Altman, "United States of Narcissism," *The Daily Beast*. Last updated July 17, 2011. *http://www. thedailybeast.com/newsweek/2011/07/17/narcissism-is-on-the-rise-in-america.html* (August 31, 2013).

you think superficiality and surface-level relationships abound? People have forgotten what it's like to be real. Honest. Open.

This is our current culture. I'm just curious; do you see any signs of this in you?

I don't think any of us is immune, and neither is our church. I have grown up in the church, and I love it immensely. However, during my lifetime, I have seen incredible damage done by keeping up this persona of perfection. We have greatly mistreated God's Word by equating perfectionism with spiritual maturity. And in doing so, we have created a barrier between the unchurched and ourselves. It is no wonder that the church has been marred by the title of "a place filled with hypocrites." I have watched pastors fall to adultery, Sunday school teachers with alcohol addictions, divorces take place in our deacons and elders, sexual immorality and pornography within church leaders, our young daughters having abortions—yet a word was never said. They continue on as if nothing ever happened. The great cover-up is pursued. *Hush* is the word.

It comes as no surprise to hear the words "I'm fine" in reply to "How are you doing?" when I know full well this is untrue. Marriages are crumbling. Children are rebelling. Anger is lingering. Bitterness is ensuing. Idolatry is lording. Laziness is corrupting. Self-righteousness is impeding. Pride is pressing. But no, we will not tell.

Jeff Magnum, pastor at Austin Stone Community Church, recently preached a sermon discussing the importance of "community apologetics." He stated that there might be nothing more powerful than when an imperfect community of believers proves to the world of unbelievers (and non-committed church goers) what God has done. There should be no such thing as a *private* life if you are a believer. Yes, it is *personal*, but it should not be kept private. When we remain silent, we do not give credit to the work that God has done on our behalf.

Do you agree or disagree? Why or why not?

Please read Proverbs 28:13. What are we given as a result of confession?

If we could more fully understand the mercy that has been granted us, we would not hesitate in confession. My friend recently commented, "I confess my sins because I know I'm a sinner. And I also know God loves sinners!" Unfortunately, what causes hesitation before an honest, sincere confession is our pride. If we think we are just kind of bad, we don't give grace enough credit. If we realize we are really bad, we have a better grasp of grace. To put it bluntly, we are all worse off than we ever imagined. May we all heed the following warning: "So, if you think you are standing firm, be careful that you don't fall!" (1 Corinthians 10:12).

There is no such thing as a secret sin . . . sin is discoverable. Read Hebrews 4:13 and Luke 12:2–3. Where will our secrets be proclaimed? And why?

We are unwilling to bear our secret sins because we are consumed with ourselves. We are worried about our self-image. We are afraid of what others will think. We have put up barriers in hopes that no one would be able to peer inside to see who we really are. Our superficiality has inflated. However, in doing this, we are hindering the proclamation of the glory of God. We are failing to recognize our own need for mercy and for allowing God to use our sinfulness for His glory. Our connection point with unbelievers is that we need a Savior too. We are not perfect. Strive as we might, we cannot work our way into heaven. It is by God's grace, and grace alone, that we have received eternal life. Why then are we working so hard to look so perfect? There is a Puritan prayer that says, "Oh the things I don't deserve, yet you give me."

I believe that you will experience liberation and freedom as you confess your secret sins (not the sins of your spouse, friend, or neighbor—but *your* sins). Healing will come. As others open up and share their sins, too, be mindful that this is difficult and painful. Your job is to be a steward of mercy. It is not your job to judge or cast blame. We all are in dire need of God's mercy. We all are broken. It is, however, your job to pray. Regardless of the mess that you've made in your life, remember that God is still able to use you. You have a story worth telling! And He's not finished with you yet!

Lord, I didn't want to be that girl hiding a secret.

Go ahead. Don't be afraid. Begin confessing your secrets today.

But in your hearts revere Christ as Lord. Always be prepared to give an answer to everyone who asks you to give the reason for the hope that you have. But do this with genteelness and respect.

—1 Peter 3:15

WHERE ARE YOU?

Week 6: Day 2

My husband grew up in Oregon, and every other summer we get together with his family in a wonderful part of the country—Bend, Oregon. One of our family bonding experiences is to endure (and I do mean endure, after our last summer adventure, but that is for another place and time) a whitewater rafting trip. This trip takes place on the Deschutes River. This whitewater excursion is ranked a "three" which makes it a perfect family outing. There have been years when the river has been low, and we have had to get out of our boat and push ourselves over the twists and turns, rocks and crannies. Then, there have been other experiences, where this calm current has become a raging monster. Whether calm or crazy, though, I would never attempt this journey without a guide. I rely on the guide's experience to get me safely back home.

Wouldn't it be great if you could get a guide for other parts of your life besides white water rafting? For example, if you were dating, wouldn't it be great if you could get a guide to walk you through the dating process? "No, not that one! He's a total loser. Date this guy instead!" If you got in an argument with your husband, wouldn't it be wonderful to pull out a strategic guide, one that would tell you how best to defend your logic and give you the cutting edge? Or a Magic 8 Ball that you could pull out and shake whenever you needed an answer, such as "Without a doubt" or "most likely" or "outlook not so good"? We may not always like or agree with the answer—but oh, the sweetness of having an immediate response. No more waiting or hedging this way or that. I can't even imagine the impact that this would have on our lives.

Many have misused the Bible in this same way: as a toy that can be manipulated, twisted, and turned to get the responses that they want to hear. The Bible is pulled off a dusty old shelf when we find ourselves in an urgent crisis. When the pressures of this world are caving in and we need an immediate response, only then do we pull out the Bible. Exclusively in our acts of desperation, do we cry out to Him. That's, if we're truly honest, what we all want the Bible to be: a quick read; an answer book. Let me tell you, sisters, that this is not how the Bible works. It's not how God works, either. He is not meant to be a Magic 8 Ball. When we use Scripture in this manner, all of a sudden we turn the Bible into a book that is all about us. This may knock your socks off this morning—but the Bible is a book that was written *for* us, not *about* us.

If you've grown up in Sunday school, as I have, then you've probably been told a time or two that God created us because He desired to have fellowship with human beings. This makes God out to sound like a lonely old guy sitting around in heaven kind of bored. Here is a guy who can have anything . . . He can create anything imaginable. Do you really believe He became bored with the lions, monkeys, and giraffes, the majestic mountains and deep valleys, the great expanse of the sea, the dense rainforest, the moon, and the stars . . . and out of His boredom, He decided to create human beings? No, that train of thought is ludicrous! God did not create us because He needs us. And furthermore, we were not created for His amusement, thrill, or entertainment. We were not created to be His puppet toys. God did not need more to do! Nor was He lonely. We were created for God's glory, as was all of creation. God's glory is the reason we exist.

With that being said, let's begin today with our hearts in the proper position, in a place of humility. Remember the high calling of low humility.

The smaller we become, the more we will behold of God. Begin today by reading Isaiah 40:21–26. Write out your thoughts about these verses. What is God speaking to you right now?

It is important to have a proper perspective on our lowly position before resuming our study of Eve. Most of us, even on bad days, think more highly of ourselves than we ought. It is easy for us to think that we are our own masters, that we are calling the shots, and that we control our own destinies. But, in fact, we do not. Our lives are but a vapor (Psalm 144:4). Meditate on that for a moment. Let that thought really sink in.

Now, we are ready to allow some powerful truths to sink in today. Open your Bible with me to Genesis 3:8–9, and let these words penetrate.

Where do we find God? _____

Where do we find Adam and Eve? _____

I am just days away from celebrating my twenty-first wedding anniversary. I am blessed to say that over the years, my heart has grown fonder and fonder for this man. I am more in love with him today than I was twenty-one years ago. Although it has been years since my husband proposed to me, I can vividly recall the moment as if it were yesterday. At the time, I was living in Tulsa, Oklahoma, working as an accountant for a public accounting firm. Coby was in the process of moving to Houston, Texas, to begin medical school at Baylor College of Medicine. We were on the verge of attempting a long-distance relationship, and the thought of being miles and miles apart made both of us uneasy. After dinner, we went for a walk on the River Park's trail along the Arkansas River. We found ourselves out on a walking bridge overlooking the river when

Coby made his move. His arms were wrapped around me when suddenly he surprised me with his proposal. He opened a ring box right in front of me and uttered the words, "Will you marry me?" It took me a while to gather my composure (as if I had any) and utter back yes. That was one of the best decisions I've ever made in my life!

Now imagine if Coby had followed his proposal with, "I want to be with you one day a week for the rest of my life." Or, "I want to include you on the big decisions of my life." Worse yet, "I want to be with you when I feel like it." I can tell you right now that my response would not have been the same. I probably would've taken that ring and thrown it right into the river.

We find ourselves on the set in the garden of Eden. In this scene, we see God Himself taking a walk in the garden. I don't believe that this was an infrequent reality. I love that God is real and personable! And not only was this the case for Adam and Eve, but it is also the case for us as well. Read Leviticus 26:12. Write out the verse below.

God is calling us into a relationship with Him, not because He has to. Not because of anything we have done or not done. Not because He is lonely. He has done it simply because He wants to. He wants to have a relationship with you. He wants to be involved in your day to day. He desires to carry on a conversation with you . . . just as you would with your best friend. Better yet, He wants to be your best friend. He wants to be your everything. Is that what you are giving Him in return? Or have you compartmentalized your relationship with Him and only left Him time once a day? Once a week? Once a month? When you feel like it? As an emergency call? If that's the case, then maybe it's time to reevaluate what we are putting into this relationship. Maybe it's time to rethink why He's not our everything. How much time are you giving God?

We can busy ourselves with going to church and Bible study after Bible study. We can get so caught up in all the things we are doing for God that we never slow down to hear if that is where God wants us to be. We fill our daytime with "good things," things that help God and promote the gospel. This may sound confusing to you, but have you learned to listen to God's voice for *you*? Are you staying attentive long enough for Him to speak to *you*? Are *you* doing what He has called *you* to do?

Read James 1:22. What does it tell us to do?

I believe the Bible is the primary way that God speaks to us and personally directs our path. The will of God will never be in conflict with His written Word. Never. And second, along with and in communion with God's written Word, we have the Holy Spirit. You may be thinking to yourself that Eve had it so much easier because she could physically see and hear the voice of God. If she could see God and hear God's audible voice and still screw this whole thing up, how do you even stand a chance? Listen to God's promise, and let these words be an encouragement to you: "Though you have not seen him, you love him; and even though you do not see him now, you believe in him and are filled with an inexpressible and glorious joy, for you are receiving the end result of your faith, the salvation of your souls" (1 Peter 1:8–9).

Read Romans 8:14. Who will be led by the Holy Spirit?

I know it can be frustrating sometimes to be sure that you are hearing the voice of God. It sure would be nice if there were instant pop-up billboards or service announcements that would interrupt our station to announce to us the will of God. It would definitely make our lives a whole lot easier, without all the second-guessing about whether or not that was God. I wish I could give you a magic formula to uncover the secrets for the future of your life or a map that clearly tells you which way to go. I do wish it would be easier to figure out. That is an honest confession.

With that being said, however, I know that I would quickly excuse myself from God if it were that easy. I would not feel compelled to spend time with Him and search His Word for answers. I would not run to Him in my times of need. I would not desperately cling to His words if my road map of life were available at the click of a button. I would not diligently seek His voice or even attempt to listen. That's how decrepit I am. And even more, how selfish I can so easily become. I don't think I'm alone on this one. And that's why these words penned by John Calvin hit me between the eyes today: "There is no worse screen to block out the Holy Spirit than confidence in our own intelligence."[49]

The Bible is counterintuitive to our way of thinking. It goes against every grain of my flesh. That's why it is imperative to challenge our natural way of thinking to ensure that it conforms to Scripture. I have learned that I cannot trust my emotions or feelings because I am too easily swayed. The only thing I can trust is God and the truths set forth in Scripture. See if you can fill out the table below with additional examples of how God's way is counterintuitive to our way.

---

[49] John Calvin, "Quotes by John Calvin", *Calvin 500*, n.d. *http://www.calvin500.com/john-calvin/quotes-by-calvin/* (September 1, 2013).

Examples:

Our Way of Thinking	A Biblical Approach
to be served	to serve
to be first	to be last (humility)

I wonder how often I miss out on what God has to say because I fail to listen. I hastily jump to my own conclusion before giving Him a chance to speak. There are days I don't even spend time with Him. I tell myself I have too many things to do. This picture of God walking in the garden, looking for Adam and Eve, has hit me profoundly. He wants to spend time with us each and every day. How often do we preoccupy ourselves with the things of this world? We hit snooze on the alarm clock ad nauseam, we run late to work, we have TV shows that take priority, our kids tug on our arms for attention, we take vacations and forget entirely about God, workouts take priority . . . why are there so many things that become more important than spending time with God? Can you hear Him now calling to you, "Where are you?"

Lord, I didn't want to be that girl who refused to walk in the garden with You.

Are you spending time with God? Is He your top priority? Are you listening to what He has to say?

I instruct you in the way of wisdom and lead you along straight paths. When you walk, your steps will not be hampered; when you run, you will not stumble.

—Proverbs 4:11, 12

Send Out a Search Party

Week 6: Day 3

As we pick up from yesterday, we see our two characters, Adam and Eve, making a beeline for a cover-up. They hear the footsteps of God in the garden, and rather than come forth with the truth, they dart to hide. I guess we can at least give Adam and Eve credit for the invention of the game "hide and seek." What they failed to recognize is that their pursuer had an unfair advantage. He is omniscient (all-knowing) and was already aware of their sin. *Omniscience* is the "capacity to know everything there is to know."[50] Scripture makes it very clear that God sees and hears everything we do. Why, He even knows our thoughts before we think them. We may try to hide things from our kids, our spouse, our families, and/or our friends—but we cannot hide anything from God. We belittle our God if we fail to understand this attribute. Allow God's Word to speak to your heart more on this topic. Read the following verses, and jot down your thoughts regarding God's omniscience.

Psalm 139:4 _____

Psalm 147:5 _____

Isaiah 46:9 _____

Isaiah 55:9 _____

Matthew 10:30 _____

Hebrews 4:13 _____

1 John 3:19–20 _____

Which one of these verses spoke most to you and why?

---

50   "Omniscience." *Oxford English Dictionary* (3rd ed.). Oxford University Press. September 2005, s.v.

The question God posed, "Where are you?" was rhetorical. There is no way for Adam and Eve to outsmart God. The question He was asking was not for His good, but for their own. As we wander away from God, there comes a time when we must ask ourselves, "Where am I? What in the world am I doing here? Why have I wandered away from the One I love?"

I want to make sure you pick up on a very important point. Notice that it is not Adam and Eve who go looking for God, but God who mercifully pursues them. Despite what we have done, God still wants us. He still comes looking for us. Does that not just give you the chills? Look up the following verses and note what each one says about God's pursuit of us.

Joshua 1:5 _____

Luke 15:3-7 _____

The Bible is chock full of believers who have totally blown it. Moses killed a man. Rahab was a prostitute. Jacob was deceitful. Sarah was a liar. Joseph was arrogant. David committed adultery. Jonah ran from God. Thomas doubted. Peter was prideful. Paul was a rampant murderer. Yet God pursued them and forgave them. Not only did He forgive them; He went on to use them for the advancement of the kingdom of God. There is nothing too big for God. Let's not forget that.

To get a better grasp of the loving God we serve, let's take a look at the life of King David. David is a man of God who really blew it. He committed sins you never would expect a man with a "heart after God's own heart" (1 Samuel 13:14) to commit. And it wasn't one of those where he accidentally or unknowingly committed a sin before he realized what was going on. No, he put a great deal of thought and effort into committing his sin, and then he went to even greater trouble to cover it up (much like Adam and Eve). His sin was intentional. The events in his life read more like a soap opera than a Bible story. When the smoke finally cleared, two people were dead, and two families were destroyed. However, and please simmer on this thought, the man behind it all was not ruined. He was able to recover from his mistakes and get back up on his feet.

Since I've already had you tossing and turning through your Bible today, allow me to acquaint you with the story that begins in 2 Samuel 11. One evening, King David has a difficult time going to sleep, so he goes out on the balcony of his palace to take a walk. Off in the distance, he sees a beautiful woman named Bathsheba taking a bath. When he finds out that her husband, Uriah, is a soldier and away at war, David sends for her and seduces her, and adultery is committed. Sometime later, she tells him that she is going to have a baby, and to no surprise, he is the father. In an attempt to cover his tracks, David has Uriah brought in from the battlefield for what appears to be some "R & R." David suggests that Uriah go home and spend time with his wife. Uriah politely refuses; going home to his wife during a time of war would be an act of disloyalty to his fellow soldiers. Since Uriah can't be persuaded to compromise, David sends him back to battle with a letter to deliver to the commanding officer. Uriah doesn't know it, but he is delivering his own death warrant. The letter tells the commanding officer to put Uriah on the front lines and withdraw the other troops so Uriah will surely die. This is exactly what happens. Uriah is killed in battle, and David marries Bathsheba. No one at the time knew the story behind the story, but the Bible goes on to say, "But the thing David had done displeased the Lord" (2 Samuel 11:27).

Turn to 2 Samuel 12:1. What happens next in our story?

Despite David's sin, God graciously pursues him by sending the prophet Nathan. Due to his loving-kindness, He does not let David dig further into his pit of sin. Rather than allow David to continue to hide, He sends a harsh rebuke through a parable that entices David to pronounce his own condemnation. A harsh rebuke may be the best thing that ever happened to him. In 2 Samuel 12:7, we see Nathan proclaim, "You are the man!" Read 2 Samuel 12:7–12. Look at all that God gave to David. Look at all that He gave to Adam and Eve. Look at all that He has given to you. What are some things that God has given to you?

I'm stuck on the words at the end of verse 8: "I would have given you even more." At these words, my heart is in anguish. Why does my own soul wander? I have been given so much, and yet my heart doth wander. I can almost hear these words being uttered by God in my own circumstances, in my own situations, in my own living room. As a parent, I am often disappointed in the disobedience of my children. How often, I must wonder, is my heavenly Father disappointed in me?

David breaks down and finally confesses, "I have sinned against the Lord." The next few words are absolutely astonishing. Nathan replies (verses 13 and 14), "The Lord has taken away your sin. You are not going to die. But because by doing this you have shown utter contempt for the Lord, the son born to you will die." Are you kidding me? Bathsheba is raped. Uriah is murdered. The baby will die. What about David? He lied. He covered up. He "despised the word of the Lord." He "scorned God." He even showed "utter contempt for the Lord." Why does he get to keep living? Adam and Eve, well, they just took a bite into an apple. But, David, why does he deserve a second chance?

Thankfully, the apostle Paul puts some of these puzzle pieces together for us. Yes, I'm going to ask you to turn to one more Scripture reference. But in order for us to wrap up today, I think it's worth your time. Read Romans 3:21–26. Like David, God gives us a chance at redemption. How has God given you another chance?

I hope you paid close enough attention to notice that in order to show God's righteousness, because of His divine forbearance, He *passed over* unpunished sin. Let me put it another way. If David were alive today and his testimony were before the court, we would be outraged about what he had done. If God were simply sweeping David's sin under the rug, we would similarly be outraged. We would yell out, "That's not fair!" Fortunately, that's not what is going on here. You see, from the time of Adam and Eve, and forward to David, and forward to all the characters in the Bible . . . for centuries the plot was building and thickening until the death of God's Son, Jesus Christ. Jesus Christ was a propitiation for David's sin. He died in David's place. Remember earlier today how we discussed God's omniscience? God was all-knowing that David's sins would be counted as Christ's sins and that David would, and could, be considered righteous because of the righteousness of Jesus Christ. God is vindicated in *passing over* David's adultery, murder, and lying because of the blood of Jesus Christ.

Jesus, once and for all, paid for our sins and provided us reconciliation with God. We have nothing to contribute to this purchase. It is by faith, and faith alone, that we are declared righteous, and undeservingly so. With the comprehension of God's undeserved mercy, we see David's reaction to unconditional forgiveness in Psalm 51. If you have the time, I highly recommend you read it. David did face the music. He made things right with God and got his life back on track.

We often mistakenly think that God hates us because of what we've done. The truth is, He loves us no matter what. When we sin, even when we sin big, He wants to forgive us and help us get back on track.

God is interested in our complete healing, and He will bring situations and circumstances into our lives to accomplish this. Just a few weeks ago, I had the privilege of being a junior high counselor at our church's youth camp. I was surprised how similar my recent journey was to that of one of my girls. We both had experienced painful friend rejection. I don't believe in coincidences. To do so would be to lessen the size of our sovereign God. I believe God had her there for a reason—and there was a lesson for me to learn as well. I was able to share with her what God had intimately taught me over the past year and half. God sometimes allows rejection as His hand of protection. A deep connection with that twelve-year-old girl was certainly unexpected. Another surprise is the rich blessings that have come from a painful experience. God can use difficulties to redirect our paths and draw us closer to Him. Now that I am on the other side of it, I can say that this season of suffering was one of the best things that ever happened to me. I'm also thankful that God allowed me to be a part of this young lady's healing. Certainly, I have been "blessed to be a blessing" (Genesis 12:3). And so have you.

Can you think of a time when God brought about healing in your life in an unexpected way, such as when a messenger or a friend was used in the process?

There may be someone in your circle of influence whom you need to reach out to. Open your eyes so that you may see. Take the time to be a blessing. Even blessings can come wrapped in unusual packages. Nathan didn't say no to God, even though the task was difficult. By saying yes, he became part of David's redemption story.

Lord, I didn't want to be that girl who hid from You.

Think of someone today whom you can be a blessing to.

Suppose one of you has a hundred sheep and loses one of them. Doesn't he leave the ninety-nine in the open country and go after the lost sheep until he finds it? And when he finds it, he joyfully puts it on his shoulders and goes home. Then he calls his friends and neighbors together and says, "Rejoice with me; I have found my lost sheep."

—Luke 15:4–6

Passing the Buck

Week 6: Day 4

Let's remind ourselves again: what was the one command that God gave to Adam and Eve? (If you need a hint, look at Genesis 2:16–17).

Can you imagine if this scene were playing out today? Just go there with me. The headline reads, "Man Takes Fruit from Garden." If that was the tagline that interrupted your favorite TV show, I can't help but think you would say, "What is the big deal? What are they getting so heated up about? How could it possibly be that bad? I mean, injustices are happening all around the world, and this one is making headlines?" You may quietly think that society is not that bad. Life is generally okay for you. You know there is violence in this world, but as long as it doesn't touch your life, you prefer not to think much about it, let alone deal with it. You've decided it's just the way things are.

But to God, obedience is a big deal. He saw what Adam and Eve and the serpent did, and it crushed Him. If we could get a glimpse of looking at our world and seeing what God sees and knowing what God knows and feeling what God feels—sin would crush us too. We really don't want to know the truth about what our sin has done in our lives and to our world. We would prefer not to know, because it makes us uncomfortable. So, I have some bad news for us today, sisters. Today's lesson is all about sin, and it may make us a bit squeamish.

Let's continue reading our account in Genesis 3:8–12. Remember it was just an apple that enticed Adam and Eve away from God. Sin is a topic that we don't like to talk about, let alone address. But if we are honest with ourselves, so many things entice us away from God.

Studies show that it is really difficult for us to retrain our brains once we've been taught something. That is why we must be diligent to study God's Word, the only absolute truth. We all have a bent toward sin; it is what comes naturally. In other words, we have been born to sin. Since the fall of Adam, we have an inherited sinful nature. It is in our DNA. When you're frustrated, maybe you have inadvertently been taught to let a curse word slip out now and then. When you're tired, maybe you've been shown it's okay to be irritable or agitated just a little. When you're frustrated with the flow of traffic, maybe you've grown accustomed to becoming mad occasionally; perhaps you slam on the steering wheel a bit (as if that will get the flow going again. I've tried it before, and it never seems to work . . .). Maybe when you don't get your way and things are not turning out according to your plan, you complain. The serpent (Satan) and our American culture will always tell you that it's okay. It's not a big deal. "Everyone else is doing it." "No one will ever even notice—especially Uncle Sam." "You deserve to have that." "You have more important things to do." "You've had a tough day—you should just kick back and relax and forget all about spending time with God today."

The only absolute truth we have is God's Word. The only place you will find what is right and wrong is in His Word. I wonder how often we challenge our thought patterns, our actions, our intentions, our motives, our plans, and our behaviors against the Word of God. Just because we have responded well in the past does not ensure that we will respond well the next go around. We must not trust ourselves. In Philippians 4:8, we are challenged to think differently. It says, "Finally, brothers and sisters, whatever is true, whatever is noble, whatever is right, whatever is pure, whatever is lovely, whatever is admirable—if anything is excellent or praiseworthy—think about such things." Do you challenge yourself in regards to how you spend your time? Are your thoughts in line with God's Word? What is it that consumes you or motivates you?

Is there any area in your life that needs to be addressed, or have you become a creature of habit by thinking, *This is okay . . . my friends are doing it, my parents did it this way, my grandparents lived this way, my neighbors are okay with this, why—I even see people at church doing this*? Sin . . . s-i-n. Sin has always been appealing. Sin doesn't even faze us anymore, because it has become so much a part of our current culture. It is so in our face that I'm afraid we have become immune to some forms of sin. I know that I'm as guilty as anyone reading this. The other night I was watching a live TV show with my children, and I could not even keep up with how many times they bleeped out the cuss words. By the end of the show, I just laughed. I was sort of in disbelief over what I had just seen. But I'll confess to you, my response was wrong. It should have been one of remorse and sadness that our current culture has hardened its heart to God (that I have become immune to it).

The media have really caught on to this. Advertisers know that even if you don't like a product at the onset or disagree with the way the product is presented, the more you are exposed to it, the more comfortable you become with it. I can remember when Ugg boots first came out. I recall thinking, *What is so special about them? Ugg must be short for "ugly."* But about a year later, after everyone was wearing them, I found myself also purchasing a pair. (The same is true with my craze for TOMS.)

According to Wikipedia, "The mere exposure effect is a psychological phenomenon by which people tend to develop a preference for things merely because they are familiar with them. In social psychology, this effect is sometimes called the familiarity principle. The effect has been demonstrated with many kinds of things, including words, Chinese characters, paintings, and pictures of faces, geometric figures, and sounds. In studies of interpersonal attraction, the more often a person is seen by someone, the more pleasing and likable that person appears to be."[51]

A sin is an act that violates a known moral rule. Sin sounds deliberate—like *I meant to do it*. And I typically don't want to accept my wrongdoing. Our culture has renamed a *sin* as a *mistake*. It sounds more palatable. An "Oops! I didn't mean to. I didn't mean to hurt anyone." I certainly like how *mistake* is defined: it means "an error in action, calculation, opinion or judgment caused by poor reasoning, carelessness, insufficient knowledge, etc."[52] I can hear Adam's response now (verse 12): "The woman you put here with me—she gave me some fruit from the tree, and I ate it." The implication: *God, it is Your fault. You put that woman here, and I made a miscalculation in judgment.*

Very few of us like to fess up to our sins, because it makes us look bad. It's really hard for us to take a deep look in the mirror and see our own sin staring back at us. Adam is directly confronted by God regarding his sin, and rather than taking a look in the mirror, he passes the buck and blames his wife. He indirectly blames God, too, by saying "the woman *You* gave me" (Genesis 3:12, emphasis added). He fails to confront his own flawed identity. He fails to take the blame himself. When Adam took a bite from the apple, he wanted to make himself God. In a matter of seconds, the apple became his idol.

Not many of us would consider an apple an idol. Idols tend to be described as golden or carved images. A lot of people think of a little fat Buddha as an idol. We typically think that *idolatry* is a word that only applies in a historical context—maybe to undeveloped people groups of long ago, or if you've been in church long enough, you may think back to the Israelites melting down their jewelry and crafting up a cow. Paul K. Moser, head of the Department of Philosophy at Loyola University, has defined idolatry as "the universal human tendency to value something or someone in a way that hinders the love and trust we owe to God. It is an act of theft from God whereby we use some part of creation in a way that steals honor from God."[53] If the shoe fits, wear it. We have to throw our preconceived notions of an idol completely out the window. An idol can by *anything* that steals our attention away from God. It can be a person, place, or thing. It can even be consuming thoughts—as simple as our mind being so full of other stuff that we have no time to think about God.

---

51 "Mere-exposure effect," *Wikipedia, The Free Encyclopedia*, Last updated July 13, 2013. http://en.wikipedia.org/wiki/Mere-exposure_effect.

52 "Mistake." Def. 1. *Dictionary Online*. The Random House Dictionary, 2013. http://dictionary.reference.com/browse/mistake.

53 Paul K. Moser, "Idolatry," *Idolaters Anonymous: Stealing God's Glory*. Last updated August 9, 2007. *Loyola University of Chicago Department of Philosophy: http://www.luc.edu/faculty/pmoser/idolanon/Idolatry.html* (June 28, 2013).

Consuming thoughts are thoughts that pervade our minds so that we can't even worship on Sunday morning; thoughts that overtake our prayer life so that we lose focus on Him. They are the "self talk" and "inner chatter" that consume us. We read into the last spat we had with our husbands. We try to imagine what everyone else in the room is thinking about us. We rehearse situations over and over in our heads, playing out every minute detail. We read between the lines. We think the "apple" is what we have to have. We spend our minds on so many useless things. At the end of the day, there are so many time wasters that have nothing to do with God, and certainly nothing to do with eternity.

Read 2 Corinthians 10:5. What are we to do with this mindless, endless inner chatter?

Before Adam even took a bite, he thought that the apple would make him like God: he would have God's wisdom and knowledge and foresight. Billboards of greatness appeared in his head. He convinced himself that he could not live without it. He thought it would be his answer to everything.

Why do we chase after God's created things rather than delight in our Creator? Why do we turn from a love relationship with Him?

We worship the musician rather than the true *Composer*. We worship our great works rather than the great *Orchestrator*. We worship our minds rather than the first *Creator*. We take our eyes off of Him and place them on a substitute—the musician, our great works, our minds. Be honest with yourself today: have you taken your eyes off of God? Does He remain your top priority? Or has something as simple as an apple come in the way? What is it you are seeking that is more important to you than God? Why are you afraid to tell others about your love for Him? What is holding you back? Are you more concerned about what others will think of you than God Himself? Cite evidence in your life that reveals this behavior.

We don't obey God, and therefore, He loves us. No, He loves us, and therefore, we obey Him. God is vehemently opposed to sin and evil because He is holy and righteous (Habakkuk 1:13). Yet, we so easily and readily make excuses for our sin. *I don't have time. I don't feel like it. I'm too tired. I'm scared. I don't know what to say. I'm not educated. I haven't been a Christian long enough. They may not like me anymore.* Can you name any more? Do any excuses in particular hit home today?

Lord, I didn't want to be that girl who had to take responsibility for her own sin.

In closing, read Psalm 73:25–26. Allow the Holy Spirit to speak personally to you today, and write a prayer in response below.

If you bet on the existence of God and find at death he does not exist, then you have lost very little. But if you bet instead on God's nonexistence and discover at death that God does exist, then you have lost everything eternally.

—Blaise Pascal, seventeenth-century philosopher

A FLAWED IDENTITY

Week 6: Day 5

Our passage today is short . . . but unfortunately, it's not all that sweet. Yesterday we left off with Adam passing the buck. Today we will see his wife do the same. To skip over these passages lightly would do all of us a great injustice. We do ourselves a great injustice if we fail to understand the depravity of our own sin. Today our main text is found in Genesis 3:12–13: "The man said, 'The woman you put here with me—she gave me some fruit from the tree, and I ate it.' Then the Lord God said to the woman, 'What is this you have done?' The woman said, 'The serpent deceived me, and I ate.'"

Read the words of Abraham Heschel, a Jewish theologian and student of the Old Testament. "The shallowness of our moral comprehension, the incapacity to sense the depth of misery caused by our own failures, is a simple fact of fallen humanity which no explanation can justify or hide."[54] We see Eve follow in her husband's footsteps, and rather than take ownership for her own actions, she blames the serpent. She refuses to take responsibility for her own sin. Yes, Satan will come and tempt us. He receives glory when we fall. However, it is not the act of being tempted that is called sin; it is our response to it (1 Corinthians 10:13). We will be faced with temptation continually, and yet, the ball is in our court. How will we react? What will be our response? Can you think of a recent temptation to which you responded without sin?

Recently I confronted someone I love dearly about some apparent sin in her life. Her response was one of defensiveness and blame. It's almost as if I could hear her words exclaim, "The Devil made me do it" (except the "Devil" had a person's name). She had justified her actions and had even found biblical support. Let's face it: we can twist and turn God's Word to justify anything we want. Taken out of context, God's Word can say what we want to hear. This becomes even more challenging when we feel as if we are justified for our reaction.

This world is filled with injustices. We don't have to look too far or watch an hour of nighttime news to see our fallen world. We easily see Satan covering the horizon of the earth from east to west. All around us is the waste of death, murder, blood, robbery, violence, pillage, affliction,

---

54   Abraham Heschel, *The Insecurity of Freedom: Essays on Human Existence* (New York: Macmillan, 1955), 10.

pain, and misery. Satan seems to color the whole creation. We can grow immune to it—to the pain, suffering, and injustice. Just like wearing a watch every day or knowing the location of the furniture in the house . . . we can get used to it. We can walk around our homes without any lights on and not take a misstep. We can grow unaffected by injustices in this world. That is, until they hit close to home.

It is difficult to treat others justly when you have been mistreated. It is almost painful "to turn the other cheek" and walk away. It is difficult to be kind when you so clearly have been wronged, when everything within you wants to fight back, and/or when you want to have the final word. After all, that is the example Eve gives us in verse 13: "The devil deceived me and I ate." *It's all his fault. He made me do it.* Thankfully, with God's intervention and help, we can forgive even in the most difficult situations. Colossians 3:2–4 says, "Set your mind on things above, not on earthly things. For you died and your life is now hidden with Christ in God. When Christ, who is your life, appears, then you also will appear with Him in glory." We get to the point of forgiveness by keeping our gaze steadfast on the cross. After reading these verses, respond to the question: How can these verses help us when we are faced with temptation?

We can pretend and act confused about what God wants from us, but His expectations are clearly spelled out in His Word. From the very beginning, God has been quite clear about what He wants from us. He wants our all. We need to beware and not think of God's Word as merely good teaching. If it is just teaching, then we will become quickly frustrated that we do not have the means with which to attain our own salvation. All our good works combined are not enough. His goals are too lofty for us.

So how do we respond? What should we do? Should we be paralyzed by the immensity of injustice in this world or even in our own lives? Should we just sit around doing nothing but feeling intense guilt because of our own complicity in it? Read Micah 6:6–8. Pay particular attention to verse 8. What three things are we told to do?

In the Old Testament, God had established a systematic way for the atonement of sin by the offering of a blood sacrifice. From the very beginning, God made it known that our sin has a price. Notice the escalation in the text. Everyone could afford burnt offerings. Not many could afford a calf that is a year old. As for a thousand rams, only the king could offer that. Ten thousand rivers of oil are well beyond what anybody could do. The sacrifice of a firstborn child is a pagan ritual that surrounded Israelite culture. Is that what God wants? Yes or no? _____

I sure hope you responded *no!* It is easy to see that none of us can measure up to the demands given in Scripture. Unfortunately, however, our pride can quickly swell over all the good things that we do. One of the biggest temptations the church has succumbed to is a work-based theology.

We compare our lives to those around us and stand up proudly exclaiming, "I'm better off than so and so. Look at what I have done. See what I have accomplished." We compare our kids to those in our inner circle. We take pride in their accomplishments. We dress up for Sunday church and brag about our consistent attendance. We polish our exteriors, detaching ourselves from any wrongdoing. We brag about our good behavior and think in our minds that we are better off than those around us. We can look so good on the outside. We become law-abiding citizens and have no qualms elevating ourselves above others. We ride that elevator up, up, and up. We obey an unwritten, human-made code of dos and don'ts.

This game of compare and contrast is a dangerous slope. There really is not a win-win situation. When we measure up, those around us are inappropriately pushed down. We see ourselves better than we ought. We detach ourselves from the world around us because we don't want to be faced with the fact that we are just like them. We don't want to admit that we need a Savior, because in our minds, we have convincingly argued that we are just fine on our own. We brag about our health, our accomplishments, our good looks, our abilities, our talents, our kids, our jobs . . . never admitting our weaknesses or pride. We can look pretty darn good on the outside.

For years I was part of a women's Bible study and accountability group where we confessed our sins to one another, in accordance with James 5:16. Week after week, there was a woman in our group who could never think of any sin in her life to confess, while the rest of us bared our souls. Interestingly, she said that she would reflect on her life daily and could not think of any sin she had committed or was wrestling with. In her mind, she was doing just fine. You could check off the Christian to-do list, and she was doing it all remarkably well. Daily quiet time: check. Prayer time: check. Church attendance: check. Attending Bible study: check. Being proficient in the Scriptures: check. I can remember marveling at this woman, even wishing I could be more like her. She seemed to have everything in her life in such order. However, I realize now that she had a huge struggle with pride. She was more deceived than the rest of us in the room. The wool had been pulled over her eyes because she was living a lie. She had been deceived to the point that she believed that she no longer struggled with sin. Living above the rest of us, she was difficult to identify with, and her personal relationships began to struggle. I have to admit that it came as little surprise to hear that years later her marriage had crumbled and ultimately ended in divorce. Sadly, she was using the wrong checklist.

What is on your checklist? How does it stack up against biblical truth?

When we elevate ourselves above others, we pay an expense. If you find yourself with a growing list of people who get on your nerves or irritate you to no end, it may be time to take a look inside. Maybe the problem does not lie in others, but rather it lies in you. I've often discovered that the people I struggle to love are much more like me than I readily admit. As a mirror reflecting a flawed image, what I often see in others are the same things I do not like in myself.

Rather than take pride in ourselves, what does Scripture teach us to do? Read 1 Peter 5:6.

If we are constantly comparing ourselves with those around us and not measuring up, we are robbed of our joy. How often have we wished that we could have something that we don't? Fill in the following blanks: If only I could do _____. If only I could have _____. If only I could go _____. We have established this imaginary list of things that we believe will make us happy. The people in our lives who have these things seem so happy. We convince ourselves that we must have them too.

I haven't met a mother who hasn't fallen for this trap. Every daycare or church nursery, school classroom and athletic field quickly becomes a haven for jealousy. It begins from the time our children are born. We compare and contrast our children from the onset, secretly wishing they would sleep through the night sooner, walk more proficiently, advance academically, be popular and well liked by their peers, obtain a full-ride college scholarship, excel in their careers, and the list goes on and on.

It doesn't end there. Women are notorious for critiquing each other to death. We look at the designer labels a woman wears, the handbag she carries, her outside appearance, her manicure, the size of her diamond, her résumé of accomplishments, her country club membership, and whether she made it on the recent "Who's Who List." We brag about our circle of friends. If we're not rich and famous, we tell about the time we at least had a brief encounter with someone who is. We have this burning desire to be liked by others and to fit in. This is called an *approval idol*, this innate desire to be accepted by others and receive their accolades.

I recently commented to my daughter that she might want to change her outfit for the activity she was about to attend. In my opinion, she looked okay, but I thought she could do better. She is absolutely gorgeous in whatever she is wearing, but I wasn't sure her outfit choice would win friends and influence people. She would be with her friends from school, and I secretly wanted her to be considered popular. I thought I was covering my secret motives when I nonchalantly made a comment that went something like this, "Are you sure you want to wear that today?" (Yes, feel free to read with much inflection in your voice. That's exactly how I sounded.) My daughter was clearly on to me and responded, "I don't care what others think of me. I'm not looking for people to be my friends because of the kind of clothes I wear." Ouch. I hate it when my sixteen year old teaches me a lesson.

Rather than look to man for approval, we are to look to God. Read Colossians 3:17, 23-24. Have you ever been guilty of an "approval idol"? What is it, and how can you change?

Eve fell prey to the idea that God was cheating her out of something. If God wasn't willingly going to give her access to the tree of knowledge of good and evil, then she was going to take action into her own hands to get it for herself. Rebellion stems from our attempt to take what God doesn't freely give. We then work out ways in our flesh to get it. When we begin to seek the approval of man, it's because we've been duped into thinking that God's approval isn't enough. When we are fooled into thinking that we don't measure up, our attempts to get more will lead us to death. In other words, we have deformed desires that always want more. However, even when we get more, more is not enough. If you view God as holding back on you, or taking away something precious from you, or not being fair to you, or being unjust, then you have an inaccurate view of God. He should not be viewed as a big minus sign.

I pray that as you read the following Scripture, the Holy Spirit will begin to give you an accurate perspective of God: "Every good and perfect gift is from above, coming down from the Father of the heavenly lights, who does not change like shifting shadows" (James 1:17).

We tend to see our lives from tinted glass windows. Little do we realize that *every* good and perfect gift comes from above. We fail to realize the good in the unforeseen circumstances and random events that come blazing toward us without warning. Rather, we picture ourselves as victims in an unfair world. Hold on with me for one more second. What you may not be able to see coming, God foreknew of long ago. Your unforeseen circumstance is no accident; it is intentional. It is also personal. God handpicked it just for you. And by God's amazing grace, what seems so horrific and unjust and unfair and imperfect can be turned into something good. God plans for it to turn into something good, even when we can't imagine how.

Finish by reading James 1:2–4 today. What is the purpose of facing trials of many kinds?

The ultimate goal is that we mature and grow up in our faith. God desires that we be made "mature and complete, not lacking anything" (James 1:4). The Greek word for *perfect* in this text is *teleios*, which means "mature or full-grown, having arrived at an end or objective."[55] In Matthew 5:48, Jesus says: "You must be *teleios* as your heavenly Father is *teleios*." May we come to realize that there is a lesson to be learned in the midst of our series of unfortunate events and wild circumstances. God's perfect gifts come because they are perfecting. They have work to do in us.

Lord, I didn't want to be that girl who blamed You for what I do not have.

---

[55] *Strong's Exhaustive Concordance: New American Standard Bible.* Updated ed. La Habra: Lockman Foundation, 1995. "G5046 teleios." *http://biblesuite.com/greek/5046.htm*

Spend time today thanking God for His perfect gifts in your life. I can reflect back on my life and see how God was working in some of my grayest moments. Even my utmost disappointments in key people in my life have morphed into the most beautiful gifts I could've ever imagined.

The gifts that are given with human hands often are wrongly motivated, sometimes defective, repeatedly unappreciated, occasionally miss-sized, and oh, how quickly forgotten. Thankfully, God's gifts are just what we need. Though they are not necessarily what we ask for, they are definitely "good and perfect."

Rejoice in all the good things the Lord your God has given you and your household.

—Deuteronomy 26:11b

Week 7: Sneaky Serpent

Day 1—Serious Consequences

Day 2—Mousetraps

Day 3—Crouching Lion

Day 4—Quite the Curse

Day 5—The Reason for Pain

Serious Consequences

Week 7: Day 1

I took my nine-year-old son and his friend down to Barton Creek tonight to hunt for frogs and catch some fish. I'll be honest; I don't particularly care for fishing. Considering that my husband is out of town, I thought it was the least I could do for my young passionate fisherman. We loaded up the fishing poles, fishing net, tackle box, and bug-catching jar. Within minutes, those two blond-haired boys were living their fondest dream. Faster than lightning, they had their shoes off and were knee-high in the creek bed. I could hear squeals of laughter and glee as they quickly pursued the frogs that were within an arm's reach. Before I knew it, three frogs and a lizard were in our bug-catching jar.

Then something strange happened, and we all took a step back. Just a few rocks away, two baby water moccasins were slithering in the water. Uncomfortable with the snakes' near presence, I prompted the boys to move upstream, where I thought a safe distance would be maintained. Wisely deciding not to get their feet wet anymore, the boys pursued fishing. One cast went into a grassy area and came too close for comfort. A five-foot cottonmouth slithered out, mad, mouth wide open and ready to strike. My son was so startled that tears began to fall. Needless to say, I was ready to pack up our bags and run. And that's exactly what we did.

We can be so startled and taken back by the physical presence of a snake, and yet, when the Enemy strikes like a serpent, why are we so hesitant to run? Why do we struggle to recognize him? Read 2 Corinthians 11:3. What type of person does Paul describe here?

Scary, isn't it? Paul's description here is not of the non-religious or atheist, the infrequent "Christmas and Easter only" church attendee, or even the superficial, carnal Christian. Did you catch his very descriptive adjectives? The person who can be seduced by the Enemy is one who is wholeheartedly and sincerely pursuing devotion to Christ. I believe that none is safe or off limits from the seduction of the Enemy. There are other Scriptures that support this phenomenon.

Write out the warning found in Proverbs 16:18.

In 1 Corinthians 10:12, who does Paul say is in jeopardy?

Look up Galatians 6:1. What words are used to describe the one who is spiritual?

Finally, what warning is given at the end?

Do not be fooled into thinking that just because you are passionately pursuing Christ, you have received immunity from temptation. Even the godliest people have a propensity to sin. In my lifetime, I've seen some godly people fall.

Can you think of any reasons why the Enemy may be in hot pursuit of Christians who are passionately (and sometimes also publicly) pursuing hard after God? What would the Enemy gain?

I've heard testimonies of many believers who have been taken off guard or surprised by the Enemy's attack in their lives for this one reason: "but I was pursuing God so hard." Many have been fooled into thinking that if they are diligently seeking God, they should have immunity from the onslaught of the Enemy. I want to point out that this line of thinking is not only faulty but also not scriptural. Our response to trials and tribulations and temptation should not be, "Why is this happening to me?" but rather, "Why not?" As Christians, we should be expecting difficulties to come our way.

In my lifetime, I've seen many godly people fall. They had become so busy doing the work of God that they no longer had intimacy with God. This is a slippery slope. We can have heads full of knowledge about the Word of God and yet have hearts that are miles away. After all, isn't this exactly like the example of the Pharisees and Sadducees in Scripture? Their heads were full, but their hearts were empty. Take a look at Revelation 12:9 and 12:12. What does it tell us about Satan's attitude toward the end of times?

If Satan knows his time is near, then is it any wonder that he is busy at work all around us? It makes sense that he wants to see believers falter and fail. The greater the testimony, the harder the fall—and all the more people to bring down with them. He's in a battle and still believes he has a chance to win. That's why we see the presence of the Enemy so remarkably obvious all around us. Read 2 Timothy 3:1–5. Note the descriptive adjectives describing people in the last days. Do any of these hit home with you today? Do you see these things all around you?

As I read this list, I become greatly saddened, because I can think of a person or illustration for every single one. Every single one. And what saddens me most is that some pertain to those who attend church on a regular basis. Some are my acquaintances. Some are my friends, and what really breaks my heart is that some are my family members. They dust the church pew every single week and then walk out of that building to pursue their own comfort and pleasure, "having a form of godliness, but denying its power." They love pleasure more than they love God. They love the things of this world more than they love God. How do I know this is true? Matthew 6:21 tells us the up and up. Write it down here:

Satan, as the Father of Lies, comes to deceive us into a faulty line of thinking. He knows we are prone to trust our feelings over our minds. We are swayed in our thinking by how we feel. This is exactly the trap that Eve fell for. She believed that the apple would give her knowledge that she did not currently possess. She thought she deserved to have it, and a sense of entitlement crept in. If we are going to win against the wiles of the Enemy, we will have to learn how to behave out of what we know as truth rather than out of how we feel. Read 2 Timothy 2:26, and write down what Satan's objective is:

Now read 2 Corinthians 10:5, and write out how we must respond.

The lies of the Enemy are often masked in our own lives. It may be easy for us to see the Enemy's deception in other people's lives and yet be so blinded by it in our own. Matthew 7:3 warns us of this deception in saying, "Why do you look at the speck of sawdust in your brother's eye and pay no attention to the plank in your own eye?" In 1 Timothy 4:1, Paul says, "The [Holy] Spirit distinctly and expressly declares that in latter times some will turn away from the faith, giving attention to deluding and seducing spirits and doctrines that demons teach" (AMP). Seduction can take on many forms, and Satan's goal is to have a heyday.

My goal today is not to cause fear, but rather to have you not be caught off guard by the work of the Enemy. He is alive and active all around us. He desires to bring us down. Remember, he still thinks he can win. Tomorrow we will discuss additional traps of the Enemy. However, before going there, I want to ensure that fear does not gain a foothold in your life. There is no reason for us to live in fear. Although Satan may inflict us for a season, he will not ultimately win. Those who are genuinely saved cannot continue to sin. Please read 1 John 3:9, and write it in your own words.

This verse can certainly be confusing, and you may be asking yourself a pertinent question: "Well, am I really a Christian? Because I certainly struggle with sin!" In the preceding verse, John states that anyone who sins is of the Devil (1 John 3:8). If taken out of context, this verse can be devastatingly alarming! Therefore, let's get to the meat of the matter. I John 3:9 says, "No one who is born of God will *continue to sin*, because God's seed remains in them; they cannot *go on sinning*, because they have been born of God" (emphasis added). Numerous verses in Scripture indicate that Christians will continue to struggle with sin. The difference, however, is that we don't continue to willfully and persistently sin. Anyone who repeatedly pursues sin, making it a consistent pattern of life, may not be a follower of Christ. Followers of Christ will be subject to God's corrective discipline. As the Bible tell us, "We know [absolutely] that anyone born of God does not [deliberately and knowingly] practice committing sin, but the One Who was begotten of God carefully watches over and protects him [Christ's divine presence within him preserves him against the evil], and the wicked one does not lay hold (get a grip) on him or touch [him]" (1 John 5:18, AMP).

We may feel defeated, snared, gripped, or even touched by the hand of the Enemy. However, we will not be destroyed. Jesus Christ has guaranteed us of that!

Let's finish today by reading Genesis 3:13–15. I imagine that Adam and Eve were a little stunned as this once beautiful creature, the serpent, was sent slithering away. To this day, there is a natural aversion to snakes, especially in the heart of a woman!

Paying particular attention to verse 15, we see the first prophecy of the virgin birth. Genesis 3:15 has been called the *protoevangelium,* the first gospel. Martin Luther said of this verse: "This text embraces and comprehends within itself everything noble and glorious that is to be found anywhere in the Scriptures."[56] The antagonism between man and snakes provides us with a symbolism of the battle between God and Satan. The offspring of the woman (Eve) would eventually crush the serpent's head, a promise that was fulfilled by Christ's victory on the cross. Jesus, in becoming man, brought Himself near Satan's domain so that Satan could "strike his heel." But the Messiah, Jesus, would "crush his head" in ultimate victory.

---

56 Herbert Carl Leupold, *Exposition of Genesis: Volumes 1 and 2* (Wartburg, 1942), public domain at http://www.ccel.org/ccel/leupold/genesis.txt.

Romans 16:20 says, "The God of peace will soon crush Satan under your feet." This verse confirms that we also share in this victory and that Satan will one day be defeated once and for all. Satan thought he had won the upper hand when Adam and Eve sinned. However, we can be assured that God will be victorious in the end! God's foreknowledge of Satan's plans reveals that ultimately He is the one in control. God's plans were not thwarted when Adam and Eve sinned, because God's plan was to bring forth something far greater than man in Eden's innocence. God wanted to bring forth redeemed man.

Don't you see? A redeemed man is far better than an innocent man. A redeemed man has something to be redeemed from and comprehends his need for a Savior, while an innocent man fails to experience the enormity of emotion. The innocent man lacks tremendous appreciation because he does not know the work that has been done on his behalf. He doesn't get it. It's God's glory that is at stake here. That's why the woman at the well, in John 4:39, excitedly exclaimed, "He told me everything that I did!" Despite her scarred past and tremendous sin, she did not feel ashamed. She had been confronted, touched, and healed by Jesus. He had taken authority over her past (and our past too) and exchanged it with dignity. She knew what she had been saved from. And now she could shout it from the rooftops. Can I hear an *amen?*

Lord, I didn't want to be that girl who was thrown off track by the attack of the Enemy.

The dictionary defines *redemption* as "deliverance, rescue, and atonement for guilt."[57] Spend time today like the woman at the well, praising God for rewriting your past as a story of His glory.

For we do not have a high priest who is unable to empathize with our weaknesses, but we have one who has been tempted in every way, just as we are—yet was without sin. Let us then approach God's throne of grace with confidence, so that we may receive mercy and find grace to help us in our time of need.

—Hebrews 4:15–16

---

57   "Redemption." Def. 2, 4. *Dictionary Online.* The Random House Dictionary, 2013. http://dictionary.reference.com/browse/redemption.

MOUSETRAPS

Week 7: Day 2

Satan, according to 1 Peter 5:8, is "like a roaring lion, seeking whom he may devour." According to my research, lions have developed two main hunting methods. The first is a version of grandmother's footsteps, in which the lion stalks from cover to cover with a final burst of speed at the end. (If spotted, the lion will sit up and stare nonchalantly into the distance.) The second method is to find a bush close to something its prey needs—usually water—climb in, and wait. This has the great advantage that the lion can catch up on sleep while technically "out hunting."

There certainly are those times in our lives when we go looking for trouble and willfully sin out of rebellion toward God. But what I have found more often to be true in my own life is that the trouble finds me. I don't wake up in the morning with intentions to be angry or bitter or resentful or jealous or depressed or impatient or frustrated or filled with gossip (trust me, I could keep going and going here). Those are not my intentions. That is not the person that I want to be. And yet, I find myself unintentionally sinning, and yes, even at times in seasons of sin, because I have been caught off guard. I have allowed my circumstances and certainly my emotional reactions to get the best of me.

What I fail to realize at those times is that there is a lion out chasing me. Did you notice in the hunting methods described above that he is just lurking out in the bushes, waiting to pounce and have a good meal? He is waiting to seize the day. Just like a real lion, Satan is often patient, waiting for the right moment and just the right circumstances to be placed in our way.

Importantly, 1 Peter 5:8 begins by saying, "Be alert and of sober mind." Girls, if we want to have a chance to stand against the Enemy, then we need to be on the lookout for his sneaky schemes. Today and tomorrow, I want to take a look at eight common mousetraps that the Enemy has set for our destruction.

1. That Would Never Happen to Me

I've watched the false belief that "that would never happen to me" play out time and time again in my own life and in the lives of others. I am reminded of a friend who discovered her husband was having an affair. One of her first remarks afterward was, "I never thought this would happen to me." She loved the Lord, her husband was a prominent leader in the church, and they both were actively involved in their community. Their kids were healthy. They were financially well off. They're very attractive. From the outside looking in, one would think they were the perfect family. They had everything going for them. They were living the American dream. And then one day she woke up and discovered that her world had been turned upside down. How did this happen?

We are easily caught off guard if we remain naive about the way the Enemy works. A common claim by many who have been seduced into having an affair is, "I never set out to have an affair. It just sort of happened." Whether or not this statement foregoes responsibility, I don't really know. But I do think there may be some truth in it. We can be caught in a seasonal onslaught of the Enemy. He works in such a way that we feel enticed by our temptation. Like a fish taking the bait, we can't let go of the hook.

Read Galatians 6:1. In Greek, the word for *caught* (*prolambano*) means "surprised, to take one by forestalling (i.e., before he can flee or conceal his crime)."[58]

The Enemy can work in such a way that we can feel trapped, as if there were no way out, no hope, or no end in sight. We do not see the light at the end of the tunnel, and before we know it, our hope has diminished.

2. It's No Big Deal

Although hindsight is twenty-twenty, it is worth noting how easily a little sin can creep into our lives and become a much bigger problem. At first, it seems like nothing. It often escapes unnoticed. We see it as acceptable because everyone else is doing it. Or we excuse it as "no big deal." However, this line of thinking can eventually lead us into trouble. Galatians 5:9 tells us that "a little yeast works through the whole batch of dough." Little sins that we think are excusable, normative, and acceptable can quickly be much bigger deals. If we do not properly deal with sin in our lives, it can fester and grow.

One of the roles of the Holy Spirit is to convict Christians of their sin. If we ignore the Holy Spirit's conviction repeatedly, eventually He will stop pleading. In other words, the Holy Spirit will convict us of sin for a while, but if we continue in our pattern of sin, then it is possible for the Holy Spirit's conviction to dissipate. We will be turned over to our sin. It is possible for us to become deafened to the Holy Spirit's voice. We can condition ourselves to no longer hear Him. Look at the following verses:

> This is why I speak to them in parables: "Though seeing, they do not see; though hearing, they do no hear or understand." (Matthew 13:13)

---

58   *Strong's Exhaustive Concordance: New American Standard Bible.* Updated ed. La Habra: Lockman Foundation, 1995. "G4301. Prolambanó." *http://biblesuite.com/greek/4301.htm*

And do not grieve the Holy Spirit of God, with whom you were sealed for the day of redemption. (Ephesians 4:30)

So, as the Holy Spirit says: "Today, if you hear his voice, do not harden your hearts . . . But encourage one another daily, as long as it is called 'Today,' so that none of you may be hardened by sin's deceitfulness." (Hebrews 3:7–8, 13)

Whoever has ears, let them hear what the Spirit says to the churches. (Revelations 3:22)

How can a hardened heart be prevented?

Now read Galatians 5:16–17 and make notes below of what needs to be done to continue to hear the Holy Spirit's voice:

3. You Should Be Queen of the Mountain

I've experienced the feeling that I should be queen of the mountaintop, and the thought of it still sends chills down my spine. I can recall a time in my life when I was on a spiritual high. It was a mountaintop experience, as I had seen God work miraculously in my life. The best way I can describe it is the thrill and joy you experience on top of a roller coaster. There are a lot of twists and turns before you get to the top. It takes some effort and hard work and a whole lot of prayer. Through the climb, you begin to see things from God's perspective, and you witness Him answering prayer. Then you arrive at the top. The view is spectacular, and you relish in the moment as you try to take it all in. You feel so close to God. But what you don't see is the bottom about to fall out from beneath you. You don't see the train headed your way around the next bend. And the ride going down is the scariest one of all!

My mountaintop experience was quickly followed by a bombardment of testing from the Enemy. It came like an unexpected tidal wave that quickly engulfed me. I wish I would've recognized it as that at the time. Unfortunately, for a season, I fell to despair, much like the prophet Elijah in 1 Kings 19. Go ahead and turn with me there.

In the preceding chapter, we see Elijah boldly preaching the word of God, courageously taking on a difficult battle in the hearts of the Israelites. This chapter concludes with these words: "The power of the Lord came on Elijah and, tucking his cloak into his belt, he ran ahead of Ahab all the way to Jezreel." We see a supernatural empowerment in our first Olympian, as Elijah's sprints are record speed. After the queen receives word of what Elijah has done, he becomes afraid and runs for his life. Read 1 Kings 19:3–5. What did Elijah want to do after his mountaintop experience? What may be some reasons why Elijah responded this way?

One of the biggest life lessons we can glean from Elijah's response has to do with expectations. Elijah, after witnessing God working in great and powerful ways, expects God to continue to do the same for him. He may have planned out how God was going to take Jezebel out of the picture. He was envisioning something more powerful than running for his life with her hot on his tail. He was expecting his roller coaster ride to continue the ascent upward, not down. What we see is that his mountaintop experience may have led him to a sense of command, a position where he could tell God what to do.

Being an idealist, I can relate. It is easy for me to plan out what I think God should do and how He should intercede on my behalf. However, life is full of disappointments, and things don't always work out as I have planned. If we are not careful, our expectations can become demands of the heart. It certainly is not wrong for us to hope for the best. After all, 1 Corinthians 13:7 says, "Love always protects, always trust, always hopes." But it doesn't stop there. How is that verse finished? Love always _____.

What God requires from us is obedience. We are not responsible for the outcome. We cannot manipulate and control other people; nor can we alter our circumstances. Rather than usurp God of His sovereignty, may we realize that God is working all things together for our good (Romans 8:28) and come to trust that we may not know or understand what is best for us. Expectations can easily slip into demands if we are not careful, being mindful that the results are in God's hands, not ours. When we become focused on results rather than God, our significance and happiness become thwarted by outcomes. It is for this reason that after a mountaintop experience we may dip to an all-time low, resulting in a tidal wave of failure, frustration, and fear.

4. Loneliness Is a Friend of Mine

When hunting its prey, a lion often looks for prey that is weak in the herd or that has wandered astray. He might as well pick off the easy meal so he can get back to napping. Nothing pleases the Enemy more than to get us off on our own. He is well aware that God says, "For where two or three gather in my name, there am I with them" (Matthew 18:20). Don't be fooled into thinking that Satan doesn't have a copy of the Scriptures. That's why one of his best tactics is to allow isolation to lead to desolation. Desolation is defined as (1) a state of complete emptiness or destruction and (2) anguished misery or loneliness.[59]

---

59   *Oxford Pocket Dictionary of Current English.* 4th ed. New York: Oxford University Press, 2009, s.v.

This tactic should not take us off guard, as we see him use it even against Christ Himself. We see Jesus being baptized by John the Baptist followed by God the Father declaring these words, "This is my Son, whom I love; with him I am well pleased" (Matthew 3:17). Fast-forward to the very next scene; we watch the Enemy leading him out to the desert: "Then Jesus was led by the Spirit into the wilderness to be tempted by the devil" (Matthew 4:1). Jesus was able to endure this time of testing without sin, but make no mistake; the experience was still difficult and brutal.

Thankfully, God understands whatever situations and circumstances we are currently undergoing. He has promised us in 1 Corinthians 10:13, "No temptation has overtaken you except what is common to man. And God is faithful; he will not let you be tempted beyond what you can bear. But when you are tempted, he will also provide a way out so that you can stand up under it." With that in mind, it is imperative that we push ourselves to pursue healthy relationships that will continuously point us to God. We are commanded in Hebrews 10:25 to "not give up meeting together" because we can encourage each other to stay the course. When we feel ourselves slipping into a secretive, unbiblical, or unhealthy practice of isolation, it should be a red flag to us that it is time to get plugged in with fellow believers.

Can you think of someone who may be struggling with loneliness or isolation? What can you do today to encourage that person?

5. What's Done in Secret Stays in Secret

You've probably all heard the ad, "What happens in Vegas, stays in Vegas." Oh, how the Enemy loves secrets. He wants to make you think that you have something special between him and you. He gives you a false sense of security that hinges on a faulty trust. Lies of deception come lurking out that sound something like this: "You'll never get caught," "You deserve this," "No one will ever know," or "What you don't have is what you need—and this is how you get it." When we are unable or unwilling to openly disclose all areas of our hearts before God, then we have been fooled into some level of secrecy. If we think we can get away with this because our parents can't see, our friends can't see, our pastor/elders/deacons can't see, our spouse can't see, or our kids can't see, then we'd better look out, as we've got a lion on our tails. Deception involves some level of secrecy.

The moment you feel as if you have to lie (even if you feel it can be justified as only a "little white lie") to explain your behavior, you've been caught in a tangled web of deception. It may be masked for a bit, but let me tell you something: what you think is done in secret cannot be hidden from God, "for God will bring every deed into judgment, with every secret thing, whether good or evil" (Ecclesiastes 12:14).

We've covered a lot of ground today, and we've uncovered several of Satan's schemes. May we not end today being disheartened, for God is at work in the midst of our circumstances. Take hope, then, my dear sister, that you are able to "stand against the wiles of the Enemy" (Ephesians 6:11). Let's learn from our mistakes so that we can be more prepared the next time around and also an encouragement to others.

I love this excerpt written by C.S. Lewis in *Mere Christianity*. May it give you fresh wind and fire today too:

> "Imagine yourself as a living house. God comes in to rebuild that house. At first, perhaps, you can understand what He is doing. He is getting the drains right and stopping the leaks in the roof and so on; you knew that those jobs needed doing and so you are not surprised. But presently He starts knocking the house about in a way that hurts abominably and does not seem to make any sense. What on earth is He up to? The explanation is that He is building quite a different house from the one you thought of - throwing out a new wing here, putting on an extra floor there, running up towers, making courtyards. You thought you were being made into a decent little cottage: but He is building a palace. He intends to come and live in it Himself."[60]

Lord, I didn't want to be that girl stuck in the mousetrap.

Did any of the mousetraps discussed today especially speak to you? If so, which one?

From the west, people will fear the name of the Lord, and from the rising of the sun, they will revere his glory. For he will come like a pent-up flood that the breath of the Lord drives along.

—Isaiah 59:19

---

60   C.S. Lewis, *Mere Christianity* (New York: Touchstone, 1996), pp. 175–176.

Crouching Lion

Week 7: Day 3

Yesterday we addressed some of the unsuspecting lies that the Enemy has successfully used against us to entice us to sin. My hope in addressing some of his tactics is that we will be better prepared to ward off his wicked schemes. God instructs us to be separated to God yet not separated from people. (For further study, read John 17:13–21.) Watching this lived out among the church during my lifetime, I've witnessed a whole lot of "holy huddling." The church is afraid to be engaged with the world because it becomes messy. The church has segregated itself from the world out of fear. There is fear that the world will rub off on it and its families—and in many cases, this looks to be arguably true. However, I'm afraid that we lose our spiritual sharpness if we are not continually evangelizing to unbelievers. Eventually, we can become spiritually dead. Additionally, if we, the church, will not be a light to this world, who will? True love for others, the kind that Jesus talks about when He says, "Love your neighbor as yourself," requires true sacrifice, the same kind of sacrifice that Jesus gave to us.

We are called to be a light to this dying world. We cannot hide our lamp stands under bushels of apathy or indifference. That would be contrary to Jesus' teaching in Matthew 28:19–20 that specifically calls us to "therefore go and make disciples of all nations, baptizing them in the name of the Father and the Son and of the Holy Spirit, and teaching them to obey everything I have commanded you. And surely I am with you always, to the very end of the age." Yet, as we go, we cannot allow Satan to blow our lights out. This, my sisters, sounds like quite the confusing conundrum. Let's unravel some more of the Enemy's trickery today and pick up where we left off yesterday.

6. Live in a Holy Bubble

Wouldn't life be simpler if we lived in a holy bubble? I've watched many of my peers pick this route because life seems so much easier without the conflict and confusion that this world can evoke. It sounds so enticing to surround yourself with Christian influences and shelter your families from the "evils" of this world. But I'm afraid that, more often than not, we have removed ourselves so much from this world that we are no longer any earthly good. What I mean by that is we become so focused on our own comfort and behavior modification, that we lose sight of what our existence here in this temporary sphere is really for.

Philippians 3:18–20 tells us, "Many live as enemies of the cross of Christ. Their destiny is destruction, their god is their stomach, and their glory is in their shame. Their mind is set on earthly things. But our citizenship is in heaven. And we eagerly await a Savior from there, the Lord Jesus Christ." Colossians 3:1–3 says, "Since, then, you have been raised with Christ. Set your hearts on things above, where Christ is seated at the right hand of God. Set your minds on things above, not on earthly things. For you died, and your life is now hidden with Christ in God." We are also instructed to "fix our eyes not on what is seen, but on what is unseen, since what is seen is temporary, but what is unseen is eternal" (2 Corinthians 4:18). These verses seem to be instructing us to live separated lives. But actually, the contrary is true. All of these verses are exhorting us to be "heavenly minded," but in the backdrop of an earthly setting. We are called to set our minds on things above, things unseen, things eternal. We are called to live as aliens or strangers in this world. We are told that our citizenship is in heaven, not here on this earth. We are told to pray for God's kingdom to come, and His will to be done. We are told that this earth is fading away, and not to focus on the temporary, but rather the eternal. So what then should our perspective be?

Truly "heavenly minded" people will be of more and more earthly good. We will see our purpose and calling with an eternal perspective. Our views will no longer be ours, but rather those that only God could have placed in us. We will see this lost world through God's eyes, not our own. And when this happens, we will become the "salt of the earth" (Matthew 5:13). "But if the salt loses its saltiness, how can it be made salty again? It is no longer good for anything, except to be thrown out and trampled underfoot."

7. You Will Never Be Hurt

God never calls us to naïveté. He calls us to walk wisely. There is a very big difference between the two. The biblical concept of wisdom emphasizes mature innocence, not childlike ignorance. We must be aware of what is out there before we walk into the middle of it. We must recognize situations that demand an extra degree of consecration, preparation, and protection.

Write out Matthew 10:16 below:

Traps are set in places where we least expect. Often Satan will look for ways to get to us through people we trust. The last thing I want to do is make you skeptical of every friendship and relationship you are in. That certainly is not what I want to accomplish here. However, I do want to point out to you that some of the most dangerous pitfalls may come from people you trust. Not everyone who appears to be trustworthy is. Not everyone has good intentions. As women, we are very relational. Therefore, the only way to survive this pitfall is desperation for discernment. A little crack in the door may be all the Enemy needs to allow an unhealthy relationship to get in. In his book, *Walking with God*, John Eldredge writes, "An old saint told me years ago that the devil doesn't so much care what particular thing he gets us to fall prey to. His primary aim is simply to get us to do something outside of Christ, for then we are vulnerable".[61]

Imagine your life as a teacup. In light of what we have learned today, we should have healthy, godly relationships that pour into us and fill us up. We then are prepared to go out into the world and pour out into the lives of others. We return to our Christian friends to once again be filled up and poured into by encouraging one another (Hebrews 10:25), so that we can go out again and be poured out. In this manner, we become living examples of Genesis 12:3: "we are blessed to be a blessing."

Are you putting this concept into practice in your own life? Does the definition of "holy huddler" apply to you? If so, what can you do to change?

8. You Are Powerless and Will Fail

Because we see most clearly with our physical sight, it is easy to lose sight of the fact that we are engaged in a spiritual battle. Ephesians 6:10–12 says, "Finally, be strong in the Lord and in his mighty power. Put on the full armor of God so that you can take your stand against the devil's schemes. For our struggle is not against flesh and blood, but against the rulers, against the authorities, against the powers of this dark world and against the spiritual forces of evil in the heavenly realms."

"Put on" is literally a dressing term. Used as an idiom, it can also mean to assume the office, manner, character, disposition, or perspective of another. We must "put on" Christ, meaning we must conduct our lives as closely to the way He would were He in our position. We are to practice His way of life because it is eternal life—the way God lives His life. It will help prepare us for His kingdom, and it enables us to glorify Him here and now.

The Enemy wants to render us powerless. The very first instruction in Ephesians 6:10 is "be strong." Too often we stop right there and assume that we must somehow muster up our own strength to fight our battles against the Enemy. We take our situations into our own hands and try to fix them on our own. In doing so, we become our own masters, thinking that we are invincible

---

[61] John Eldredge, *Walking with God* (Nashville: Thomas Nelson, 2008), 89.

and capable of getting ourselves out of the messes we find ourselves in. But then the day comes when we can't find the strength within to change, and we cannot even fathom a way out—so we crater. We crater because we fail to finish the first instruction, which reads, "Be strong in the Lord and in His mighty power."

It is only through surrendering to God's power that we can expect to win the spiritual battles of this life. If we enter into the battlefield alone, there's no telling what will happen. But, if we enter in His power, we are guaranteed to win. As John said in 1 John 4:4, "You, dear children, are from God and have overcome them, because the one who is in you is greater than he who is in the world."

How would you describe a spiritual battle?

Every time you are presented with the opportunity to entertain a lustful thought, you have entered a spiritual battlefield. Every time you have the chance to do something vindictive, you are on the battlefield. Every time you have the chance to say something harsh and hurtful, you are in the midst of battle. Every time you toy with the notion that you're just a little bit better than most of the people you know, you are surrounded by Enemy fire. Every time you want to satisfy the flesh, you are engaged in conflict.

Life is a spiritual battlefield, and there is a force at work in this world that does not want you to do well. There is a force at work in this world that does not want you to live for Jesus. There is a force at work in this world that does not want you to minister to others in His name. There is a force at work in this world that does not want you to bear the fruit of the Spirit. And that force will do whatever it takes to ensure you don't do these things.

Did you have a spiritual battle this week? Who won?

Now, let me make this perfectly clear: our Enemy might be strong, but our Savior is stronger. Don't get the impression that a fight between God and the Devil is a close match. The Devil has been defeated. Beaten. Stomped. Humiliated. He has no power in your life, so you don't have to moan and groan about how oppressive the Devil is. This feeling of powerlessness or fear of failing is a lie.

Lord, I didn't want to be that girl who was snared.

Recount some lies from the Enemy that you have fallen for in the past. What have you learned from them?

So do not fear, for I am with you; do not be dismayed, for I am your God. I will strengthen you and help you; I will uphold you with my righteous right hand.

—Isaiah 41:10

QUITE THE CURSE

Week 7: Day 4

Find a pregnant woman in the room and ask her how many child-birthing horror stories she has been told during the course of her pregnancy. Oh, how we women love to talk. And there certainly are some stories to tell. Considering that my husband is a physician, I have probably heard more than my fair share. There are many stories that can cause our sides to split in pure laughter and, sadly, others still that empty the tissue box. Knowing full well that there are sisters struggling with the pain of infertility, may we not take lightly our text for today. Please read Genesis 3:16, and write it below.

The difficult truth is that there are consequences for our sin. Eve's sin had far-reaching ramifications. But did you realize that we are on her team? One of the most difficult lessons I have had with my own children is that of group discipline. There have been many times when one or two kids will ruin it for the entire class. There will be just a few that are disobeying the class rules, which results in the teacher laying down the law for all. Benjamin Franklin has said, "The rotten apple spoils his companion." Repeatedly I've tried to explain this concept to my kids. That's why the coach has the entire team run extra laps or do fifty push-ups when an error is made by a teammate. It's because we are in this thing together. We are all on the same team. So, let's quit pointing fingers and laying blame. We're no better than Eve. It's time we take one for the team.

Yes, *difficult*, *grueling*, *heart-wrenching*, or *painful* only go so far to describe the adversity that we as women face in child bearing. I'm right there with you—it is certainly hard. Adam and Eve sinned, and the curse is stark—for both women and men.

The second curse given to women is as follows: "Your desire will be for your husband, and he will rule over you." Oh how I can attest that both of these statements are certainly true. There was a deep, innate desire within me to be married. This word *desire* is strong, inferring an unquenched craving or addiction. So much of a woman's self-esteem can be said to be dependent on a man. But did you know that this is all part of the curse? Women change the way they dress to catch the attention of a man. Women's self-esteem will be tightly woven to what a man thinks of them. How many of us spent hours fixing our hair, trying on various outfits, hanging out with certain friends, and adjusting what we did in our free time, just in order to meet a boy? Be honest—they make us crazy. I recall a friend of mine taking up golf just so she could meet a man. I know of others who have learned the rules to football, tried co-ed sports, or taken on new hobbies and interests in the hope that they would meet the men of their dreams. Sometimes he is caught—and sometimes he is not.

Here's the crux of the curse: we have this void inside us as women that we have been fooled into thinking must be filled with a man. If you are single, I'm especially speaking to you. This void, or emptiness, was ultimately meant for God. Don't you see why it's called a curse? As women, we have been fooled into thinking that we have to have men in order to be happy. As soon as a woman gets a man, however, she comes to the realization that he doesn't make her happy, either. We end up with unmet expectations that can only be filled by God. If we enter into our marriages expecting our spouses to make us happy, we are setting them up to fail.

Let's not forget the final words of the curse: "and he will rule over you." Due to the curse, women have to fight an innate desire to be the head of their homes, which would subvert God's ordained order for the home. Since the fall, women have had difficulty submitting to their husbands' authority, and men have had to fight for the authority in their home. Sin has affected the willing submission of women and the loving headship of men. Women battle to usurp the divinely appointed headship of their husband with plows of domination, manipulation, and control.

Over the course of my lifetime, I have watched the effect of this curse come true. The liberation of women's rights has led to an American culture of female dominance in the home and a feminization of men. I was sickened last week when I opened a popular magazine to see a teenage boy dressed in woman's clothing and wearing makeup. It made my stomach turn. Is that the future of America? And I have to wonder if we, women in the church, have contributed to the problem? Have we diminished the lordship of men even in our own homes? As the Bible says, "Each one of you also must love his wife as he loves himself, and the wife must respect her husband" (Ephesians 5:33).

What do you think it means to respect your husband?

Notice that in this verse we as women are instructed to respect our husbands. Do you find it interesting that we don't have to be reminded to *agape* love them? That's because we don't have to be told. Genesis 3:16 tells us "our desire will be for our husbands." It is natural for us to be sensitive, nurturing, compassionate, and kind. It's the respect part that doesn't come so naturally. We are born wanting to trump our husbands. As soon as we take hold of the wheel, we send our cars into tailspin. You've probably heard the saying that "men are from Mars and women are from Venus." Yes, we are very different, and learning how to decipher mixed signals that we send each other may help all of us stay on the road. Let's dive into a few excuses of why we have so quickly jumped into the driver's seat of our marriages.

My Husband Doesn't Want to Lead

Considering the feminist-dominated culture in which we live, the idea that men don't want to lead doesn't surprise me. After a few generations of women dominating in the home, men have lost sight of what it means to lead. Because it has not been modeled well to them, they have opted out of leading in their own homes. As a result, many of us women are willing to get up and drive. And do you blame these men? We have belittled their abilities, critiqued their talents, been unsupportive of their endeavors, resisted their intimacy, refused their counsel, and undermined their decisions. Do any of these hit home this week?

I have one word for how you should respond: *encourage!* You are your husband's biggest advocate. If you've never been one before, it is time to squeeze into that high school cheerleading uniform and try it on for size. I believe you can do it, and so can he. Notice that the root word in *encourage* is *courage*. It may mean standing out on a limb so that the course of action will be changed in your home. Start believing that your husband can lead. He is capable. With some urging, I believe he will also be willing to give it a try.

Here's how this may look in the beginning: praise him for his accomplishments. Communicate thankfulness to him. Allow him to have the final say—and don't hem and haw about it. Keep your mouth shut when necessary, and always respect him in front of the kids. Be gracious when he makes mistakes (listen, you make mistakes too). Don't obey begrudgingly (he will see right through you). Ask him for counsel and advice. Lean on him to be your pillar of strength. Tell him how much you appreciate him, not just for what he does for you but because of who he is. Disagree graciously and gently. Applaud loudly when you begin to see him lead. What other steps can you take in your home to allow your husband to lead?

He Doesn't Know What He Is Doing

We can quickly fall into a trap of critiquing our husbands' every move and decision. Even our good intentions to "speak the truth in love" toward our spouses can go dangerously awry. What I have learned slowly (and yes, I mean slowly) over the years is that when I speak negative criticism toward my husband, he can translate my words as contempt for who he is as a man. Even my best attempts to correct my husband and mold him into the man I wanted him to be were total

179

failures. I had to come to a breaking point where I realized that it was not my job to be his Holy Spirit. It was not my job to correct, teach, train, and discipline my husband. My best attempts became my greatest nightmares.

In her book entitled *Love & Respect*, Dr. Emerson Eggerichs encourages women to show unconditional respect for their spouses: "A simple application is that a wife is to display a respectful facial expression and tone when he fails to be the man she wants. She can give her husband unconditional respect in tone and expression while confronting his unloving behavior and without endorsing his unloving reactions".[62] In other words, it's not so much what we say, but how we say it. Showing respect to a man is like showing love to a woman. It lights him up and feeds his soul.

How are you doing on a scale of one to ten in showing unconditional respect to your husband?

I Can Do It Better

Many women are afraid to take the risk of showing their husbands unconditional respect. There is a common fear that they will be treated as doormats, rendered powerless, or lose their own identities. They fear that this subservient attitude will lead to them being walked all over. Thus, in order to protect themselves, they react with negativity, constantly correcting their husbands' mistakes or smothering them with mothering. They've bought into the notion that they can do it better. This train of thought may win you a few battles, but it certainly won't win you the war. You will end up with a malfunctioning marriage. In marriages, a little humility can go a long way.

God Created Us Equal, So It Doesn't Matter Who Leads

The argument that it doesn't matter who leads, since God created us equal, is fueled by Galatians 3:28, which states, "There is neither Jew nor Gentile, neither slave nor free, nor is there male and female, for you are all one in Christ Jesus." Peter concurs with this theology and tells husbands: treat your wives "with respect as the weaker partner and as heirs with you of the gracious gift of life" (1 Peter 3:7). In light of the grace of God, women are to be valued by their husbands and perceived as equal before God. This equality, however, does not mean that we have the same roles. It is a man's job to honor and cherish his wife, just as he does his own flesh (see Ephesians 5:28–29). Called to be the head of the household, he is to lay down his life for her. It is his calling to protect the house and to love his wife as he loves himself. When men do this for us, we feel incredibly honored and valued. Bottom line: we feel loved.

---

[62] Dr. Emerson Eggerichs, *Love & Respect: The Love She Most Desires, The Respect He Desperately Needs* (Nashville: Thomas Nelson, 2004), 42.

When we honor and respect our husbands (in and away from their presence), they feel important and willing to lay down their lives for us. In return, when we feel cherished and loved by our husbands, we are willing to show them respect. As counterintuitive as it may seem, putting these biblical principles into practice really does work.

I Don't Need a Man to Tell Me What to Do

Many women have resolved to a position that they do not need a man to tell them what to do. Their husbands have done unthinkable things (whether it be straying away from the Lord, falling into seasons of sinfulness, or merely treating them in an unloving way) and lost their respect. Rather than respect them out of obedience to the Lord, they have chosen the path of least resistance and determined that they will live their lives the way they please, regardless of what their husbands say or do. I typically see this kind of response when women are struggling to show respect to their mates because they view them as undeserving of respect. Their husbands may be unbelievers or alcoholics or unemployed or struggling with anger, pornography, adultery, or other detestable sins. These situations have resulted in women feeling dishonored and unloved, and the natural reaction is to fight the tendency to be hurt again. A wall therefore is put up to protect the heart. Rather than go through the motions and say things that they don't sincerely feel, to put it simply, to act "hypocritically," they resolve to live life independently of their spouses. This kind of marriage looks like two ships headed in opposite directions.

He hunts; she shops. He watches sports; she works out. He reads; she bakes. He vacations with his friends; she vacations with hers. Ignoring the real issue at hand, they begin living very separate lives. Neither of them is willing to take the first step toward reconciliation, so they move further and further apart. The wife refuses to show respect to her husband because she doesn't feel like it. Her emotions and feelings are ruling the roost. Yes, her husband has hurt her. His actions and words have been uncaring and unkind. He, in her opinion, does not deserve respect. If she were to show respect to her husband, she thinks she would be a total phony.

What would you tell this woman to do? Does your advice align with Scripture?

Has anyone told you that reading God's Word is more than mere teaching; it is dangerous? It is dangerous because it *reads* you and evokes a response in you. Being obedient to God is never hypocrisy. We must start realizing that we cannot trust our feelings and emotions. When the alarm clock goes off in the morning, we have to get up whether we feel like it or not. That is called being responsible. Let's start acting like responsible women of God and take ownership of our own reactions. Let's begin trusting God that He can do a good work in our marriages, despite what our history has shown, and in spite of what we feel. Maturing in Christ begins with you and your actions, not those of your spouse, "for the eyes of the Lord are on the righteous and his ears are attentive to their prayer" (1 Peter 3:12a).

One final thought, because I know that there are many struggling marriages out there and that the thought of reconciliation may seem impossible to you right now. Maybe you cannot even fathom your marriage improving at this juncture. You've lost all hope. May you be reminded of Paul's words in 2 Corinthians 12:9: "My grace is sufficient for you, for my power is made perfect in weakness." My friend, I truly believe that God's grace is sufficient for you. And I also want you to know that "there is now no condemnation for those who are in Christ Jesus" (Romans 8:1). Don't beat yourself up over past mistakes. Allow God's grace to sink in. He is your portion. He is your strength.

Lord, I didn't want to be that girl who ruled the roost in her home.

Maybe today you had difficulty confessing those words because deep within, you want to be the ruler in your home. You are not willing to give up that responsibility to your spouse. You are deeply afraid to surrender control. Ask God for help today. Ask Him to change your heart.

All to Jesus I surrender; all to him I freely give;
I will ever love and trust him, in his presence daily live.

—*"I Surrender All," J. W. Van Deventer*

THE REASON FOR PAIN

Week 7: Day 5

I woke up today not feeling well. I have a fever combined with aches and pains. It is *no bueno* for me. My whole body hurts right down to the bone, and ibuprofen and Motrin are not cutting to the core. How funny that I picked up our text for today and found the curse of pain leaping out of the page. Read it with me, and let me know if you can feel my pain. See Genesis 3:17–19. What one word is used to describe the type of toil that man will face *all* the days of his life?

I've been told many times that fever is a way to notify the body that something is wrong. There is an infection being fought within. Fever is not a bad thing. It's our bodily thermostat informing us that it's time to take a break and possibly even call the doctor. However, pain is a much louder warning sign. I love the way C. S. Lewis puts it into perspective by saying, "But pain insists upon being attended to. God whispers to us in our pleasures, speaks in our conscience, but shouts in our pains: it is His megaphone to rouse a deaf world."[63]

Reflecting back over the past few weeks, we begin to see a story unfolding. Here we have a sovereign God that creates this beautiful, magnificent world, and throughout the creation process God stops and remarks that "it is good." At this point in the story, there is no pain, no fever, no suffering, no remorse, no bitterness, no envy, no strife, no death, and not even a hint of evil. But then this sly creature appears in the garden and leads Eve down this disastrous path. And not only does she fall, but also she brings along Adam with her. This perfect world is all of a sudden faced with the calamity of sin. Sin results in unprecedented suffering and thus begs the question, "Why do bad things happen to good people?" We also might ask, "Why does God allow pain and suffering in this world?" You certainly don't have to look too far to see that this world is full of pain and suffering.

Let's turn to Romans 8:20 for an answer: "For the creation was subjected to frustration, not by its own choice, but by the will of the one who subjected it."

It is a difficult concept for us to digest that God, who we are supposed to trust, who is the source of goodness, would also allow pain and suffering to be a part of this world. Knowing, however, that my thoughts are not God's thoughts (Isaiah 55:8), there must be a reason. There must be a

---

[63] C.S. Lewis, *The Problem of Pain* (New York: HarperOne, 2009), 91.

greater purpose at work that I cannot readily see. There must be a reason that God would allow the "creation to be subjected to frustration," which is so obvious in the natural disasters and calamities that this world experiences. Natural order was not seduced; man and woman were. It was a human choice that resulted in sin. Why then is the whole creation subjected to such futility?

John Piper says, "God put the natural world under a curse so that the physical horrors we see around us in diseases and calamities would become vivid pictures of how horrible sin is. In other words, natural evil is a signpost pointing to the unspeakable horror or moral evil."[64]

Pain and suffering in this world serve as reminders to us of just how repugnant our sin is in the eyes of God. Otherwise, how quickly we forget. We get so caught up in our own little worlds that we so easily tune out God. It becomes easy for us to forget that our "little white lies" are a big deal to God and the sins that we want to sweep under the rug really do matter. I doubt any of us truly understands the agonizing affect of our sin upon a holy God. If we did, we would be more abhorred by our own evil.

Do you feel you are truly remorseful for *all* your sin? (Pay particular attention to the word "all," for there are many sins that we justify or blow off.)

Pain is simply a reminder to us of the depravity of our sin. We pay more attention to removing the stain on our favorite blouse than eradicating sin from our lives. If we could for a second grasp the pain that we cause in the spiritual realm through our abhorrent, vile, repulsive, disgusting, and repetitive sin, we may be more conscientious in stamping it out of our routines. We don't like the ringtone of those words, period. Therefore, we like to sugarcoat our sin and heavily douse it with perfume. We attempt to make it more palatable through justification, entitlement, or blame. In doing so, we fail to recognize that a sin is a sin, and all sins are painful reminders that we have fallen away from God.

Do we realize that when we become angry at our children we are actually sinning against God? When we harbor sins in our hearts (may it be bitterness, anger, resentments, or jealousy) we are choosing to sin against God? Our anger directed toward a person or thing is in actuality directed straight at God. Look up the following verses and write down the name of the sinner and the sinned-against:

Genesis 39:8–9 _____

---

[64] John Piper, "The Triumph of the Gospel in the New Heavens and the New Earth," (sermon), Desiring God Foundation. Last updated September 12, 2010. *http://www.desiringgod.org/resource-library/conference-messages/the-triumph-of-the-gospel-in-the-new-heavens-and-the-new-earth* (August 31, 2013).

Psalm 51:4 _____

Luke 15:21 _____

Acts 5:3–4 _____

May the gravity and depravity of our sin sink in a little bit today. We don't get into trouble because we think too little, but because we think too much. What we value outweighs the things that are important to God. His precepts, His values, His commands, and His perspectives go to the wayside as we determine the way that feels right to us in our hearts. But my heart so often gets me in trouble. My heart chooses to watch TV rather than spend time with God. My heart wanders to jealousy and bitterness rather than the things of God. My heart decides how I spend my time, my money, and my energy—often without any consideration of God. Scripture tells us, "The mind governed by the flesh is death, but the mind governed by the Spirit is life and peace" (Romans 8:6).

Please read the account of the Israelites in Exodus 32:1–10. Remember that just a few pages back (in Exodus 14 to be exact), the Israelites were miraculously delivered from the hands of the Egyptians. God did amazing things in their sight. How quickly we see that they had forgotten. Who do they attribute this act to in verse 4?

Their act of disobedience seems so despicable to me. How in the world could they possibly attribute this incredible act of God to a little "g"? How dare they forget what God had done for them? Note how God responds (verses 9 and 10):

We are beings that were created to worship; how quickly our attention can twist and turn to an alternative. So quickly we erect idols in our lives that become the epitome of our attention rather than God. We wake in the morning with our minds twirling with all the things we have to do. We rush to work, thinking of what we need to accomplish that day. We have very little time for God because we have so much on our calendars, and our agendas are jammed full of things that bear no eternal consequences. Like the Israelites, we have consumed ourselves with the pleasures of the here and now. We take our eyes off of God and observe what we can physically see. We replace the intangible with the tangible.

Think for a moment—have any idols been erected in your life recently? An idol is anything that replaces God.

There will be numerous times when we are faced with the seductive traps of the Enemy, and we will have to deliberately choose obedience instead. This determined obedience does not come from our own willpower and self-righteousness. We can muster up all our courage and, after a few days, be utterly defeated. (It's why the last piece of chocolate cake in the refrigerator calls my name, and I am often rendered helpless). Our motivation for victory over the Enemy and his lure of idols is anchored in something far greater than inner resolve.

Read the following verse: "I have hidden your word in my heart that I might not sin against you" (Psalm 119:11). Our commitment to long-term, lasting obedience must first be rooted in our love for God. It is only through a consistent relationship with Him that we will find the power to defeat the Enemy. Can I ask you a tough question today? Why do you study God's Word? Do you whole-heartedly intend to obey? Or are you skimming the text merely to fulfill a daily ritual? If so, is this a waste of your time? God's Holy Word was intended to be transforming to us. Therefore, in order for it to be radically effective, we need to begin to listen *and* obey. We need to be not merely hearers of the Word, but also doers (James 1:22).

Can you identify any weaknesses in your faith, trust, or love for Christ that are affecting your resolve today? Are there any disappointments, pains, or areas of suffering that are getting the best of you or causing you to doubt your faith in God?

It's convenient to fool yourself and justify your behavior when you are not fully committed to God. When our hearts erect "idols," the things of this world cloud our judgment. In order to turn away from temptation and sin, we may have to step away from our current circumstances. If our lives are surrounded by seduction and we are having difficulty taking a stand, then God may be directing us to a new path, a new set of friends, a new direction. When we grab hold of God and the truth and liberty of His Word, we will willingly change our circumstances in order to fully obey Him.

Do you need to take action toward changing your environment to preserve obedience to God (for example, maybe you need a new set of friends rather than the "girls night out" group that drinks heavily and talks poorly about their spouses. Over time, you have noticed that rather than being a light for Christ, you have begun to chime right in)?

We began today by looking at the curse of Adam in Genesis 3:17–19 and how pain and suffering serve as a reminder of the pain that our sin causes God. Let's not end on that note, though. I want to also paint a picture for you of tremendous encouragement and hope. Read the continuation of Romans 8:21: ". . . that the creation itself will be liberated from its bondage to decay and brought into the freedom and glory of the children of God."

The calamities of this world serve as a picture of the judgment that sin will one day receive. We just see a glimpse of it now, but a day is coming when pain and suffering will be no more. God promises that this world will one day be freed from the curse. Be encouraged by the following verses:

> See, I will create new heavens and a new earth. The former things will not be remembered, nor will they come to mind. (Isaiah 65:17)

> Repent, then, and turn to God, so that your sins may be wiped out, that times of refreshing may come from the Lord, and that he may send the Messiah, who has been appointed for you—even Jesus. Heaven must receive him until the time comes for God to restore everything, as he promised long ago through his holy prophets. (Acts 3:19–21)

> I consider that our present sufferings are not worth comparing with the glory that will be revealed in us. We know that the whole creation has been groaning as in the pains of childbirth right up to the present time. Not only so, but we ourselves, who have the firstfruits of the Spirit, groan inwardly as we wait eagerly for our adoption to sonship, the redemption of our bodies. For in this hope we were saved. But hope that is seen is no hope at all. Who hopes for what they already have? But if we hope for what we do not yet have, we wait for it patiently. (Romans 8:18, 22–25)

A day is coming when creation will be liberated from its bondage and decay. A day is coming when we will experience the freedom and glory of the children of God. Yes, there will be a day when pain and suffering will be no more.

Lord, I didn't want to be that girl experiencing pain.

Find hope in the fact that your current pain and suffering will not last for eternity. Thank God that your body will be redeemed and that creation will be restored. Our current sufferings are not even worth comparing to the glory that will be revealed in us.

We all know people who have been made much meaner and more irritable and more intolerable to live with by suffering: It is not right to say that all suffering perfects. It only perfects one type of person . . . the one who accepts the call of God in Christ Jesus.

—Oswald Chambers, *My Utmost for His Highest*

WEEK 8: A FRESH START

Day 1—A Godly Heritage

Day 2—Wrapped Up in Vanity

Day 3—The Danger of Anger

Day 4—From Generation to Generation

Day 5—He Made Me Something Beautiful

A GODLY HERITAGE

Week 8: Day 1

I want to say how thankful I am for each and every one of you. You have been so faithful in showing up every day to spend time with God. I am praying for you, even though I may not know you by name. I believe that God has a plan for your life and will be faithful in carrying it out. He has begun a good work in you. His desire is that your faith be mature and complete, not lacking anything. That being said, I also know that you may be in a place where you cannot see the forest through the trees. Your circumstances, pain, and suffering are engulfing you, and right now, you cannot imagine your life being better. It seems impossible. You hear about God's goodness, His provision, His blessings, and His outpouring of the Holy Spirit in other people's lives, and you stop and wonder why can't that be true for you. *Why don't I see God working in my life?* you wonder.

You hear verses like James 1:3–4: "because you know that the testing of your faith produces perseverance. Let perseverance finish its work so that you may be mature and complete, not lacking anything." You stop and wonder, *Why am I stuck on the "testing of faith" part? When do I get to move on? When will things let up for me and improve? Because Lord, I am ready to finish this work. I am lacking one thing . . . and its name is patience!*

Often our unmet expectations can turn into a deep sense of longing, or jealousy, for what we do not have. Warren Wiersbe, pastor and Christian author, once said, "How sad it is when people only *hear* about God's blessing, but never experience it, because they are not in the place where God can bless them."[65]

Our hearts are not in a place to receive and accept God's good gift. We are unable to see it as "good" because it doesn't meet our expectations. We would not have planned for things to turn out this way. Our heart's strings may be pulling us in a different direction.

---

65   Warren Wiersbe, *Be Committed (Ruth and Esther): Doing God's Will Whatever the Cost* (Colorado Springs: David C. Cook, 1993), 22.

Recount a time when you pursued your desires rather than accepting God's direction:

We are easily thrown off course when things don't go as expected. Now imagine yourself sitting in Eve's shoes. She sinned. She led her husband to sin. She was disciplined. Her husband was disciplined too. To add to her misery, her punishment not only included herself but also the entire female race for generations to come. Just think of it. For years and years to come, women would blame her for their pain and agony.

When the anesthesiologist cannot make it to the hospital room in time, who are we to blame for our childbirth pains? Yes, we blame Eve! Imagine the weight of that label. Does it seem a bit unbearable? What would your reaction be if you were Eve?

Many would resort to anger toward God, thinking that the punishment did not fit the crime. Others would pass blame on to the Devil, saying, "He made me do it." Some would choose bitterness or resentment. Wallowing in despair or self-pity may be more your cup of tea. Here's what I find absolutely breathtaking—the response of Eve's very own husband. I think I may have to begin calling him Prince Adam. He has rolled out the red carpet for his wife. Look at what he does in Genesis 3:20. He calls his wife Eve, in Hebrew *Chavah,* because she would become the mother of all the living[66]. Prior to this, her name was woman, or *Isha,* because she came from man.[67] The Septuagint, a Greek version of the Hebrew Scriptures, translates this verse to say, "And Adam called his wife's name Life." I love that! He did not look at her in anger and resentment. He did not see her for what she had done. He looked at her and through God's eyes was able to see her forgiven, walking in newness of life. What we see unfolding here right before our eyes is the gracious act of forgiveness between a man and a wife. He did not bring out the laundry list of her past deeds. He did not get upset that the Lord also disciplined him. He did not wallow in his own self-pity, being self-absorbed. He did not walk away from the situation, or leave Eve abandoned. Instead, Adam stepped up, and he led.

Ladies, when we let a man lead, it is the sexiest thing in the world! (Can I use that word in a women's Bible study?) Adam manned up and led his family through the process of forgiveness

---

[66]   Weil, Biblische Legenden der Muselmänner, "Eve" *Jewish Encyclopedia* (New York: Funk and Wagnalls, 1901), http://www.jewishencyclopedia.com/articles/5916-eve.

[67]   John Wesley, "Genesis 3:20" (commentary), *Wesley's Explanatory Notes. http://www.biblestudytools.com/commentaries/wesleys-explanatory-notes/genesis/genesis-3.html.*

and acceptance. He gave his wife a new name. It is a beautiful thing! He confesses out loud not who she was or deserved to be, but who she would become. She would become the mother of life!

This is such an astonishing statement, because at this point, what Eve truly deserves is death. She has sinned before a holy God, and now her seed of sin has infected all humankind. Look at these verses:

> For the wages of sin is death. (Romans 6:23a)

> For all have sinned and fall short of the glory of God. (Romans 3:23)

> Indeed, there is no one on earth who is righteous, no one who does what is right and never sins. (Ecclesiastes 7:20)

> What shall we conclude then? Do we have any advantage? Not at all! For we have already made the charge that Jews and Gentiles alike are all under the power of sin. (Romans 3:9)

However, despite Eve's sin, we see Adam give her a new identity. He is able to move past her sin and not allow it to be connected with her anymore. He doesn't play that game. Remember, he could name her anything. The name game was left up to him. He, however, chooses a name to identify her that has nothing to do with her past sin (we are all fully aware that she is a sinner) nor with her accomplishments. For up to this point, her accomplishments are noteworthy for history's sake but certainly not for becoming well admired or respected. One should also note that Eve is not even a mother, yet Adam chooses a name describing the one she will become.

We see Adam not thinking about himself anymore (remember, just a few verses back he was passing the buck). Rather, he has moved away from his self-obsession (*Will this woman make me look bad?*) and self-absorption (*What will my wife think of me if I don't eat of the apple?*) and has started to put others before himself. In *Mere Christianity*, C. S. Lewis describes this as gospel-humility: "If we were to meet a truly humble person, we would never come away from meeting them thinking they were humble. They would not be always telling us they were a nobody (because a person who keeps saying they are a nobody is actually a self-obsessed person). The thing we would remember from meeting a truly gospel-humble person is how much they seemed to be totally interested in us. Because the essence of gospel-humility is not thinking more of myself or thinking less of myself, it is thinking of myself less."[68]

True gospel-humility is translated as not thinking about oneself. You don't need to walk into a room worried about whether or not you will fit in. You don't have to be consumed with making people like you or accept you. No longer is your identity based on whom you know or what you have accomplished. You can have joy whether you win or lose the game, in rain or sunshine, and in sickness or in health. Your joy comes from being a participant. Life no longer is all about you.

---

68 Timothy Keller, *The Freedom of Self-Forgetfulness* (Chorley: 10Publishing, 2012), 31-32.

Rather, it is about those who are around you. The secret is that you find your identity in Christ. It is not *who* you are, but *whose* you are that really matters.

I wonder how long it took Eve to accept her new identity. Did she obsess over her prior sin? As women, we tend to be excellent at obsessing. We fret for hours over the things we've said or done. We can carry on entire conversations within our own pretty lil' heads. We can rehash history and change the way the story ended. In fact, it can be difficult for us to let things go. Since it is excruciatingly difficult to compartmentalize our thoughts, we tend to lose sleep over situations quite easily. The slightest bit of criticism can send us in a whirlwind. Why is that? Because we care too much about what others think of us.

On the contrary, if we blow off other's criticism entirely, downplaying the significance of any sort of feedback, we are consumed with pride. When we assume no one else has any insight into our lives or that others don't know what they are talking about, we become subjected to our own pride. How then can we not think too much or too little of what others say to us? Is there a way to experience such freedom?

I believe there is. I believe we can live in total freedom from human-made expectations and the expectations that we place upon ourselves through one simple word: *acceptance.* If we accept who God says we are, we are no longer bound to measure up to a worldly value system. A performance-based system is no longer in place. In God's value system, it is not behavior first and love second. He loves us; therefore, we have a deep desire to please Him. Love always comes first and behavior second. This is why Jesus was able to say to the convicted felon who made a public profession of faith on the nearby cross, "Truly I say to you, today you will be with me in paradise" (Luke 23:43). This man's forgiveness was not based on anything that he had done. It was based solely on what Christ had done for him. The Bible tells us, "Therefore, there is now no condemnation for those who are in Christ Jesus, because through Christ Jesus the law of the Spirit who gives life has set you free from the law of sin and death" (Romans 8:1–2).

Accepting God's forgiveness for our sins allows us to move past our sinfulness. This self-forgetfulness provides us with a haven of freedom and joy. We will no longer continually beat ourselves up for our failures or past mistakes. Nor will setting expectations too low victimize us. Both of those result in zapping our joy.

My husband complimented me the other day for the way I looked. Quickly, I shrugged off his compliment and made it sound as if it were no big deal. I commented on how I had bought the new outfit on sale, and I discounted the way my hair looked. For in my eyes, I didn't feel that I measured up. I felt unworthy of his praise. My reaction caused irritation, which was readily apparent by his next comment of "I was just trying to give you a compliment." I quickly realized how difficult it is for me to accept a compliment. How much more difficult it must be for me to accept God's forgiveness and praise.

Lord, I didn't want to be that girl who refused to accept forgiveness.

Have you accepted God's forgiveness ? And if so, does your life reflect it?

For the LORD *takes delight in his people; he crowns the humble with victory.*

—Psalm 149:4

Wrapped Up in Vanity

Week 8: Day 2

I have some trepidation about discussing the topic at hand today. Therefore, I would like to begin a little differently. Please put down your pen or pencil, put your Bible study aside, and spend a few minutes in prayer today. Spend some time asking the Holy Spirit for your ears to be receptive to His voice and for your heart to be prepared to listen. I also want you to ask the Lord to search your heart and bring to light any uncovered darkness (Psalm 139:23). If you would like, journal what the Lord is speaking to you:

As we continue with our story of Eve, I hope you realize that we are not just reciting history. This story is alive and active because it is part of God's Word. I pray that the Holy Spirit has been speaking to you personally all along this journey. And I also pray that you take the courage to begin applying what you have learned, "for the word of God is alive and active. Sharper than any double-edged sword, it penetrates even to dividing soul and spirit, joints and marrow; it judges the thoughts and attitudes of the heart" (Hebrews 4:12).

We will jump into Eve's life story, all ready full of twists and turns, by reading Genesis 3:21–4:2. Go ahead and chronicle the next events in her life below:

We see Adam's prophetic name for Eve come into fruition with the birth of her two sons, Cain and Abel. She beautifully acknowledges that God is ultimately the source of all life. So many times we think we hold the destiny for our lives in our own hands. If we eat better, see a doctor regularly, exercise routinely, and use good hygiene, we will somehow have control over our number of days. I don't want to negate any of those things. I try to take good care of myself as well and believe that my body is the temple of the Holy Spirit (1 Corinthians 6:19). I want to provide the Holy Spirit with a pleasant environment in which to live. As Martha Stewart would say, "It is a good thing." However, I also have watched many people turn their health into idolatry.

There may be many reasons why this occurs. Some want their bodies to look fit in order to attract the opposite sex. For others, working out improves their self-esteem. They figure if they are tone and fit and can bench-press more than the person next to them, they are pretty darn good. I look better than the person next to me, so I'm all right, and I feel good about myself. Still others work out and eat stringently because they are afraid of dying. They want their lives to be extended for as long as possible because they don't know where they will spend eternity.

Do any of these scenarios apply to you? Or maybe you can think of another reason we become so focused on our health.

Thinking too much of ourselves and how we look and how long we will live only turns our focus onto ourselves (as does eating too much, by the way). I believe that indulgence is also a sin—but that's for another time and place. Dieting is a multi-billion dollar industry in the United States. It is no wonder that there is so much attention placed on how we look . . . and how the food we eat makes us feel. I am wary about even addressing this issue because I know that my words can easily be misunderstood. What I am trying to address here is when the focus of our health becomes overindulgence. When we begin our days consumed by our exercise routines, our fitness regimens, our health food addictions—we must begin to wonder if we are on the right track. If our focus is on the food we can or cannot eat for the day, rather than on consuming *the bread of life* (Jesus), then we've missed it. Our thoughts are obsessed with fitting into our skinny jeans and drinking our skinny lattes, all without a thought of indulging in God's Word. We've traded in a godly value system for that of the world.

If we are focused too much on any one thing other than God, it is a sin. When we get out of whack, so to speak, is when our minds are consumed with achieving or acquiring something for ourselves. Our hearts become tainted to be a certain size, look a certain way, or fit in with a certain crowd. When our minds become focused on this goal (an inward focus on self) rather than on others, we lose sight of our purpose in this world. Scripture even warns us that such things will occur in the last days. Paraphrase 1 Timothy 4:1–4:

Many years ago, when my children were younger, I began running with a group of neighborhood friends. I had recently quit working to be a stay-at-home mom and looked forward with great anticipation to my daily runs. I would wake up at 4:30 a.m. just so I could spend some time with them (since several of them worked, we had to run in the break of dawn). After a few months, I was convinced that I should run a marathon. One successful marathon quickly turned into another and another. I had retired from my job in a suit and traded it in for running shoes. At the time, I thought this newfound passion was great! I was so excited to have something to talk about in group settings and found myself diving all the way in. Who knew the pats on the back one could receive for merely being a runner? It became a challenge for me to break my personal best, constantly striving to improve. I cross-trained. I did triathlons. I invested in an expensive treadmill. I subscribed to a running magazine. What I failed to realize is that slowly, it was becoming my life. I didn't even see it happening.

My passion no longer was waking up to see what I could do for God that day or what He wanted to say. No, my passion had become meeting my girlfriends to run. I would jeopardize time in the evening with my husband because I had to get to bed . . . so that I could get up in the morning again to run. I missed out on time with my kids because I was so exhausted by mid-day that all I wanted to do was take a nap. I lived for a couple of years in zombie mode.

I had a friend who spoke up and said she thought I was running too much, but I didn't want to listen. I didn't want to hear what she had to say. The thought of giving up running seemed unbearable to me. Who would I be? What would I do? Would people find me interesting? What if I gained weight? Would my husband still be attracted to me? It was such a slow fade that I didn't even recognize it at the time. Five years in, I suffered a hip injury that took me permanently off the marathon trail. I thought it was the worst thing that had ever happened to me. I could not understand why God would allow such a thing. It took me a long time to recognize that in actuality, this was one of God's gifts. My "little bit" of running had taken up a place in my heart that was only meant for God. He had to slow me down to see. The problem was not in the running. The problem was that it meant too much to me.

What about you? Where do you find your identity?

There is a lot of fear about whether or not our identity in Christ is enough. *Will He really be there for me? Is He really all I need? Does He truly love me, even when I mess up really bad? Does He honestly know what is best for me? Is He watching right now? Does He see my misery?* It is at these times of doubt that we must stretch ourselves to trust Him. Look up the following verses and note what they tell us about God:

2 Samuel 22:31 _____

Psalm 9:10 _____

Psalm 118:8 _____

Isaiah 26:3 _____

Nahum 1:7 _____

There is one more fear I want to address today, and that is the fear of death. Sisters, I want you to know that if you are a child of God, you have nothing to fear. Your eternity is locked and sealed. The Bible says, "And this is the testimony: God has given us eternal life, and this life is in his Son. Whoever has the Son has life; whoever does not have the Son of God does not have life. I write these things to you who believe in the name of the Son of God so that you may know that you have eternal life" (1 John 5:11–13). And in regards to the number of days we will live, our sovereign God has that figured out. Acts 17:26 says, "From one man [referring to Adam] he made all the nations, that they should inhabit the whole earth; and he marked out their appointed times in history and the boundaries of their lands."

Returning to Genesis 4, we see that Eve names her second son Abel. His name means "breath" or "temporary" or "meaningless," hinting at his shortness of life. The Hebrew word for Abel is used only two other times in Scripture. Please look up both Ecclesiastes 1:2 and 12:8. What is the author describing as meaningless? _____

In this short book, we see the "affecting and minute description of old age and death is concluded by the author with the same exclamation by which he began this book: O vanity of vanities, saith Koheleth, all is vanity. Now that man, the masterpiece of God's creation, the delegated sovereign of this lower world, is turned to dust, what is there stable or worthy of contemplation besides? All—All is Vanity!"[69]

Read James 4:13–17. How does James describe our lives? _____

We get so consumed by the things of this world. I can remember times when I was so anxious about things in junior high . . . and then in high school . . . and again in college . . . only to repeat my anxious behavior as a newlywed. Over and over again, I have given myself over to anxiety and worry. As I look back, did those thing really matter? In my lifetime I have lost so much sleep over things that were outside of my control. I have spent time making up my mind about how I wanted a situation to turn out. Rather than resting in the fact that God is in control, I made plans to do this or that. It is so much better to trust God with our plans, our agendas, and our dreams. What if we woke up each day and asked God what He wanted us to do? Would it change the way we live?

Lord, I didn't want to be that girl wrapped up in vanity.

---

[69] Adam Clarke, "Ecclesiastes 12:8." (Commentary), *Bible Hub*. Last updated May 18, 2013. *http://biblehub.com/ecclesiastes/12-8.htm* (August 31, 2013).

Where is your focus today? Is it on eternity?

Store your treasures in heaven, where moths and rust cannot destroy, and thieves do not break in and steal.

—Matthew 6:20, NLT

THE DANGER OF ANGER

Week 8: Day 3

My kids have discovered a particular "hot button" with me. I can feel the hair rise on the back of my neck every time one of them brings the subject up: our move. My husband and I felt the leading of the Holy Spirit in such an outpouring and miraculous way in regards to our move. In ways we've never experienced before, God made it very clear that my husband was to leave his job of the past twenty years and that we were to be rooted up to go. Our move was not to the other side of the world, although it surely has seemed like it at times. Our move was merely from Houston to Austin, but it has been the toughest sell for my three kids. I can point out to them all the amazing things that we've seen God do. I can remind them of all the unexplainable circumstances that led up to our move. I can point them back to Scripture and our obedience in hearing God's voice and following through. I can see God working in us, around us, and through us every single day. His hand upon us during this transition has been nothing short of extraordinary. But then, one of my kids will speak up in the car about hating it here, missing old friends, or feeling that this place still just doesn't quite feel like home.

I do my best to acknowledge their feelings. I can understand where they are coming from. It is difficult, and possibly impossible, to find those "soul" friends. I get that. I've struggled with the move in regards to that too. Yet, as a mom, I know we are supposed to be in Austin. I know in my heart of hearts that this move has been good. Yes, God is good. Try as I may, though, I've come up short in convincing my kids wholeheartedly of the same. I have failed to change their hearts. I cannot seem to get to the root of the matter and fix the hurt.

We're going to look at another heart issue today. From the onset, you may think that God is not being fair. From the outside looking in, it appears that these two brothers are doing the exact same thing. As you read, may you be reminded, however, that God looks at the heart. We are reminded of this throughout Scripture, such as in 1 Samuel: "But the Lord said to Samuel, 'Do not look on his appearance or on the height of his stature, because I have rejected him. For the Lord sees not as man sees: man looks on the outward appearance, but the Lord looks on the heart'" (1 Samuel 16:7, ESV).

In Genesis 3, we saw the root of disbelief and disobedience in the lives of Adam and Eve. Today we will look at the fruit of their sin being displayed in the life of their firstborn son. We now vividly see the sinful nature that has been ingrained in their offspring. Yet, God has not abandoned them or turned a deaf ear. In fact, just the opposite is true. He is continually revealing Himself to them while, at the same time, holding each one individually accountable. Read our text today in Genesis 4:3–7.

We quickly notice that God's sight penetrates much deeper than what we see on the outside. Both Cain and Abel offer sacrifices to the Lord, which, from the outside looking in, appear to be appropriate. An act that appears to be good and satisfactory, however, can be ugly in the sight of the Lord. This is because God looks at the outside behavior as an extension of the condition of the heart. To put it simply, God peers within, past all the shenanigans, and sees the inner motives. Turn to Hebrews 11:4.

Why is Abel's sacrifice considered acceptable to God?

Upon the instant disapproval of his sacrifice to the Lord (Genesis 4:5), we see Cain become angry with God. His sinful anger is a result of an interpersonal battle. We see Cain wanting to take the place of God. Satan's trickery in Genesis 3:5, "For God knows that when you eat from it your eyes will be opened . . . and you will be *like God"* comes to fruition (emphasis added). When we think too highly of ourselves, we feel justified in our anger. The more exalted we become in our own eyes, the more difficult it becomes to take blame. We feel we are always right. What we fail to realize is that when we become angry, we are fighting to protect ourselves. We have, in fact, tried to take the place of God.

Think about it for a moment. What makes you angry? What really sets you off?

We become angry when we don't get what we want. When I have to sit in an unexpected traffic delay, I become angry because it interferes with *my* plans. When my kids are fighting in the backseat of the car, I get angry because it affects *my* peace and quiet. When my husband doesn't put away the dishes or leaves his clothes all over the floor, I get furious because now the burden lies on me to clean up his mess. He has affected *my* time. When my boss wants things done a certain way, but I think my way is better, I become angry. He has failed to recognize *my* worth. When my family makes plans for where we should eat dinner or travel on our next vacation or spend some extra money, and they don't even ask me, I get angry. That's not what *I* wanted to do. They changed *my* plans. Sinful anger yells at the top of its lungs: "You are not giving me what I want! I am not pleased with you!"

One of Satan's most effective ploys is to get us to step into the courtroom. We are looking for a verdict each and every day. *Have I done enough to measure up? Am I good enough to be accepted? Will I be considered valuable enough to survive to the next round?* We are constantly behaving as if we are on trial in a courtroom and the jury's vote is still out. The way we too often live is based on our approval rating in the courtroom. This self-evaluation process lies in limbo as we attempt to justify whether or not we measure up. Our self-esteem, whether good or bad, becomes a living yo-yo during the process. When we perform good deeds or have good behavior, our self-esteem is up. When we struggle with sin and anger, our self-esteem plummets downward.

We judge others, and in a similar fashion, we judge ourselves. However, did you realize that in doing so you are acting as judge? When you match behavior (whether it be yours or someone else's) to your own happiness, then, in effect, you are taking the verdict into your own hands. You are saying that when someone acts the way you want or does things you like, then the verdict is in, and that person is "not guilty." But, when the opposite is true, and someone's performance does not measure up, causing you to be offended or angry, then guess what? "Guilty" is the call.

Christianity is the only religion where we receive the verdict "not guilty" before any performance at all. In fact, it goes even one step further than that and declares us completely innocent! Romans 8:1 says, "Therefore, there is now no condemnation for those who are in Christ Jesus." From the moment of salvation, we are considered "not guilty" and are made free to walk in this newness of life. Since we have been made free, we do not have to carry the burden of judgment. It is not our job. The load of carrying around vengeance and anger is not our responsibility. We do not need to be wasting our time holding onto bitterness. We should not allow it to take up one more thought. Why? Because we have been given a substitute. There is someone else to take care of that for us. Someone else to carry our burdens and to take our place in the courtroom. His name is Jesus. Jesus is our sacrifice; He has taken the condemnation we deserve. All we must do when we are offended is look to the cross. I always remind myself that His opinion of me is all that matters. His opinion of others is not up to me.

Look up the following verses. Jot down how they help you understand this biblical truth.

Matthew 7:1–2 _____

Romans 2:1 _____

Romans 14:10–12 _____

I Corinthians 4:3–5 _____

James 4:12 _____

Romans 12:19 says, "Do not take revenge, my dear friends, but leave room for God's wrath, for it is written: 'It is mine to avenge; I will repay,' says the Lord." Our response of anger reveals that we do not believe that God is a just God. When we take matters into our own hands and step back into the courtroom, we are making it our business to act as judge. Unjustifiable anger takes the responsibility back into our own hands. The grievance is no longer against God, but against the self.

In Genesis 4:7, God says to Cain, "Sin is crouching at your door; it desires to have you, but you must rule over it." The secret to victory over sin is to keep our gaze focused on Jesus. Comparing and contrasting to those around us are only mudslides from the Enemy. Therefore, we must be vigilant to keep our attention on Him. The book of Hebrews tell us, "Therefore, since we are surrounded by such a great cloud of witnesses, let us throw off everything that hinders and the sin that so easily entangles. And let us run with perseverance the race marked out for us, fixing our eyes on Jesus, the pioneer and perfecter of faith. For the joy set before him he endured the cross, scorning its shame, and sat down at the right hand of the throne of God" (Hebrews 12:1–2).

Lord, I didn't want to be that girl who was stuck in the courtroom.

Are you wasting your time hanging on to anger? Are you ready to accept that that is not your job to do? Write your response to God below:

Fools give full vent to their rage, but the wise bring calm in the end.

—Proverbs 29:11

FROM GENERATION
TO GENERATION
Week 8: Day 4

Looking back at my family photos, I easily recognize the family resemblances. It is easy to see that I am my mother's daughter. Likewise, the same could be said of her. We have an uncanny resemblance in our eyes and our smiles. Now that I have two teenage daughters, I can see it in them as well. They have so many similarities that even though they are two and a half years apart, they look nearly identical. Repeatedly they have been mistaken as twins. Through Scripture today, we will take a look at our resemblances to our parents, the least of which are physical.

Parents are meant to have a lasting impact on their children, but unfortunately, it's not always good. I can remember growing up with this idealism that my parents were perfect, that they could do no wrong. After all, I was taught to adhere to a strict code of ethics, to never question authority, and to obey at all costs. I cannot recall a time that my parents expressed any record of wrong. They never asked for my forgiveness. Strangely, I accepted this notion for years. And that is why it has taken me years to recognize and accept the fact that they were in fact not perfect. Not everything that I had been shown was ideal. Not every bit of advice they have given me was right. I'll be completely honest, because I love my parents immensely, that it has been a struggle for me to admit that they were wrong. I had to come to the realization that I was carrying some baggage, that when I left my parents' home, I left with my suitcase packed full. It may have just been a carry-on (just in case, Mom, you are reading this), but no doubt, I had it maxed out.

This irony became apparent to me when I became a parent. I set out with the intention to be the perfect parent. I read several parenting books and attended parenting classes and had purposed that I would do things right. I had plans to follow this parental wisdom to a T. But try as I might, and despite my best intentions, I still failed. I still made mistakes. I love my kids beyond measure, and I so desire what is best for them. I tried my best to cooperate with God and walk with my children toward restoration and healing by reflecting my relationship with Christ. But I would be a fool to think that I haven't passed on some junk in the trunk to my own children. If I left my home with a carry-on, my kids will probably leave with an oversized camper. I don't want to be prideful or naive. My hope is that we have some freedom in addressing the negative strongholds that have taken root in our family trees. We've *all* made mistakes. For goodness' sake, let's not be afraid to deal with them—and give our children the liberty to do the same!

We have been taught to "honor our father and mother" (Ephesians 6:2), so for years I thought this meant that I should not reflect back negatively on my childhood. I interpreted this verse to mean that I had no right to recognize the sin that had been passed down to me. "Honor" in this verse means to show respect, reverence, and admiration. Imagine sitting at a formal dinner at the White House, and when the President walks into the room, everyone rises to show their respect. This is exactly what is due to our parents, regardless of the baggage they have passed down. We show the President honor whether we agree or disagree with his diplomacy. In the same manner, we show our parents respect for their love, affection, hard work, and efforts. Every parent has something that we can pay tribute to. Let's not throw out the baby with the bath water. But let's be deliberate in rooting out any of our parents' destructive habits and tendencies so that we can put a stop to them being passed down.

Has the Holy Spirit already revealed any baggage that has been passed down either to you or from you? Please share.

For some, facing the past may be one of the scariest experiences. We have tried to blot out our history and remove it from our memories. There are things in our pasts that haunt us that we have tried to overcome. When that sin rears its ugly head, we become frightened. When we see traits in our children, the mirror oddly reflects our own image. Be it a sarcastic voice, a resistance to share, a moodiness that manipulates, a demand to be right—how quickly I am reminded that I have shown them this. They are mimicking me. The blessing of children is that we can see our sinful selves in and through them. So ladies, let's buckle up our bootstraps today. Don't shy away. The reason for us going here today is to shed some light on the deception that the Enemy has kept in the dark. Read our text for today, Genesis 4:8–26.

Taking into consideration what we discussed yesterday, we must be mindful not to put our parents or ourselves back in the courtroom. The purpose of today is not to play judge. We do not want to tally up our inherited sins by keeping score and pointing out records of wrong. Going there will do no one any good. In fact, it would do more harm than good. The key to reflecting back is so that we can cover our past with God's mercy. We can look back and see what we've been saved from and shout *hallelujah* for how far we've come. Please keep this on the back burner today as you do some reflecting on your own family tree.

How does Cain handle his anger toward his brother?

The Bible has much to say about how we are to handle our anger. There are two types: righteous anger and sinful anger. Righteous anger stems from when somebody is violating God's standards of justice. A perfect illustration of this is when Jesus throws the moneychangers from the temple (Matthew 21:12–13; Mark 11:15–18; John 2:13–22). Jesus' actions are pure because they are rooted in His concern for the protection of God's holiness and worship. It is not centered on His self. Sinful anger, however, is all about the protection of the self. We are therefore not taught to eradicate anger completely from our lives. But we must be careful to only display a righteous anger. A few quick pointers to differentiate between the two:

- Be sure that your anger has the right motives. Is it to protect God or to protect the self? Jesus did not get caught up in petty disagreements or hurt feelings over His self. He had a much bigger perspective in mind.
- Keep anger in focus. In other words, Jesus showed anger toward sinful behavior and true injustices toward God. He was angry at the behavior, but He still loved the sinner. He did not allow a person's sin, a person's weaknesses, to affect His pursuit after him or her. His deep love and compassion for others brought Him to anger. He was concerned about their spiritual welfare. However, in the example of Cain, we see his deep hatred and jealousy as the driving force behind his deep-rooted anger. He clearly wasn't concerned about Abel's well being.
- Remain self-controlled. Be mindful to keep your emotions in check. Ask yourself whether you are controlling your emotions or they are controlling you.
- Keep it short. Don't remain angry for long or let the sun go down on your wrath. By doing so, you're just allowing the Enemy to have a foothold. Remember Genesis 4:7: "sin is crouching at your door." It is up to you to subdue it and not allow it in.
- Ask yourself, "What will be the results?" Jesus' anger was in line with God's Word and continued the purposes of God. Cain's anger only resulted in death.

In Ephesians 4:26–27, we are taught the following: "In your anger do not sin: Do not let the sun go down while you are still angry, and do not give the devil a foothold." All the Enemy is waiting for is a little crack in the door to come in. Unaddressed sin can creep in and become a much bigger problem if not properly attended to. In today's text, we see Cain's grudge against God and his brother wreaking havoc on him and the future generations to come. Don't be blindsided into thinking that a little grudge, resentment, or bitterness is no big deal. Your intention to hurt the person who has wronged you is only hurting yourself.

Notice that Abel did not intentionally harm his brother. There is no mention of any wrongdoing on his part. Abel's only claim to fame was that "the Lord looked with favor on Abel and his offering." As a quick side note, I want to point out that there will be times when you will be a victim for doing what is right. God's blessing on you can create tension and jealousy in the hearts of others, even though you've done nothing wrong. Others may even reach the point of hating you because they see the outpouring of the Holy Spirit in your life. For Abel, this meant someone in his own bloodline. May I encourage you to not let that stop or dwindle your passion for the Lord. Please continue your sold-out, radical love for Him, keeping in mind that your faithfulness will one day be rewarded (Hebrews 11:4).

Look back at Genesis 4:23–24. We now see the lineage of Cain, a restless wanderer. What sin does Lamech commit? _____

How often have we carried on the traditions of some of our parents' bad decisions? I can recall a sermon I heard my previous pastor give about a woman who would chop off the ends of her honey ham every Easter. She would cut off a good two inches or so from each end. Stunned by her crazy carving, and after years of marriage, her husband finally got up the courage to ask her why did she cut off the ends of the ham. She replied, "Because that's what my mother did." She instantly called her mother to inquire what the purpose was in lopping off the ends of the ham only to discover that her mother did so in order for it to fit in her roasting pan. How often when we are tested do we respond in the same way as our parents? If our parents modeled a wrong behavior, has it become acceptable for us to react inappropriately too?

We fail to realize that the gifts we are giving our children may not be good for them. What exactly are we passing down? If you grew up with parents who became worried or anxious whenever facing an unexpected circumstance, then it is very likely that your response will be the same. Those who grew up practicing deception or manipulation, watching it modeled by a parent, find it contagiously attractive as an approach to life. When honesty is not held in high regard in a home, dishonesty quickly can become a way of life. Another attractive approach is flying off the handle with anger. You are quick-tempered and easily lash out at those you love. With a flash of the tongue, you say many regrettable things. Unless we start diving into the crux of the issue, we will easily carry these traits of our parents into our adult lives. These are behaviors that we've accepted as "all right." We've assumed because our parents modeled them, they are excusable. We've been deceived into thinking that the truth of God's Word only applies in part.

Let's be diligent in applying the whole truth—nothing but the truth, my dear sisters. Ask the Holy Spirit to reveal to you today any sinful tendencies that seem natural to you. Allow me to begin by asking a few pointed questions: Did your parents live a very different public life from their private life? Was it difficult to reconcile the two? Were your parents easily angered or always justifying their anger? Did your parents openly and readily lie for you? Were they trying to cover up your mistakes or make you appear better before others? Now boldly ask God to free you from any deception that has been pulled over your eyes.

One of the greatest things about gifts is that they can be gifted back! If you've been given a gift that is out of line with God's Word, then go ahead and give that gift back. You do not have to accept it. You do not have to accept the sins of your lineage and continue to live that way. There comes a time when, regardless of your history, your ancestry, and your parents, you will have to take ownership of your own sin. The buck will have to stop here. You will be held responsible for your actions and your actions alone. Half in the room may be shouting *amen!* for the burden this alleviates them from while a deafening silence has overcome others. As much as we would like to blame others for our sinful choices, we still will be held accountable for our own reactions and responses. We may have a strong propensity to sin in certain ways because of what we've been taught; however, a sin is a sin and is inexcusable.

In light of what we have learned today, may we be reminded of God's incredible mercy to "cover a multitude of sins." God is the perfect parent, and let's not confuse Him with human beings! He loves us unconditionally and forgives us repetitively. It is so exciting to see our text end up here: "At that time people began to call on the name of the Lord" (Genesis 4:26).

Let's join them today and call on His name. He is the one who is able to take our flawed past and turn it into a beautiful spiritual heritage. Let's allow that to be written down in our family trees. I pray that my family tree looks like a bunch of nuts, nutty for Jesus.

Lord, I didn't want to be that girl who gifted my children with baggage.

Pray today for your spiritual lineage. Whether you have biological children or not, you are planting seeds. What kind of seeds are you planting?

Yet to all who did receive him, to those who believed in his name, he gave the right to become children of God—children born not of natural descent, nor of human decision or a husband's will, but born of God.

—John 1:12–13

HE MADE ME SOMETHING BEAUTIFUL

Week 8: Day 5

A year ago, after a speaking engagement in Houston, a friend whom I highly respect sought me out of the crowd. Looking me squarely in the eyes, she posed the question, "When are you going to write a book?" A bit bewildered by her statement, I began to seek the Lord to see if this was the path He was directing me to. I've taught adult Sunday school classes for years and have been heavily involved in women's development, but that's about all I have to hang my hat on. I don't have a seminary degree. I don't have all the answers. In fact, since my move to Austin, due to my newness, I have had even fewer responsibilities in the church. Yet I took this petition of writing a book before the Lord and specifically made my request to Him.

Two weeks later, a friend who lives in Boston called and point-blank asked me, "Sue, when are you going to write a woman's Bible study? I miss your teaching so much." At that moment, I knew it was a direct answer to my prayer request. Still, the barriers to writing seemed insurmountable. My doubts came barging in like a tidal wave. I tried to find every imaginable excuse to discount that I had heard an answer directly from God. When God calls you to do something new, doubt may be your biggest enemy. I found myself in a new home and a new church body, with new friendships and a shaken identity. It is thanks to God that I have finished this book. There were many times when I wanted to put the computer aside and finish up shop. I thought I was done. This task seemed so hard.

Several months into my writing adventure, there came a time when I was especially downhearted, wondering if I would ever be allowed to teach again. Did I really believe that God had placed on me a calling to teach? Was I really supposed to be writing a book? Had God given me this gift of teaching only to take it away? I am familiar with the words of Job 1:21: "The Lord gave and the Lord has taken away." Was that what had happened to me? Would I take the blessings from His hand so freely but not allow Him to also take them away? Of course I asked Him many times, "Lord, have I sinned against You? Is there any reason why my voice that so longs to give glory to You has been shut up? Open my eyes, Lord, that I may see my own sinfulness."

I prayed that the Lord would again remind me of my calling. If I were to continue to write, I needed Him to be faithful in telling me. I made my request in the morning, and in the middle of the afternoon I received a phone call with the request to come speak at a woman's conference in Houston. God did not give up on me. In the midst of my doubt and the crisis of my identity, He pursued me. To Him and Him alone be the glory.

> But God chose the foolish things of the world to shame the wise; God chose the weak things of the world to shame the strong. God chose the lowly things of this world and the despised things—and the things that are not—to nullify the things that are, so that no one may boast before him. It is because of him that you are in Christ Jesus, who has become for us wisdom from God—that is, our righteousness, holiness and redemption. Therefore, as it is written: *"Let the one who boasts boast in the Lord."* (1 Corinthians 1:27, emphasis added)

I bare my heart and my soul before you today so that you may know that I, too, am broken. I am weak. I have my good days and my bad. I have doubts, and I have fears. Many times I put more focus on self than I do God. There are days I put on my label of sinfulness and shame. But God . . . but God lifts up my head so that I can shout His name from the rooftop. He is the lifter of my head: "But you, Lord, are a shield around me, my glory, the One who lifts my head high" (Psalm 3:3).

But God . . . I don't know how anyone survives without Him. Despite our sinfulness, our brokenness, our stubbornness, our pride and weaknesses, He has chosen to include us as part of His much bigger plan. The Bibles tells us, "In a well-furnished kitchen there are not only crystal goblets and silver platters, but waste cans and compost buckets—some containers used to serve fine meals, others to take out the garbage. Become the kind of container God can use to present any and every kind of gift to his guests for their blessing" (2 Timothy 2:20–21, MSG).

How are you making your life available to God to be used as a blessing?

At the end of the day, we all fall short of perfection. When we reflect back on the life of Eve, we know in our heart of hearts that we would have sinned too. This imperfection has been passed down to us, and despite our good deeds and well-intended behavior, we still cannot measure up on our own accord. Just like Eve, we didn't want to be *that* girl. But despite our best intentions, we are. Yes, we all are. As is written in the book of Romans, "Therefore, just as sin entered the world through one man, and death through sin, and in this way death came to all people, because all sinned—To be sure, sin was in the world before the law was given, but sin is not charged against anyone's account where there is no law. Nevertheless, death reigned from the time of Adam to the time of Moses, even over those who did not sin by breaking a command, as did Adam, who is a pattern of the one to come" (Romans 5:12–14).

According to God's law, the wages of sin is death. The first Adam introduced sin into the world. What was needed was a new Adam, one who knew no sin or deceit (see 1 Peter 2:22). Like Adam, Jesus was a perfect man. Entering into this world, He knew no sin. But unlike Adam, Jesus did not sin, even though He was tempted. He led a perfect life so that the scales could be balanced and our ransom of indebtedness could be paid. The book of Hebrews tells us, "But when this priest [Jesus Christ] had offered for all time one sacrifice for sins, he sat down at the right hand of God, and since that time he waits for his enemies to be made his footstool. For by one sacrifice he has made perfect forever those who are being made holy" (Hebrews 10:12–14).

We can all rejoice for the work that has been done on our behalf. We know that death will have no sting. The pains of this world will not last forever. We have the perfect Adam, who has rescued us from sin and death! "So it is written: "The first man Adam became a living being; the last Adam, a life-giving spirit" (1 Corinthians 15:45).

Share with your group what has impacted you the most during this study on the life of Eve.

Lord, I am so glad that I'm that girl!

Thank the Lord that despite your failures, your sins, your history, and your weaknesses, you are a girl who has received life!

However, I consider my life worth nothing to me; my only aim is to finish the race and complete the task the Lord Jesus has given me—the task of testifying to the good news of God's grace.

—Acts 20:24

I'm Yours, Lord. Everything I Got!

Sue Allen lives in Austin, Texas, with her husband of twenty-two years and their three children. She desires to show other women that with God, ordinary women can be extraordinary. Her husband is a pediatric emergency room and infectious disease physician. In humble obedience, the Allens have tried to live a surrendered life to God. They are in the process of adopting a child from Haiti and have faithfully served their church in various capacities, including short-term missions, youth ministry, and adult ministry. Sue is an author, Bible teacher, and speaker at various women's conferences. This is her first book.

The Allens' decision to adopt from Haiti was inspired by a heartfelt conviction that they have been blessed to be a blessing to others (2 Corinthians 9:8-12). With that in mind, Coby and Sue have made a decision to donate all proceeds from this book to orphan care in Haiti. Coby is the medical director of a clinic located in the city of Neply, Haiti. With their recent involvement there, Sue and Coby's eyes have been opened, and their hearts have been burdened to do all that they can to help. For more information about their efforts there, please go to www.myLIFEspeaks.com.

Printed in the United States
By Bookmasters